ASKARI

A story of collaboration and betrayal in the anti-apartheid struggle

Jacob Dlamini

Jacob Dlamini
27 October 2014

JACANA

First published by Jacana Media (Pty) Ltd in 2014

10 Orange Street
Sunnyside
Auckland Park 2092
South Africa
+2711 628 3200
www.jacana.co.za

ISBN 978-1-4314-0975-4

Front cover images:
© Gille de Vlieg / South Photographs / Africa Media Online
© Paul Weinberg / South Photographs / Africa Media Online
Map by Sue Abraham

Cover design by publicide
Set in Sabon 11/15.5pt
Printed and bound by Creda Communications
Job no. 002270

See a complete list of Jacana titles at www.jacana.co.za

For Natali Hava, Mbali Marie and Naledi Eveline,
and in memory of Maki Skhosana

Contents

Abbreviations

ALN	National Liberation Army (Algeria)
ANC	African National Congress
Apla	Azanian People's Liberation Army
Azapo	Azanian People's Organisation
CIS	Criminal Investigation Service
COIN	Counterinsurgency strategy
Cosas	Congress of South African Students
DCC	Directorate of Covert Collection
DINA	National Intelligence Directorate (Chile)
ESMA	Naval School of Mechanics in Buenos Aires
Frelimo	Mozambican Liberation Front
MK	Umkhonto we Sizwe
MNR/Renamo	Mozambican National Resistance
MPLA	People's Movement for the Liberation of Angola
NIS	National Intelligence Service
NP	National Party
NSMS	National Security Management System
PAC	Pan Africanist Congress
PC	Communist Party (Chile)
RPMC	Regional Politico-Military Council
SADF	South African Defence Force

SAP	South African Police
Saso	South African Students' Organisation
SB	Security Branch
Swapo	South West Africa People's Organisation
TRC	Truth and Reconciliation Commission
Unisa	University of South Africa
Unita	National Union for the Total Independence of Angola
Zapu	Zimbabwe African People's Union
ZCC	Zion Christian Church

We are in fact convinced that no human experience is without meaning or unworthy of analysis, and that fundamental values, even if they are not positive, can be deduced from this particular world which we are describing.

– Primo Levi, *Survival in Auschwitz*

N
ZIMBABWE
Beit Bridge
BOTSWANA
Louis Trichardt
MOZAMBIQUE
Pietersburg
Turfloop
TRANSVAAL
Penge
Hoedspruit
N1
Steelpoort
Burgersfort
Pilgrim's Rest
Bushbuckridge
Matibidi
Lydenburg
Letlhabile
Hammanskraal
Zeerust
Soshanguve
N4
Vlakplaas farm
PRETORIA
Mamelodi
Nelspruit
Rustenburg
Atteridgeville
Verwoerdburg
Middelburg
Barberton
Tembisa
Krugersdorp
Kagiso
Johannesburg
Soweto
Josefsdal
Piggs Peak
Namaacha
Lomahasha
MAPUTO
Katlehong
Duduza
Emelo
MBABANE
Potchefstroom
Bhunya
Manzini
Klerksdorp
Mankayane
SWAZILAND
Piet Retief
Bophuthatswana
Lebowa
BOTSWANA
MOZAMBIQUE
Pretoria
TRANSVAAL
NAMIBIA
SWAZI-LAND
ORANGE FREE STATE
NATAL
LESOTHO
Durban
CAPE PROVINCE
Cape Town
Port Elizabeth
N2
NATAL
INDIAN OCEAN
Pietermaritzburg
Chesterville
Durban
Umlazi
0
200
KILOMETRES

Introduction

Sometime in 1988 I came across an article titled 'The strange saga of Mr X1' in the anti-apartheid magazine *Work in Progress*.[1] The article told the story of a senior member of the then-banned African National Congress (ANC) and its armed wing, Umkhonto we Sizwe (MK), who had defected to the Security Branch of the South African Police (SAP). The defector had testified in February and March of that year against his former ANC comrades Simon Dladla, Ebrahim Ismail Ebrahim and Mandla Acton Maseko in a terrorism and treason trial in which the three faced the death penalty.

Mr Justice Henry Daniels, the presiding judge in the trial, had ruled that the defector be referred to only as Mr X1 to shield his identity.[2] There was to be no mention in court or in the media of the defector's real name or of the various *noms de guerre* he used while in the ANC; there were to be no pictures of him or cartoons of his likeness published in the newspapers. The trial, which was held in the Transvaal Supreme Court in Pretoria, was billed by the media as South Africa's biggest political case since the 1964 Rivonia Trial, in which Nelson Mandela was sentenced to life on Robben Island.[3] And Mr X1 was the state's star witness.

This book is about Mr X1. It is about his conversion from freedom fighter to apartheid agent. Mr X1's appearance on the witness stand in 1988 was but one episode in an eight-year period during which he turned collaboration into a career choice, becoming one of apartheid's most notorious turncoats. This, then, is a story about collaboration in apartheid South Africa. It is also about how we in the 21st century might understand Mr X1's acts of betrayal, situated as we are at some historical (and perhaps ethical) remove from when he decided to become one with his former enemies. It is about a man and his circumstances, what social scientists like to call agency and structure. It is about Mr X1's choices and the conditions under which he made them.

The book looks at collaboration and complicity to see if such examination might yield new ways of approaching South African history. How different would the history of apartheid sound if told, not as the story of a racial war, but of what we might call, after Njabulo Ndebele, a 'fatal intimacy' between black and white South Africans?[4] This book seeks to contribute to efforts to render South Africa's contemporary history in a manner that does not take race and apartheid's language of race at face value.[5] It does not buy into apartheid assumptions about how race determined the moral choices and political loyalties of individuals.

To be sure, Mr X1's metamorphosis from insurgent to counter-insurgent was not a straightforward transformation in which black became white, night became day, and wrong became right. In fact, his actions form but one layer in a sedimentation of betrayals in which he himself was betrayed by the Royal Swazi Police, and may have been sold out to the Swazis and the Security Branch of the SAP for 'sordid monetary gain' by some of his own comrades in the ANC.[6]

The story recounted here does not have a reliable narrator. Mr X1, whose voice can be heard in snippets throughout the book, told so many lies that he cannot be trusted. As the author, I cannot be considered a reliable narrator because I was not 'there', nor have I achieved the balance between explaining and understanding that these events require. I have known about Mr X1 for more than half my life, and researched the topic extensively, but I am not sure that I understand it all. Furthermore, I cannot say I have not judged him.

Nor can the primary source materials on which the book relies be trusted. These include slivers of official archives from the South

African conflict, the bulk of which have yet to be opened to the public.[7] Among the remnants are files that survived what Terry Bell and Dumisa Ntsebeza called apartheid's 'paper Auschwitz'.[8] This analogy, overstated though it may be, refers to the industrial-scale destruction of at least 44 tonnes of the apartheid state's security archive by the military, police and intelligence services in 1993, shortly before the advent of democracy.[9] The destruction amounted to what Achille Mbembe called a 'denial of debt', a refusal to settle apartheid's accounts.[10] But the attempt to wipe away the stain of history was stymied by the problem of sheer volume.[11] The archive was simply too big to be destroyed *in toto*. As Ray Lalla, a former ANC intelligence operative with knowledge of the apartheid archive, remarked of his former adversaries, 'They were like the Germans. They kept files on everything. When they tried to destroy the archives, they discovered it was a mammoth task. There was so much material, they could not destroy it all.'[12]

My archival sources include a copy of Mr X1's confidential Security Branch file, dated 1987; the transcript of his 1988 court testimony against Dladla, Ebrahim and Maseko; and Mr X1's evidence given in camera in 1990 before the Harms Commission of Inquiry, appointed by President F.W. de Klerk to look into 'certain murders'. These murders referred to a string of assassinations for which Dirk Coetzee and Almond Nofomela, ex-members of a Security Branch death squad, had claimed responsibility in a sensational public disclosure. There are also personnel files covering the period 1988–1990 from Vlakplaas, the secret police death-squad base from which Mr X1 operated for four years after his defection. These files were salvaged by the Truth and Reconciliation Commission (TRC) during its investigations into the state-sponsored violence of the apartheid era.

Of the individuals from both sides of the political divide who knew and worked with Mr X1 – from his comrades in the ANC to the Vlakplaas commander Eugene de Kock – none is entirely reliable. Their recollections are tainted by fear and the desire to give apartheid secrets an afterlife in the democratic South Africa. Equally suspect are many of the books and newspaper articles that speak about Mr X1.[13] Written by activists, scholars and reporters, they contain factual inaccuracies – not to mention a perennial misspelling of Mr X1's real name – that call into question their worth. One book even gives two dates for when Mr X1 died.[14] There is also Mr X1's family. Staunchly ANC, except for one brother who belongs to the Azanian People's Organisation (Azapo), they accepted without question Mr X1's explanation for why he defected.

Glenn Moss, who wrote the *Work in Progress* article about Mr X1 in 1988, could not say who Mr X1 was without being in contempt of court. But he did offer clues to show what made this a strange tale. Mr X1 came from a 'struggle family' and had a brother who had served five years as a political prisoner on Robben Island. Mr X1 was also a highly trained MK operative and had received specialised military instruction in East Germany and the Soviet Union. Why, Moss asked, would such a man switch sides? Moss hinted at possible reasons for Mr X1's defection, pointing out, for instance, that when Mr X1 took the witness stand against Dladla, Ebrahim and Maseko, he bore scars from what looked to have been a savage beating. But Moss, himself a former political detainee, could not ask if Mr X1 had been 'turned' through torture without running the risk of a lawsuit – or worse.[15] Mr X1, for his part, blamed the Swazi police for his scars, claiming they had assaulted him shortly before he defected to the SAP in August 1986.[16]

Moss's question – Why did Mr X1 switch sides? – was to be my question, too, for 26 years. I cannot say what interested me in the account of Mr X1. Perhaps it was the sense of mystery evoked by his pseudonym. Maybe it was the idea that someone so senior in the ANC could abandon ranks in such a spectacular fashion. When I first read the Moss article, I had yet to be introduced to the literature on the complexities of collaboration and resistance. But as I immersed myself in this literature, my fascination with Mr X1 grew. It took on various forms and assumed different emphases along the way. But its overall shape was always determined by that original 'Why?' This book tries to answer that question. Only it does so cognisant of the fact that, as the Hungarian scholar Istvan Rev says, the historian is always late and cannot for that reason record 'what in fact happened exactly in the way it happened'.[17] As Rev writes, the job of the historian is to 'demonstrate the inherently uncertain character of any representation of the past'.[18] And to do so, I would add, without assuming a position of innocence or objectivity, whatever that may be.

* * *

It is 1986 and I am a Standard Six pupil at Ponego Secondary School in Katlehong. Schooling in state institutions has been disrupted more or less since the 1976 Soweto rebellion. By the 1980s, there are constant class boycotts and township schools are under military occupation. Four white military conscripts are stationed at Ponego, which has been surrounded by barbed wire. All entrances to the school are closed except one, manned by soldiers who patrol the school grounds in pairs. Students must produce IDs to enter. The Congress of South African Students (Cosas) has called for a semi-permanent class boycott. The majority of the students heed the call and do not come to school. But I don't believe in class boycotts. I defy the call, as do a handful of other students. The teachers, being government employees, have no choice but to show up for work. This is not to say they are conscientious about their jobs. A good number, poorly qualified as they are, can hardly be bothered to teach the few of us who turn up. But others try.

Many of the students who come to school in defiance of the class boycott wear ordinary clothes, not the grey-and-white uniform that would mark them out on the streets. I wear my uniform. My mother insists on it. Occasionally, the school is pelted with rocks while we are in class, so we sit away from the windows during lessons. Once, during a lunch break, rocks rain down on the roof of the school. I am standing outside with some of my classmates. I cannot see who threw the rocks but I know the direction from which they were hurled. Two soldiers rush towards us. Their rifles cocked and raised, they ask where the rocks came from. 'That way,' I say, pointing at a row of houses to the south of the school. The soldiers walk towards the houses. But whoever threw the rocks is long gone. The soldiers know this, hence their half-hearted walk in the direction of the stone-throwers. They resume their patrol around the schoolyard. It occurs to me later that 'helping' the soldiers might not have been such a smart idea. I rush home at the end of the school day. I am afraid the rock-throwers might have seen me pointing in their direction. Thankfully, nothing happens to me. But were these the actions of a collaborator? Why did I answer the soldiers' question? Had I been overcome by what Jean-Paul Sartre called an instinctive 'humanitarian helpfulness', referring to the random help that Parisians would give their German occupiers during the Second World War?[19]

The year is 1987 and I am a Standard Seven pupil at Ponego. I am taking a dull class called Biblical Studies, which requires little study. All you have to do is memorise words like 'apocrypha', which are written up on the board. But it is a popular subject, especially with a group of student activists who like to sit at the back of the room. A great many young people are fighting apartheid at this time – in ways both large and small. Readers will understand when I say that such activism in general was not necessarily represented by these activists in particular. For these classmates, school starts on Tuesday and ends on Thursday. This is not to say they do not come to school on Mondays and Fridays. They come late on Mondays and spend the day basking in the sun, nursing their hangovers; they always leave before school ends on Fridays so they can start partying early. Their other favourite day is Wednesday, sports day, which means that classes continue only until lunchtime. That's just the way they roll. These 'activists' are much older than the rest of us; some are about the same age as our teachers. They tease the young teachers constantly, especially the women. But the latter give as good as they get and tease these students about being *dom* – stupid.

One day, the Biblical Studies teacher announces that we are going to have an exam. She tells us the date and the work to be covered. On the appointed day she comes to class early and asks us to remove everything from our desks except our pens and writing pads. She is about to write the questions on the blackboard when she is interrupted by a baritone from the back of the room. 'Why?' he asks. 'Because you are about to write your test,' she says. 'No,' says the student, 'we cannot write the test. You did not tell us we would have a test today.' His friends pipe in: 'It's unfair, Mistress, to expect us to write a test we did not prepare for.' 'But I told you,' the teacher says. 'No, you did not,' the baritones reply. The teacher looks around the room for support. 'Class, did I not tell you last week that you would be writing a test today?' No answer. Finally, I raise my hand. 'Yes, Dlamini,' prompts the teacher. 'You told us,' I say in Zulu. She asks me to repeat what I just said. '*Usitshelile*,' I reply. 'Shut up, *wena*,' the big boys call out. The teacher asks if anyone else remembers her telling us about the test. No one remembers, not even my deskmate and friend Elias. The teacher says she is giving the test whether the class likes it or not. She tells me to follow her to the staffroom. As I gather my books, the big boys at the back whisper, 'Sell-out'. Some make catcalls. '*U-Dlamini uyasithengisa*.' (Dlamini is selling us out.) '*Sizomlungisa*,' they shout. (We are going to sort him out.) I am scared. But I cannot turn back now. I write the test and return to the classroom. It is tense. No one will talk to me.

Do these episodes make me a collaborator? It is possible that some readers might find here proof of my own taint. 'How could it not be?' asks the narrator in Gillian Slovo's novel *Red dust*. 'South Africa has always been about sides.'[20] In my defence, let me say that I was not collaborating with the soldiers who occupied my school. I knew what those young white men in their brown fatigues and with their R5 rifles were: occupiers and representatives of an illegitimate government. I knew what a disruptive force they were; how they would conduct random searches in our classrooms or gawk through the windows at one of our teachers, an albino, during lessons, all the while making snide comments in Afrikaans about his skin colour. And I was certainly not taking sides by writing that Biblical Studies exam. I simply believed it was the right thing to do.

* * *

I relate these experiences because, in a modest way, they suggest a need to think critically about collaboration and complicity in South African history. Despite its fixation on racial purity, apartheid generated an 'unwanted intimacy' between people that built an insidious complicity into daily life. The complexity of apartheid as a form of government and a system of social control was such that one could not simply exist in innocent opposition to it. Everyone was 'implicated willy-nilly in its thinking and practices and shaped their responsibility accordingly'.[21] This is not to say every South African collaborated with apartheid, or that the mere fact of being a South African made one complicit with a criminal system. There was a world of difference between Mr X1 and the tens of thousands of activists who fought against it. There is a yawning gap separating the collaborators who staffed apartheid's bureaucracies of repression and the millions of South Africans who had no choice but to live with its police, its soldiers and its functionaries.

To talk about collaboration under apartheid is to probe the nature of the post-apartheid political settlement. It is to ask why, beyond the fact that South Africa had a negotiated transition, the country did not have the type of reckoning with the past, apart from the TRC of course, that could have led to the purification of the public sphere and the purging from public office of those tainted by collaboration with our authoritarian past. Why did South Africa not have what some countries in Eastern Europe, notably the former Czechoslovakia, called lustration, where those who had collaborated with the repressive regimes that collapsed at the end of the Cold

War were excluded from public life, or their participation curbed by some degree of exposure or confession?[22] Why is it that, whereas the figure of the informer – however complex and ambiguous the circumstances of each case – came to stand for the depravity of the police states in the former Eastern bloc, South Africans have no comparable symbol for the criminality of apartheid, which was served by a vast network of collaborators?[23]

To be sure, South Africa had Dirk Coetzee, Eugene de Kock and Almond Nofomela – policemen right 'in the heart of the whore', to use Coetzee's own description of apartheid's most lethal death squad. But even these self-confessed killers and convicted murderers (in the case of De Kock and Nofomela) have been treated by apartheid apologists like the proverbial bad apples of any war and not as the 'public servants', however bizarre that sounds, that these men were.

To write about collaboration in South Africa means challenging a certain nostalgia that would have us believe that apartheid was essentially a well-meaning modernisation project with what Hermann Giliomee called a 'comparatively impressive' economic performance over its 46-year lifespan.[24] It means calling into question Giliomee's grotesque understatement that apartheid showed a 'gross disrespect' for human rights.[25] It is telling that in his explanation of apartheid, Giliomee has nothing more to say about death squads than that 'some operatives on the lower level of the security forces took the law in their own hands'.[26] It is equally telling that his account of apartheid leaves no (political) room for the thousands of black policemen and soldiers who fought for apartheid. 'Many white soldiers and policemen were ready to fight in what they assumed to be a showdown over which racial group would rule South Africa, confident that the white public backed them,' he writes.[27] In Giliomee's account, the political conflict in South Africa was essentially a racial one.

In truth, political conflict in South Africa has always been a racially promiscuous affair. For a country with a reputation for a

Manichaean view of politics, South Africa has produced a wide range of collaborators, double agents, *izimpimpi* (Nguni for spies or traitors) and turncoats throughout its history. From *amaMbuka* (Zulu for traitors) of the earliest clashes between African peoples and European settlers, and the *verraaiers* and 'Judas Boers' of the South African War of 1899–1902,[28] to the struggle against apartheid, political wars in South Africa have always been intimate affairs. This does not mean that there was a moral equivalence between those who, for example, fought to preserve apartheid and those who struggled against what the United Nations correctly denounced as a crime against humanity. Nor is it to suggest that words such as 'collaborator', 'double agent', 'informer', '*impimpi*', 'sell-out' and 'turncoat' are timeless terms whose meaning travels unchanged through history. They are loaded words and their meanings are always context-specific, politically constructed, contested and subject to change. Collaboration is marked by ambiguity and, as Raymond Suttner says, 'simple labels cannot explain a very complex phenomenon'.[29]

* * *

In his description of Paris under Nazi occupation, Sartre noted that complicity was widespread. The French could not 'take a step, eat or even breathe without colluding with the occupier'.[30] According to Sartre, Parisians did not have to be active collaborators; the very condition of living under occupation made them complicit. 'Every one of our acts was ambiguous: we never knew whether to condemn ourselves totally or fully approve our actions; a subtle poison infected the best of undertakings.'[31] Of course, apartheid South Africa was not occupied France. But there was something intimate about apartheid, something ubiquitous about complicity with an inhumane system.

Consider two dispensations with which apartheid can be compared: the military dictatorships of Latin America during the second half of the 20th century, and the Communist regimes of the Soviet Union and Eastern Europe. Tina Rosenberg sums up the difference between them as follows: 'The eastern European dictatorships were criminal regimes, while the Latin American were regimes of criminals.'[32] The Latin American juntas, from Argentina to Brazil, did not pretend to be ruling on behalf of grateful citizens, but they had the weapons. The generals had a pronounced rightist ideology, but they preferred an apolitical populace.[33] 'The eastern European Communist regimes, by contrast, sought political participation. They proclaimed themselves the instrument of the working class and aimed for nothing less than the transformation of their citizens.'[34]

These differences led to distinct manifestations of collaboration. While many people in Latin America supported the military dictatorships and collaboration was in fact common, 'one can point to a few men who committed the actual crimes'.[35] The Soviet bloc regimes, in contrast, claimed they were agents of history driving their societies to the highest stage of human development. In the process, they tried to turn every citizen into a co-conspirator.[36] In these societies, 'the lines of complicity ran like veins and arteries inside the human body. Even the most natural responses of self-preservation were also, in a sense, acts of collaboration.'[37]

Apartheid was a hybrid. It was a series of criminal regimes carrying out a crime against humanity. It was also a regime of criminals who presided over a massive repressive machinery and murdered their political opponents. But repression was tempered by circumstance. One needs only to compare the numbers of people slaughtered by the Argentine and Guatemalan juntas, for example, with those killed by successive apartheid governments over 40 years to realise that, as criminal as apartheid was, as a killing machine it was no match for the murderous regimes found in Latin America. The truth is that, as in Eastern Europe, apartheid depended far more on collaboration to work. In South Africa, too, the 'lines of complicity ran like veins and arteries inside the human body'. This is not to suggest that everyone was a collaborator caught up in a web of moral relativism. Far from it: individuals could still act, choose and take moral stands. They could refuse to collaborate. In fact, many did.

For most black South Africans, the face of apartheid was black. From the clerks who staffed government offices, the teachers who taught Bantu education, the 'elected' and non-elected officials who ran townships, to the policemen and -women who enforced apartheid laws, the average bureaucrat was black. These black faces were not isolated apparatchiks. They lived in the same communities they 'served'. As the anthropologist Julia Hornberger points out, the apartheid police force never lacked 'willing black recruits'.[38] She asks, 'Why would black people voluntarily submit to a system that systematically discriminated against them and which, in addition, made them complicit in the oppression of other black people?'[39] There are, of course, many reasons why the apartheid police never lacked willing black recruits.

Almond Nofomela was a bricklayer and a high-school drop-out when he joined the SAP in 1979. 'I needed money to help support my family,' he said.[40] Johannes Koole, a member of the SAP and, like Nofomela, a key member of its death squads, joined the police in 1966. Asked in February 2000 during his appearance before the TRC's Amnesty Committee why he had served the death squads so diligently, and whether he had an opinion about apartheid itself, Koole claimed he had no independent political views. 'I was just doing the job that I was given by the then-government.' Koole's attempt to sound like some banal bureaucrat merely doing his job stumped Ramula Patel, a lawyer for the Amnesty Committee. 'Alright,' said Patel, 'I have no further questions for you except merely to state, Sir, that it almost defies logic for me that you didn't have a political understanding at the time.'[41]

Patel's remark is instructive. Collaborators upset our beliefs about who we are. They do not display the 'political understanding' of apartheid that we assume bound us together. Their lack of this understanding makes them what Mary Douglas calls polluting people – dirt. Douglas argues that to speak about pollution is to speak about morality.[42] It is to speak, in other words, about that which holds a polity together. But, as Sharika Thiranagama and Tobias Kelly ask: 'What if the accusation of treachery reveals not the presence of a venal traitor but the absence of any concrete basis for the people?'[43]

The narrator of Mongane Serote's novel *Revelations* expresses the same anxiety, thus, 'Once when we said "the people", it was almost like saying God. But who are the people?'[44] The ANC itself was aware that there might not be a clearly defined people with an identifiable set of characteristics and interests to bind them together. The organisation understood that the imagined community in whose name it was fighting was in fact far more imagined than community. In a pamphlet published sometime in the 1980s, the ANC blamed black collaborators for delaying the struggle against apartheid: 'We could have long defeated the white oppressors if it was not for the black traitors who are prepared to work for them.'[45]

For the ANC, collaboration was a disease. In a 1986 interview with the ANC journal *Sechaba*, the MK leader Chris Hani defended the use of 'necklacing' to kill suspected collaborators. This was a macabre method whereby individuals accused of collaboration would have tyres doused with petrol placed around their necks or on their bodies and then set alight. 'So the necklace was a weapon devised by the oppressed themselves to remove this cancer from our society, the cancer of collaboration of the puppets. It is not a weapon of the ANC. It is a weapon of the masses themselves to cleanse the townships from the very disruptive and even lethal activities of the puppets and collaborators.'[46] But even such gruesome sanctions as these against collaborators did not stop the fact of complicity and betrayal.

* * *

According to Giliomee, apartheid delivered dynamic economic growth between 1948 and 1994, 'accompanied by the development of a sophisticated infrastructure and a steady increase in the life expectancy of all population groups'.[47] This claim is driven by the assumption that, for all its faults, apartheid delivered the economic goods and created a functional bureaucracy. But apartheid and its bureaucracy were never the well-oiled machine of Giliomee's imagination.[48] The system was messy, inefficient and violent. Apartheid did not work and, as a result, eventually collapsed under its own weight. But the regime did create bureaucratic procedures that governed everything from the destruction of communities to the official sanctioning of political murder. By recounting the history of apartheid as in part a story about collaboration, we can show that the death squads, for example, were not freelance outfits manned by low-level operatives acting on their own. They were organised structures in which operatives had to comply with such bureaucratic commonplaces as filling out travel logs, and submitting claims for subsistence and travel after their missions of murder and mayhem.

By examining collaboration and complicity under apartheid, we are able to challenge another myth that confuses legalism with the rule of law. We are able to appreciate how apartheid's securocrats could amuse themselves 'with all the attributes of protocol and the greatest possible imitation of legality' at the same time as they were dispatching activists to extrajudicial death.[49]

Giliomee says that for all its 'gross disrespect for human rights', apartheid itself was 'never lawless'.[50] In similar vein, the journalist Jacques Pauw has written that apartheid death squads were 'especially effective where South African security legislation, harsh as it was, had failed the authorities'.[51] These claims stem from the mistaken belief that apartheid South Africa was a nation of laws. The claims call to mind an exchange between John Vorster, South Africa's prime minister from 1966 to 1978, and the Paraguayan dictator Alfredo Stroessner. Vorster, on an official visit to South America in August 1975, asked Stroessner why Paraguay had a navy when it had no seaport. Stroessner replied that it was for the same reason that South Africa had a minister of justice.[52] Stroessner was a killer, but even he understood that South Africa's tradition of legal forms was mainly for show. The truth is that apartheid operated without contradiction both within and without its own 'legal' bounds. The killing of political opponents was not, as Pauw suggests, a desperate measure arrived at when all else had failed. It was all of a piece with the bureaucratic and political workings of apartheid. To say, with Stroessner, that apartheid South Africa's 'commitment' to the law was a charade is not to say that apartheid courts did not have an independent existence or that they did not 'work'. They did, and many individuals found effective ways to win a measure of justice in a system stacked against them. In fact, the courts were a site of struggle against apartheid. But we should not confuse form and content.

Speaking about collaboration under apartheid also means examining the role and legacy of the TRC. It means acknowledging the commission's achievements while pointing out its limitations. It is noteworthy that while the commission's Amnesty Committee devoted a special three-day hearing in Pretoria in February 2000 to the story of Mr X1, it treated him as nothing more than a victim of state-sanctioned apartheid violence.[53] This was no isolated oversight. Save for a few special cases, the TRC was not interested in complex individual cases. Mr X1 mattered to the commission only for what his story said about the depravity of the SAP – not for what it said about Mr X1's choices and the conditions under which he made them. But to see Mr X1 as only a 'victim' is to hide from historical view his agency and to diminish his capacity to act, regardless of his circumstances. Being a victim of torture might help explain Mr X1's choices. It did not absolve him of moral responsibility for his subsequent actions.[54]

However, the commission does not deserve much of the criticism to which it has been subjected. In fact, a lot of the criticism has been unfair. Vusi Pikoli, a lawyer and former member of MK, who subsequently headed South Africa's National Prosecuting Authority, commented, 'The TRC only did half the job. It gave us half-truths and half-reconciliation, quarter-reparations but full amnesty.'[55] Pikoli's claim was at best unfair, considering that only 1146 (16 per cent) of the 7115 amnesty applications dealt with by the TRC were approved. The rest were rejected.[56] It was Pikoli's job (as well as that of the government of which he was a part) to prosecute those whose amnesty applications were rejected – and the National Prosecuting Authority chose not to take that road. But the commission did make possible the confessions of killers such as Eugene de Kock, the exposure of how apartheid's repressive machinery worked, and the uncovering of paper trails showing who gave the orders and, in some instances, who pulled the trigger.

While this book owes its existence in a general sense to the TRC, it avoids the simplistic binary of perpetrator and victim favoured by the commission. The TRC worked with four kinds of truth: the factual and forensic; personal and narrative truth; social truth; and healing and restorative truth. This book works with all four. But it does not do so in the hope of finding a bigger truth. There is no truth with a definite article in the world of collaborators. Mr X1 did not live long enough to give his side of the story but, for a man who spent almost his entire adult life in the shadows, he dropped enough clues about how he saw the world. I draw on those clues to tell his story. However, instead of letting Mr X1 (and him alone) stand for collaboration, I place his story in the context of other stories, other truths.

The portrait of Mr X1 needs to be painted on a larger canvas. In the background are some of the major events of the second half of the 20th century: the Cold War, the 1968 student revolts, Pretoria's wars in southern Africa, the fall of the Berlin Wall and the formal end of apartheid. The South Africa in which Mr X1 took up arms against apartheid rule was not only allied to some of the most brutal regimes of the 20th century, it was also such a pariah that even such diverse figures as the liberal philosopher Richard Rorty and

William F. Buckley Jr, the intellectual father of the neoconservative movement in the US, thought the use of violence to fight apartheid justified.[57]

This book is hopefully not the last word on Mr X1. Clare Wald, the controversial writer at the centre of Patrick Flanery's novel *Absolution*, says at one point to Sam Leroux, her would-be biographer, 'You asked the wrong questions. How do you think you can write my life? You have nothing but a skeleton of facts, which you will flesh out with your own conjectures. I have shown you nothing. Because you now think that you know why, at one period in my life, I might have violated my own elaborate ethics, you will paint a pad of muscle and skin, and say, "That is who she is, there, as I've drawn her."'[58] I, too, have nothing but a skeleton of facts, and all I can do to flesh it out is draw on many lives, mine included.

1
The insurgent

Every revolutionary ends by becoming either an oppressor or a heretic.

– Albert Camus[1]

Mr X1 was Glory Lefoshie Sedibe. He was born on 16 May 1953 in the historic gold-mining town of Pilgrim's Rest in what was then the Eastern Transvaal. Sedibe's parents were Ephraim Sedibe, a schoolteacher-turned-mining company clerk, and Lillian Mamoedi Sedibe, a housewife. Sedibe was the second son and third-born of Ephraim and Lillian's nine children. The parents had a fondness for the letter G: they gave each one of their children a name beginning with this letter, starting with Georgina (born in 1947) and ending with Gift (born in 1971). Lillian came from a farming town in the Eastern Transvaal called Frankfort. Ephraim had attended the Botshabelo Training Institute, which was part of a Lutheran mission station near Middelburg, about 170 kilometres east of Johannesburg.

Ephraim Sedibe dropped out of Botshabelo when his family could no longer pay for him to complete his training as a teacher. But the Lutheran missionaries who ran the school in the 1940s considered him so talented that they recommended him for a teaching post at a primary school in Penge, an asbestos-mining town about 400 kilometres north-east of Johannesburg, sometime in the late 1940s.[2] Teaching was then one of the only professions to which black South Africans could aspire, but the pay was poor.[3] In 1949 Ephraim

Sedibe quit teaching for a job as an administrative clerk at Penge mine, where the pay was slightly better.[4] So the Sedibe children were raised in an environment in which their father's white-collar professions (teacher, clerk) made them part of a select social group. But his paltry remuneration (supplemented by inadequate food rations issued by Penge mine) made them no different materially from the rest of the lower-working-class families whose children Ephraim Sedibe had taught and with whom the Sedibe children grew up.

This family background is key to understanding Sedibe and the enormous moral, political and geographic distances he covered in his journey from schoolboy to revolutionary to heretic. Collaborators are made, not born. This means we must understand Sedibe as he, his family and his comrades knew him before his defection. It means understanding Sedibe as a historical actor who did not come fully formed into the world as a traitor, but as a subject who emerged through a series of actions and choices.

Sedibe was 24 when he joined the outlawed ANC in 1977. He had yet to turn 25 when the ANC sent him for specialised intelligence training in East Germany. He was 30 when he went to the Soviet Union for additional intelligence training in 1983, and was 31 when the ANC appointed him head of Military Intelligence for the Transvaal, an important area of responsibility that covered South Africa's commercial capital of Johannesburg and its political capital, Pretoria. Until his defection in August 1986, Sedibe was a charismatic ANC operative and a popular commander of MK known by the *noms de guerre* Comrade September, Lucky Seme and Wally Williams. He also went by the nicknames Dois M and Sebata.[5] When he defected, he had been married for three years to Maria da Conceição, a Mozambican popularly known as Cão, whom he had met in Maputo. The couple had a three-year-old daughter.

What might have become of Sedibe had he not defected? Siphiwe Nyanda and Solly Shoke, Sedibe's contemporaries in MK, went on to become, in succession, head of the South African National Defence Force. Ray Lalla, who trained alongside Sedibe in Moscow in 1983 and worked with him in Mozambique and Swaziland, came to head the Crime Intelligence Division of the South African Police Service under the presidencies of Nelson Mandela and Thabo Mbeki. While we have no way of knowing what would have become of Sedibe, we can speculate, on the basis of the paths taken by some of his closest comrades, that he, too, might have become a senior official in the post-apartheid government, or found his way to becoming a wealthy businessman.

* * *

On 9 August 1986, three days before his defection, Sedibe attended a party at 43 Trelawney Park, a home in Manzini, Swaziland, belonging to the Masilela family and frequented by South African exiles. The partygoers talked politics and about 'home' – meaning South Africa. Save for one failed MK mission into South Africa in 1977, Sedibe had not been home or seen his family in nine years. But he made quite an impression that day with his passion for the land of his birth. Elias Masilela, an ANC sympathiser who attended the party, recalled, 'By the end of that evening, I was convinced that when South Africa became independent, September would be one of the high-ranking intellectuals in the new government.'[6]

Masilela was not alone. Ebrahim Ebrahim, whom Sedibe testified against in 1988, called Sedibe a 'very good comrade'. Thanks in part to Sedibe's testimony, Ebrahim was sentenced in January 1989 to 20 years in prison for high treason, while his co-accused, Maseko and Dladla, got 23 years for high treason and 12 years for terrorism, respectively. But Ebrahim, released in 1991 after the Appeal Court overturned his conviction on the ground that he had been kidnapped from Swaziland and brought illegally to South Africa to stand trial, still remembered Sedibe the revolutionary as 'one of the outstanding comrades' in the ANC.[7] (Dladla and

Maseko died of natural causes in the 1990s.) The ANC veteran George Nene observed: 'He had a good personality – that is why we could mix socially.'[8] Recalling his reaction to Sedibe's defection, Sam Mtileni, a member of MK who worked with Sedibe, said, 'I was stunned to hear that such a dedicated guy [had defected].'[9]

Humphrey Mkhwanazi, one of Sedibe's closest friends in MK, called him a 'trusted military genius'. Mkhwanazi, a trained physicist who went by the *nom de guerre* Gorky, described Sedibe's defection as 'too embarrassing' for the ANC. 'I think September's story is an illustration of how complex this thing [collaboration] was.'[10]

Even Sedibe's enemies in the SAP thought highly of him. Eugene de Kock said, 'MK September was well-known to the security police as an excellent and successful operative: wily, crafty and keeping to all the basic rules of security and counter-surveillance, and hard to catch. Betrayal by his own was the only way to get him. My personal opinion of him was much higher than that granted him by others in the security establishment in South Africa. His personal security police file had one piece of information that made it clear to me that he was absolutely different from all the other ANC members operating in Swaziland or elsewhere. It said: "He cares greatly for his operators and agents and takes good care of them." To me, he was a man to respect, even as an enemy.'[11]

For his part, when he was asked under cross-examination in the 1988 trial against Dladla, Ebrahim and Maseko to explain his defection, Sedibe would only say, 'I am now a policeman.' He would not answer questions about whether he still believed in what the ANC stood for.[12] Yet Sebide, as Mr X1, did tell the court about the circumstances that led him down the path of insurgency. It all began with his elder brother, Gilbert Kaborone Sedibe, nicknamed KK after Kenneth Kaunda, the Zambian leader whom Kaborone's classmates at the University of the North (also known as Turfloop) said he resembled.

Kaborone, Ephraim and Lillian's second child and eldest son, was born in Pilgrim's Rest on 23 October 1950. He matriculated in

1971 at Tutulane High School in Pietersburg in what was then the Northern Transvaal. In 1973 he began studying for a law degree at Turfloop. In September 1974 he was elected president of Turfloop's Students' Representative Council.

Kaborone belonged to the 1968 generation. He was a part of what Václav Havel, the Czech dissident-turned-statesman, called a 'decade of cultural, spiritual, and social rebellion against all establishments'.[13] As Kaborone himself put it when I interviewed him in 2014, 'We were radical. Anything that was harassing the status quo, we were for it.'[14] It was in that spirit of rebellion that in 1974 Kaborone, in his capacity as president of the students' council, proposed a student rally to celebrate the collapse of Portuguese rule in Africa. The Portuguese military had decided, following its coup in April 1974 against the authoritarian Estado Novo regime, to grant independence to Portugal's colonies, including Angola and Mozambique. The handover of power to the Mozambican Liberation Front, known by its Portuguese acronym Frelimo, was agreed to in terms of the Lusaka Accord of 7 September 1974. Sedibe proposed the rally for 25 September.

Kaborone's proposal for what became known as the 'Viva Frelimo' rally was taken up by university students aligned to the Black Consciousness Movement in other parts of South Africa, notably Durban. It became a national movement of sorts. As Kaborone explained in 1975 during a trial in which he and eight other members of the Black Consciousness Movement-aligned Black People's Convention and the South African Students' Organisation (Saso) were charged with terrorism for organising the rallies despite a government ban, 'it was really something to be happy about because for instance we were feeling really that Black people in Mozambique, after about 300 years of oppression, now they had a chance of being given the time to rule themselves. It was something of general happiness on the campus, so that was how the students received my message of holding the rally.'[15]

Asked in court if he had held any strong political views prior to going to university, Kaborone answered, 'None at all.'[16] So what had radicalised him? Kaborone replied that going to university had opened his eyes. 'I began to see the problems that were really facing our community, that is the Black community, through the problems of my father in particular.' Although Penge mine gave Ephraim Sedibe food rations to supplement his income, that still was not enough and the old man found it 'difficult to pay for school' for his children.[17] Kaborone testified that his political development also led him to think seriously about his relationship with whites, especially those who had taught him at Tutulane High School in Pietersburg. 'The attitude of the White staff towards Blacks, it was really very distressing as far as I was concerned.' He remembered in particular one white teacher with a fondness for lashing black girls on the buttocks.[18]

Kaborone and his co-accused were found guilty of terrorism on 21 December 1976, after a trial lasting five months, and given sentences ranging from five to ten years on Robben Island. Kaborone received five years. In a written plea prepared in response to the charge against him, he declared: 'On the face of the charge sheet, it is beyond any reasonable doubt that not only the Black Consciousness Movement but the whole Black Community in South Africa is on trial. This indictment is one against the freedom of my father, against the liberation of my mother, against the birthright of my brothers and sisters and against the accordance to them of recognition and humane [*sic*] dignity. This is an evil indictment. It is an indictment against God for having created me black. It is an indictment against Christ for having said that I am a free man.'[19]

In her study of the 1968 student protesters in Turin, Luisa Passerini remarked that the Italian student movement 'had speech at its centre'.[20] The same could be said of the South African students' movement. You hear the centrality of speech in Kaborone's plea, complete with its rhetorical flourishes. 'I am being charged because the weeping and lamenting of my mother urge me to stand up and defend her ebony womanhood. I am being charged for declaring the dire desire of my brothers and sisters for human dignity for liberation from oppression and for saying that my uncles in the mines, in the factories and in the building industries should be paid at least wages enough to buy their meagre food, and for demanding the right of my aunt in the kitchen to stay with the children of her Black womb; yes, I am being charged for demanding our rights as Blacks to human life, the right of my people for respect and liberation from racist oppression. I am not here because I am a terrorist. I am here basically because I am answering the call to struggle for human dignity.'[21]

Kaborone stated in his plea, 'Black Consciousness calls upon me to declare solidarity with the oppressed of this country and to struggle for their liberation. It says to me: "Blackman, you're on your own, nobody can break the shackles of your oppression."'

Kaborone's plea did not sway the court. But his prison sentence left a lasting impression on his younger brother. During his 1988 testimony against Dladla, Ebrahim and Maseko, Sedibe recalled that the five-year sentence against his brother, the first person in the family to go to university, left him 'heart sore'.[22] Kaborone spent 15 months in detention prior to his conviction. After he was sentenced, Glory visited him in prison. Kaborone recalled, 'He spoke to me about leaving [South Africa]. He told me he would leave the first chance he got. He said there was no alternative.'[23]

* * *

As the historian Kirsten Weld remarks, 'one must not confuse the rich life of a person with its thin archival record – its paper cadaver'.[24] Weld's observation is certainly apt when we look at the dry timeline constructed by the Security Branch to trace Sedibe's movements from the time he went into exile in 1977 to his return to South Africa in 1986.[25] The timeline emerged from a series of interrogation sessions that began immediately after Sedibe's defection in August 1986. When the police drew up Sedibe's timeline, they were following a particular archival logic, 'one of surveillance, social control, and ideological management'. This was a 'Cold War-inflected logic that used archives as a weapon against enemies of the state'.[26] The timeline tracks Sedibe's every move, but it is lifeless. It strips his life of substance, even though he was part of a conflict that cost thousands of lives across southern Africa. Yet, reading the timeline in the light of the collapse of apartheid, we cannot help applying another view, 'one of democratic opening, historical memory' and the pursuit of justice.[27] Applying the second logic to the timeline also means remembering the intimacy at the heart of Sedibe's decision, fresh from the sentencing of his brother, to forsake his family and go into exile.

According to the police timeline, Sedibe's political travels began in January 1977 when he illegally crossed the fence near the Josefsdal border post into Swaziland, one of the 'main battlegrounds on which the South African liberation struggle was fought'.[28] In April 1977 Sedibe left Swaziland for Matola, a suburb on the outskirts of Maputo, the capital of Mozambique. Matola was an important base of operations for the ANC: it boasted a number of properties used by the ANC as residences and transit points for members moving in and out of southern Africa. In May 1977 Sedibe moved to Dar es Salaam in Tanzania for unspecified medical attention. In June 1977 he moved to the ANC's Engineering transit camp in Angola, where his military training began in earnest. The camp, near the Angolan capital of Luanda, had been opened in late 1976 and was one of 12 ANC camps established in Angola between 1976 and 1981.[29]

Between June and December 1977, Sedibe trained at Teterow in East Germany as part of an elite group of MK volunteers who received training at a secret base about 50 kilometres from the port of Rostock on the Baltic Sea. In December 1977 Sedibe infiltrated South Africa for a day before retreating back to Mozambique. From the rest of December 1977 to February 1978, Sedibe was at the ANC's Quibaxe camp in Angola. He moved from Quibaxe to Funda camp, also in Angola, in February 1978 and was there for a month.

Between March 1978 and December 1978, Sedibe was stationed in Maputo as part of what the ANC called its Transvaal rural machinery – those units focused on military and political operations in Transvaal's farming areas. He was in Maputo between December 1978 and February 1980. Between February 1980 and September 1983, he operated between Mozambique and Swaziland. Between September 1983 and December 1983, he was part of a small group of MK operatives, including Ray Lalla, James Ngculu, Bobby Patel and Sue Rabkin, sent to Moscow for specialised training. He was in Mozambique between January and April 1984 and then moved to the ANC's headquarters in Lusaka, Zambia. After being appointed head of ANC Military Intelligence for the Transvaal, he moved to Swaziland in July 1984 and remained there until January 1985.

He was in Maputo between January and August 1985. He then returned to Swaziland in August 1985 (but continued to shuttle illegally back and forth between Swaziland and Mozambique) and was in Swaziland in August 1986 when he defected. That is where the timeline leaves his movements.

In truth, Sedibe's decision to go into exile via Swaziland was not random. He made his move in January 1977 after doing his research and having collected intelligence from migrant labourers and the many locals who were 'citizens of the blurred border, able to live within the very thickness of the line drawn on the map'.[30]

After arriving in Swaziland, he registered as a refugee with the Royal Swazi Police as required by the law in Swaziland and was sent to the Mawelawela refugee camp near Manzini, where he was officially recruited into the ANC. To mark Sedibe's formal entry into the ANC, Mongameli Johnson Tshali, an MK commander who went by the *nom de guerre* Lennox Lagu, gave Sedibe the first of his various MK names, one by which many in the ANC would know him: Comrade September.[31]

It was not inevitable that Sedibe would choose life as an insurgent over life as a student. Mzwakhe Ndlela, who joined the ANC in exile in the 1980s, commented, 'It is seldom remembered that not everyone who joined the ANC joined MK.'[32] Sedibe left South Africa in the hope of furthering his studies. But he opted for the military route after hearing one Jacob Zuma, a member of MK and a charismatic raconteur, give a lecture on South African politics.[33] Zuma, the son of a domestic worker whose father had died when Zuma was an infant, had little formal education when he was sent to Robben Island in 1963. But there he grew into one of the ANC's leaders. Ebrahim Ebrahim, who shared a cell with Zuma for ten years, helped teach him to read and write English. 'He had had no formal education,' Ebrahim recalled, 'but I have to say that he was exceptional. In six months he was reading Tolstoy.'[34]

Thula Simpson has written insightfully about the journey into exile, via Swaziland, that a volunteer like Sedibe would have undertaken.[35] Sedibe crossed into Mozambique in April 1977, most likely by jumping over the Lomahasha–Namaacha border fence – the main route for ANC operatives leaving or entering Swaziland.[36] He would most likely have been travelling with a group of fellow recruits and they would have been led by ANC escorts. The escorts would have driven the recruits over 80 kilometres on a 'poorly maintained road manned by a couple of Mozambican army checkpoints' to Maputo.[37] Sedibe would have stayed (as confirmed by the police timeline) at an ANC transit house in Matola before his transfer to Tanzania and, from there, to Angola.

We can reconstruct Sedibe's life in Angola, his time in East Germany and in the Soviet Union from several sources. James Ngculu, an MK recruit who joined the ANC at about the same time as Sedibe and trained in some of the same places, remembered that while there was always a shortage of food in ANC camps in Angola, the camaraderie among the recruits more than made up for their deprivations.[38] These being military camps, life was organised around physical exercise, military training, political instruction, drills and guard duty. Guard duties were necessary but unpopular given the fact that Angola was in the midst of a civil war in which the ANC backed the ruling People's Movement for the Liberation of

Angola (MPLA), while South Africa supported the rival National Union for the Total Independence of Angola (Unita).

The ANC tried to turn the camps into havens for intellectual exchange, complete with news monitoring services and libraries. On 2 November 1983, for example, Gladman Sello, a member of the ANC's Information Office in Luanda, wrote to Mike Terry, the secretary of the Anti-Apartheid Movement in London: 'Would you be so kind as to send us some novels, we like to encourage our comrades to read, we have some material but we would like to have something for leisure time, like love stories and so on.' Sello requested the following books: *The experiment* by Patrick Skene Catling, *Alfie darling* by Bill Naughton, *Georgy girl* by Margaret Forster, *Cocksure* by Mordecai Richler, *The naked and the dead* and *An American dream*, both novels by Norman Mailer, and *Black spring* by Henry Miller. Sello also asked for Bronislaw Malinowski's *Sex and repression in savage society*.[39]

Life in MK camps was difficult, but filled with purpose. The thousands of recruits who streamed into the camps believed they were changing the world.[40] MK member Sam Mtileni said Sedibe liked to read. 'He liked education.'[41]

We know from Ngculu and his fellow MK insurgent Neo Potsane, two of those chosen for specialised training in East Germany, about life at the Teterow military camp.[42] Here, trainees were housed in a double-storey building with a basement. They slept two to a room. No smoking was allowed.[43] Life at Teterow consisted of classes on the history of South Africa and the ANC conducted by, among others, the ANC cadres Pallo Jordan, Aziz Pahad and Essop Pahad, as well as military and physical drills held in the surrounding countryside by East German instructors with the aid of German-speaking MK veterans as translators. Recalling his time at Teterow, which trained about a thousand MK insurgents from the 1970s to 1990,[44] Ngculu wrote, 'Generally, people who were trained in East Germany came back very fit and with a strong sense of discipline.'[45] Those sent to Teterow were considered the cream of MK and were earmarked for important tasks.

The police timeline records Sedibe as being in Mozambique between December 1978 and February 1980, and says that he operated from there between February 1980 and September 1983. But it leaves out the fact that Sedibe narrowly avoided death when the South African Defence Force (SADF) attacked ANC properties in Matola on 30 January 1981. On this occasion the South African raiders killed 12 people and abducted three ANC members, including Vuyani Mavuso, who was killed by the Security Branch sometime in late 1981 when he refused to collaborate. Sedibe was injured in the thigh.

When the timeline notes that Sedibe left Mozambique for Zambia in April 1984, it does not explain that this was done involuntarily. Sedibe was among the ANC members unceremoniously kicked out of Mozambique after the Mozambican president, Samora Machel, signed the Nkomati Accord with his South African counterpart, P.W. Botha, on 16 March 1984.

The accord and the resulting expulsions were a serious blow to the ANC and to the morale of its members. Ray Lalla, who operated between Mozambique and Swaziland as an MK intelligence operative, commented, 'Nkomati unsettled a lot of people.' Speaking about Sedibe in particular, Lalla said, 'At some stage I got the feeling he was not convinced we would ever go home.'[46] The journalist Michael Wolfers, who attended the signing ceremony, wrote that under the accord, 'neither territory could be used for attacks against the other'.[47] The South Africans pressed for the agreement as part of a regional strategy to recreate the territorial buffer that apartheid South Africa had enjoyed until the collapse of the Portuguese colonies. As Wolfers wrote, 'South Africa went to Nkomati to try to close doors to the ANC, not to Mozambique. Mozambique went to Nkomati to try to stem the South African attacks and the infiltration by South Africa of MNR [Mozambican National Resistance, or Renamo] bandits.'[48] But the South Africans, who had subjected Mozambique to cross-border raids and terrorism by proxy through Renamo, had no intention of keeping their end of the bargain. In fact, while the Mozambicans went out of their way to respect the terms of the accord, forcibly ejecting ANC members from Mozambique at times, the South Africans were not faithful to their promises. Wolfers remarked that Machel made the mistake of attributing 'to the South African leaders a higher morality than they were willing or capable of pursuing'.[49]

When Sedibe switched sides, he had been a member of the ANC and MK for nine years. When he died mysteriously on 20 March 1994 at his suburban home outside Pretoria, at the age of 40, he had been working for the apartheid Security Branch and Military Intelligence for almost eight years – one shy of his time in the ANC. Various reasons have been given for his death. James Ngculu said Sedibe was 'suspected to have been poisoned by the security forces'.[50] Eugene de Kock claimed Sedibe was killed with a poison that mimicked the symptoms of hepatitis B.[51] Jacques Pauw wrote that Sedibe suffered a heart attack.[52] When Sedibe was reunited with his wife and their daughter in Piet Retief in October 1986, two months after his defection, one of the first things he said to her, as she recounted in Mozambican Portuguese, was, '*Eu estou doente, eu estou com problemas de coração*' (I am ill, I have heart problems).[53]

Sedibe's friend Humphrey Mkhwanazi confirmed that Sedibe had a weak heart. 'Sometimes we would be drinking and September would get heart palpitations.'[54] When Sedibe died, the state pathologist who conducted his autopsy identified his weak heart as a contributing factor. The insurance company with which Sedibe had a life policy used the pathologist's finding to refuse to pay out, claiming he had failed to disclose a pre-existing condition.[55] According to his brother, 'The doctor [who attended to Sedibe's corpse] had written that he had [had] a heart problem.'[56] Kaborone accused the doctor of foul play. 'He was a Boer guy working with the police. He must have known that my brother had been poisoned.'

Kaborone claimed that Sedibe had every reason to enjoy life. 'He was happy about the transition. He was busy with Joe Nhlanhla [the ANC's head of intelligence and democratic South Africa's first minister of intelligence].' Ebrahim confirmed this, saying, 'When we were unbanned, he started to make contact to say he wanted to talk to us. But he died suddenly.'[57] Kaborone recalled that his younger brother had told him, '"They want me back. They want information from me. They know there are people in the ANC working with the Boers."'[58] Sedibe did not live long enough to test whether these invitations were genuine.

It is also possible that Sedibe, who by some accounts was chronically depressed, died from alcohol poisoning. By the time of his death – in the presence of Ção and their two daughters at home in the formerly whites-only municipality of Verwoerdburg – Sedibe was drinking about three 750ml bottles of vodka a day.[59] Speaking of Sedibe's last days, his widow said, '*Ele não comia. So bebia. Era whiskey. Era vinho. Era cerveja. Era gin.*' (He would not eat. Only drink. It was whiskey. It was wine. It was beer. It was gin.) When he died, Sedibe had recently returned from Mozambique, where he had gone to seek treatment for his drinking problem. Raised a Lutheran, Sedibe had also been looking for a new church to join. In fact, one of his fellow askaris had taken him to the Zion Christian Church (ZCC), the biggest independent church in southern Africa.[60] He was, it seemed, looking for a new place in a fast-changing South Africa.

When Sedibe died, his first defining cause – fighting *against* apartheid – was about to triumph, and his second – fighting *for* apartheid – was about to lose. The ANC, which had been unbanned in February 1990, was on the verge of winning the elections that would usher in a nonracial democracy. Sedibe had fought for so long on both sides of the political divide that it could safely be said that he knew too much about the skeletons in both closets. He knew about Security Branch and Military Intelligence agents in the ANC. In fact, he had helped recruit some of them.

According to De Kock, Sedibe was poisoned by a former Military Intelligence officer who then went on to reinvent himself as a security and risk analyst advising corporations about investing in Africa. The officer killed Sedibe to protect his ANC agents. These agents returned the favour by protecting their former handler from possible prosecution by the post-apartheid government.[61]

So it was that their secrets gained an afterlife in post-apartheid South Africa.

2

The askari

ADVOCATE LEONARD GERING: How do you spell Ascari?
AARON MPOPO MTHEMBU: *S-c-a-r-e*.
GERING: Is this – what language is this word?
MTHEMBU: I think it is English.
JUDGE JOOS HEFER: Can you perhaps assist Mr Prosecutor?
PROSECUTOR: This is the name that is known by the White members of the security force. I don't know if the Black members ...
HEFER: Can you spell the name?
PROSECUTOR: *A-s-c-a-r-i-s*. Or *i-e-s*. I am not sure if it is *i* or *i-e*.[1]

When Sedibe took the stand in February 1988 for a marathon six weeks as Mr X1,[2] he was then a 'rehabilitated terrorist' being used by the South African state to put away three unrehabilitated terrorists. By employing Sedibe as a state witness, prosecutors Harry Prinsloo and Louisa van der Walt were relying on one of the oldest practices in English common law, itself one of the principal sources of law in South Africa. In English common law, the use of 'accomplice evidence' goes back centuries.[3] It even enjoyed the support of the philosopher Jeremy Bentham, who argued that 'if there be no other means, this method is good; since the impunity of a single criminal is a less evil than the impunity of many'.[4] South Africa had of course used 'rehabilitated terrorists' before, most famously against Mandela and other founder members of MK in the Rivonia Trial in 1963–1964. In that trial, the state prosecutor, Percy Yutar, relied on Mr X (Bruno Mtolo), Mr Y (Cyril Davids) and Mr Z (Patrick Mthembu) to produce accomplice evidence against the ten accused. Mtolo later claimed that he turned against his comrades because he could not stand the thought of 'dying for a stupid cause'.[5]

In its use of 'rehabilitated terrorists', South Africa appears to have borrowed from the government of Italy, which was counted among apartheid's friends in Europe. The Italians used such individuals to devastating effect against the urban guerrilla groups known as the Red Brigades in the 1970s.[6] Captured Red Brigade members who agreed to testify against former comrades in return for immunity from prosecution were officially called 'repentant terrorists'. This designation was closer to the South African idea of a 'rehabilitated terrorist' than to the British concept of a 'converted terrorist', invoked during the Troubles in Northern Ireland. The latter concept explicitly downplayed a witness's motivation and focused instead on using his or her testimony to secure a conviction. British officials acknowledged that many such witnesses were motivated by nothing more than the wish to 'save their own skins'.[7] The South African and Italian governments, in contrast, saw the rehabilitation of a 'terrorist' in grand terms as a 'public rejection of the old life coupled with the act of repentance'.[8] They also saw this as having the additional benefit of legitimising the state while delegitimising their opponents.

But Sedibe was more than a turncoat. He became an *askari*. Kiarie Wanjogu, who teaches Swahili at Yale University, says that the word 'askari' means police in Swahili. Ann Biersteker, who has taught Swahili and African literature at Yale and Michigan State universities, believes the term is an Arabic borrowing into Swahili that historically meant soldier, policeman or guard. In her understanding, the term, which now usually means security guard, has no racial connotations.[9] According to the historian Stephen Ellis, British forces acquired the word in the 'Mau Mau insurgency and transmitted [it] via Rhodesian officers to the South African Police'.[10]

By the time the word entered South Africa's lexicon of terror in the 1970s, it referred to ANC and Pan Africanist Congress (PAC) members who, through voluntary defection or torture, had switched sides to fight against their former comrades as part of a domestic counterinsurgency campaign. By 1993, when the askari project came to a formal end as apartheid was dismantled, there were between 100 and 300 men (and a handful of women) classified as askaris on the SAP payroll. After defecting from the liberation movements, many had attended the segregated Hammanskraal Police College for conversion into 'proper' police officers.[11]

At its height, the ANC in exile numbered no more than 12,000 members. Not all of these were combatants and, among the soldiers, not all were capable of military operations.[12] We might be tempted to conclude, then, that securing an estimated 300 askaris out of about 12,000 ANC members over 14 years, which is how long the askari project lasted, reflects poorly on the whole business.[13] That would be a mistake. The askari operation was never about numbers. It was about finding quick and cost-effective ways to defend apartheid.

The Security Branch had established the askari project in 1979, using a handful of defectors and captured ANC and PAC insurgents, as part of a campaign to improve South Africa's domestic counterinsurgency capabilities. The first recruits were housed at Vlakplaas, a 44-hectare farm along the Hennops River, west of Pretoria, bought specially for this purpose. The first askaris were treated as informers and paid about R200 from a secret police fund.[14] When Tlhomedi Ephraim Mfalapitsa became an askari in January 1982, a month after defecting from the ANC, the Security Branch gave him new clothes, food rations and 'some few hundred rands' as a stipend. At the end of January 1982, the Security Branch changed the askaris' status from informers to police officers by absorbing them into the police force proper at salaries ranging, according to Mfalapitsa, from R600 to R700 a month.[15]

Save for Colonel Johan Viktor, its founding commander, Vlakplaas was at first an all-black unit. Viktor was replaced in August 1980 by Captain Dirk Coetzee, a 'gangster of practically

Olympic achievements'.[16] Coetzee was demoted at the end of 1981 for passing around pornographic material among his colleagues – but not before killing a number of anti-apartheid activists on behalf of a grateful government. It was acceptable to kill for God and Country – but definitely not OK to peddle smut. In August 1981 a number of white policemen, all veterans of South Africa's counterinsurgencies in Rhodesia and South West Africa (Namibia), were transferred to Vlakplaas. The askaris on the farm were divided into four groups, each led by a white officer. Vlakplaas fell under Section C, the counter-terrorism arm of the Security Branch. By 1982 Vlakplaas and its askaris were considered the 'special forces' of the Security Branch.[17]

The Security Branch referred to Vlakplaas as a rehabilitation centre for former terrorists. But, as the TRC observed, 'there is no sign that any rehabilitation took place'.[18] Goodman Twala, an MK operative who became an askari in January 1986, said his police interrogators offered to take him to a 'rehabilitation centre', meaning Vlakplaas, if he agreed to defect. Asked what he did at Vlakplaas, Twala replied, 'I did not do anything specific there, except that it was work.'[19]

Twala was trying to make 'working' at Vlakplaas sound banal. It was anything but. When Almond Nofomela joined Vlakplaas in December 1980, shortly after his graduation from the Hammanskraal Police College, he, his fellow officers and the askaris at Vlakplaas received intensive training in counterinsurgency techniques. Nofomela recalled, 'It was a physical training and theory in how should you ambush, how should you kidnap and how should you shoot and so on.'[20]

According to Nofomela, Vlakplaas operatives were taught that 'whenever we shoot we shoot from the chest and to the head'. They were also instructed on how to use weapons made in the Eastern bloc and to handle knives of different lengths. 'Captain [Dirk] Coetzee emphasised the fact that when we, for instance, when we kidnap at times, we should use a knife to injure a person so that we would be in a position to overpower him, not to kill him and so on.'[21] Nofomela and his colleagues first applied their training on 19 November 1981 when they ambushed and killed Griffiths Mxenge, a lawyer and underground ANC operative, in Umlazi, near Durban. Nofomela, fellow cop David Tshikalanga and askaris Brian Ngqulunga and Joe Mamasela butchered Mxenge near a stadium in Umlazi. Using knives to make the killing look like a robbery, they almost severed Mxenge's head. They then stole his car, wristwatch and leather jacket as trophies.

Some claim that the askari project did not begin as a deliberate tool of state violence. Chris Mosiane, an MK operative who became an askari in 1984 following his abduction from a Swaziland jail by the Security Branch, stated, 'In the initial stages askaris were used as police dogs to sniff out insurgents with white SB [Security Branch members] as their handlers. Black SB were used to monitor the askaris.'[22] But from the very beginning askaris always did more than track their former comrades. They served as agents provocateurs, assassins, bounty hunters, double agents, informers, intelligence analysts, spies and, of course, state witnesses. Some even ran agents within the ANC and PAC, and many mounted false-flag operations, such as recruiting unsuspecting youths and then giving them booby-trapped explosives, to discredit the anti-apartheid organisations. They were assisted in the performance of their duties by a network of apartheid agents in both the ANC and PAC.

When, in January 2014, I interviewed a former askari whom I will call Judas Mpho Tladi, I asked about the biggest surprise he experienced after he became an askari in January 1988. Tladi said it was finding out just who in the ANC was in the pay of the South African police and spy agencies.[23] Tladi had operated in the ANC underground in Swaziland and specialised in illegal border crossings. His job included moving ANC members in and out of Swaziland and Mozambique. Tladi's ANC network had depended on people on both sides of the South Africa–Swaziland border. Tladi revealed that a woman named Jane Mtshali (not her real name), who had been part of his ANC network in Piet Retief, had in fact been working for the Security Branch – something he discovered only after he became an askari. When I heard this, it was my turn to be surprised.

I had met Mtshali in 2009 during a research trip to a small township outside Piet Retief. Mtshali and her fellow ANC councillors in the local municipality had been kicked out of office in a wave of protests that rocked South Africa after Jacob Zuma became South Africa's president in May 2009.[24] Mtshali boasted during our interview that, unlike the young protesters who had kicked her out of office and torched her house, she had paid her dues in the struggle. She had been a member of the ANC underground in Piet Retief, responsible for moving insurgents in and out of South Africa. Few of the protesters who had driven her out of her home are likely to have known this, and certainly none of those I interviewed suggested at the time that Mtshali might have been an apartheid agent. She offered to take me to the border area to show me where she would ferry insurgents across. I never took her up on her offer.

* * *

When I interviewed Eugene de Kock, the last commander of Vlakplaas, at Pretoria Central Prison in February 2013, I asked him to define an askari. 'A traitor,' he said.[25] De Kock, who commanded Glory Sedibe at Vlakplaas for four years after the latter's defection, insisted that Sedibe was not an askari. 'I never used him as an askari. I treated him like an officer.' When, between May 2013 and January 2014, I spoke to five former askaris, I would start our conversations by asking them to define the word 'askari', and whether they were comfortable with my using it to refer to them. Delilah Rekisa (not her real name), the only female askari I was able to interview, preferred the term 'cadre'.[26] Gregory Sibusiso Radebe, whom I interviewed in person twice at the Johannesburg Prison in May 2013, said, 'To my knowledge, the word was coined to derogatorily refer to an ex-member of the revolutionary armies [the ANC's MK or the PAC's Apla, the Azanian People's Liberation Army] who joined the apartheid regime's Security Branch counterinsurgency unit based at Vlakplaas.'[27] Not everyone could become an askari. One needed to have been a trained insurgent before one could become a counterinsurgent.

I asked Radebe if there was a better word than 'askari' to use to refer to people in his category. He replied, 'I do not know if there is a "better" word to use because that has never been a matter of choice to start with.' Asked what it took to make an askari, Radebe said, 'One had to have been a member of either MK or Apla and renounce these organisations to be a member of that unit [Vlakplaas].' Some did so voluntarily on getting back to South Africa. Others were arrested by apartheid security forces and then made to work against their former comrades, or 'kidnapped from neighbouring countries and brought back to South Africa and then forced to join Vlakplaas'. Some were 'handed over to South Africa by Swazi security forces who were in the payroll of the South African security forces'. Asked to describe the average askari, Radebe replied, 'Ordinary South Africans like you see every day were there. There were also guys of notable intelligence. It was your overall mix of South Africans, and that probably is what made that unit the spearhead in the Security Branch's fight against the ANC. I think it was the only unit that could blend in anywhere in the country and bring information in the shortest time possible.'

When I met Almond Nofomela in January 2014, he threatened to sue anyone who referred to him as an askari. 'I was never an askari,' he declared.[28] This was true: he was a policeman and, like many cops who worked with askaris, he disdained them. They were, after all, traitors, people of dubious loyalties. Except for Joe Mamasela, askaris were serious drunkards, something that did not endear them to the teetotaller Nofomela. He worked closely and socialised with askaris but he was not one of them. However, Nofomela was not averse to using alcohol against political targets.

A former activist from Piet Retief said Nofomela used to frequent a shebeen called Mary's Place in the area. Nofomela and a team of askaris led patrons, some of whom were underground ANC activists, to believe that they were members of the police Liquor Squad, suggesting that the shebeen was 'safe' from police raids.[29] 'They also bought a lot of liquor for the patrons. Unfortunately, I was one of them,' the activist recalled with some embarrassment.[30] Nofomela's cover was so intact that he even played for Thokozani All Blacks, one of the top soccer teams in Piet Retief, and used that as a cover for his activities, claiming he was going away for games when in fact he was embarking on his missions of murder.

Nicknamed Kaizer for his footballing prowess, Nofomela told me that when at a shebeen, he would always order Krest Ginger Ale, a popular South African soda that looks like beer, pretending to get drunk as he eavesdropped on conversations between activists.[31] But he was no askari. His 'threat' to sue for defamation confirmed the moral taint associated with the word. Not even a convicted killer like Nofomela, who spent 22 years in jail for murder and robbery, wanted to be called an askari.

Askaris were a breed apart. They were lethal because, as former freedom fighters, they were fluent in the rhetoric of revolution. They could identify activists in any locality and knew how to trade in fictions of racial solidarity. These fictions were assumptions founded on the myth that because every black person was formally a victim of apartheid, every black person was by definition opposed to apartheid. Askaris tapped into the incredulity of those who 'would never understand how a black South African could betray his own people, how a person could choose to help the vicious oppressor against the oppressed'.[32] Askaris took advantage of such naivety. They insinuated themselves into activist groups and underground networks. Radebe commented, without irony, 'These guys [askaris] were not impostors. They came from the outside [exile]. He knows exactly what to say. He speaks the language.'[33]

In its 14-year history, Vlakplaas had only two white askaris,

Hugh Lugg and Ronald Tokarev Bezuidenhout. Lugg was a British-born anti-apartheid activist who was part of a whites-only MK unit. The unit was made up of four men and one woman – Damian de Lange, Ian Robertson, Paul Annegarn, Lugg and Susan Westcott – and Lugg defected to the police after he fell out with one of his comrades, allegedly over a woman. Bezuidenhout was a former member of the South African Defence Force who had joined the ANC but then defected to the Security Branch in the late 1980s.

Askaris used intimacy to their advantage. Tlhomedi Ephraim Mfalapitsa, who grew up in Kagiso, a township outside Krugersdorp, west of Johannesburg, left South Africa via Botswana in the wake of the June 1976 student rebellion to join the ANC. He was accompanied by two childhood friends, both brothers from the Musi family. The three friends were so close that, as Mfalapitsa put it, 'I was actually like a member of the family in Musi's family.'[34] Mfalapitsa received military training at Novo Catengue, an ANC camp in Angola, and at Teterow. After his return from East Germany, he and one of the Musi brothers operated briefly from Botswana. The two were arrested in that country, declared prohibited immigrants and deported to Zambia. In Lusaka, Mfalapitsa was stationed at MK's headquarters, working alongside and living with the second of the Musi brothers.

Mfalapitsa, possibly the only person to apply to the TRC for amnesty for crimes committed both as an MK operative and an askari, defected to the SAP in November 1981 after participating in ANC torture of a man suspected of being an apartheid agent in Lusaka. He joined Vlakplaas in January 1982. 'Yes, I was referred to as an askari or a former terrorist or a source, or all of those names,' Mfalapitsa told a TRC Amnesty Committee hearing in Johannesburg on 4 May 1999. He had applied for amnesty in what was called the Cosas Four case, involving Zandisile Musi, younger brother of the two Musi boys who had gone into exile with Mfalapitsa in 1976. The Cosas Four case dated back to February 1982, a month into Mfalapitsa's entry into Vlakplaas. Mfalapitsa had gone to his family home in Kagiso and, while there, had visited the neighbouring Musi household. The Musis knew that Mfalapitsa had gone into exile with their two sons, but they did not know that he had defected and was working for the Security Branch at Vlakplaas.

Zandisile Musi, 18 at the time, was a student activist. He whispered to Mfalapitsa that he and a group of activist friends wanted to leave South Africa for military training abroad. He asked if Mfalapitsa could help take them out of the country. Mfalapitsa, thinking this was a trap set by his new bosses at Vlakplaas to test his loyalty, reported Zandisile Musi's request to Captain Jan Carel Coetzee, who headed Vlakplaas from 1981 to 1983, and Brigadier Willem Schoon, commander of C-Section. Coetzee and Schoon ordered Mfalapitsa to cultivate Zandisile and his friends and to offer them military training inside South Africa. Zandisile Musi trusted Mfalapitsa and regarded him as a brother. As Mfalapitsa said of his relationship with the Musis, 'it was very intimate'.

On 15 February 1982 Mfalapitsa, accompanied by the askari Joe Mamasela, posing as a fellow MK operative, fetched Musi and his friends Eustice Bimbo Madikela, Fanyana Nhlapo and Ntshingo Mataboge from outside Leratong Hospital in Kagiso. Mfalapitsa and Mamasela drove the four boys to a disused mine shaft near Krugersdorp to begin their 'training'. Unbeknown to the boys, the Security Branch had booby-trapped the mine shaft with explosives. With Mamasela standing sentry outside, Mfalapitsa led the four boys inside. He showed them a firearm and a hand grenade and told them to wait while he went back to fetch more weapons. No sooner had Mfalapitsa stepped outside than Musi, the only survivor of the incident, heard an explosion. His three friends died instantly. Musi was taken to hospital and later detained by the police. Mfalapitsa received a R1000 'bonus' from his bosses at Vlakplaas for the mission.

Asked during his public testimony before the TRC Amnesty Committee if he had anything to say to Zandisile Musi, who was in the audience, Mfalapitsa declared, 'I'm a black man, you're a black man. And I do appreciate that you are, you are intensely and profoundly aggrieved by what subsequently aspired [*sic*] from my involvement in the struggle of the past and my involvement in the situation in South Africa. But I would like to appeal that you look at this from a broader context and from the point of view of the situation in which I was at that point.'[35]

Mfalapitsa was trying to make an argument for complexity. More than once during his testimony, he referred to the 'broader context' of South Africa's political conflict, asking that his actions be understood within it. Mfalapitsa tried to elevate his actions away from the personal to something more general. Casting himself as a victim, he said, 'I was also caught up in this paradox of history. I was caught up in this situation in which the youth of South Africa were finding it difficult to make sense of their existence.'

Mfalapitsa testified that even though the police paid him R1000 for his role in the mission, he had not carried it out for money or for reasons of self-preservation. But Zandisile Musi would not buy this claim.

Asked to respond to Mfalapitsa's testimony, Musi brought matters back to the personal. Speaking through a Xhosa interpreter, he said, 'Perhaps for them to trust him he had to do this, and he did this to a family that he knew very well and he said that family was sympathising with the ANC. That action, that act in itself was going to make the police trust him.'

Peter Moleke Lengene, a student leader in Soweto and one of the organisers of the 1976 uprising, became an askari a few months after the Security Branch abducted him in February 1982 from Botswana, where he had fled into exile in 1976. In 1989, acting on orders from Vlakplaas, Lengene infiltrated a group of youth activists from Soweto whose names were Cassius Nceba, Caswell Khumalo and Richard Ngwenya. The three activists, friends of Lengene's, were members of the Soweto Youth Congress. Unaware that Lengene was an askari, they asked him to help them leave

South Africa for military training abroad. Anton Pretorius, a lieutenant-colonel in the Security Branch and member of a special outfit called the Soweto Intelligence Unit, wanted the three killed with booby-trapped limpet mines. The intention was to use 'false-flag methods', meaning that the Security Branch would carry out the operation but attribute it to ANC incompetence. Oscar Linda Moni, an askari who participated in the operation, recalled, 'Peter Lengene immediately said no to Pretorius's suggestion and he further indicated that he'll never be part of this plan. Peter Lengene stated the following reasons for his non-participation: the comrades are known to him; his family stays in Soweto; other people might link him to the comrades' disappearance since they might have seen him in contact with them.'[36]

In the event, Lengene did participate in the operation. Vlakplaas was not a moral democracy in which the occasional attack of conscience was allowed. Askaris could not opt out of operations because their scruples would not let them take part. Lengene, working with fellow askaris Oscar Linda Moni and another named only as Monyane, gave Nceba, Khumalo and Ngwenya 'training' in the handling of firearms and explosives at a hotel in Hillbrow, Johannesburg, and selected three 'targets' for them. These were electricity substations in Kliptown, Mzimhlophe and New Canada, all near railway stations in Soweto. The three youths were then given booby-trapped limpet mines. Pretorius ordered Monyane to 'work' with Nceba, Lengene with Khumalo and Moni with Ngwenya. The askaris' orders were to make sure the bombs did their job. If they failed, the askaris were to shoot their marks on the spot.

Nceba was blown to pieces by 'his' limpet mine. Ngwenya was shot by Moni (who was drunk) and only died later as a result of his injuries. Moni later claimed that he had deliberately avoided killing Ngwenya on the spot 'as a result of probably the fear of committing this heinous murder, or ... as a result of my conscience having operated'.[37] It is not clear from the TRC's records who or what killed Khumalo, but the askaris and their Security Branch bosses took his body as well as that of Ngwenya to a spot near Rustenburg. They burned the bodies with petrol and then threw the remains into a ditch alongside the road.

* * *

As with any counterinsurgency outfit, the work of askaris was driven by information. Askaris drew on intelligence from the Security Branch's network of informers, as well as their own knowledge of how activists operated. They used the information to sabotage anti-apartheid opposition, capture activists or kill insurgents. Askaris were divided into groups that were sometimes based on where each member had operated from as an insurgent. If an askari had been active in Botswana as an ANC or PAC member, he would be placed in the group responsible for the Western Transvaal, which bordered Botswana; if an askari had operated from Swaziland, he would be in the group responsible for the Eastern Transvaal. Lesotho, the Orange Free State and the Eastern Cape each had their dedicated groups. Vlakplaas was not the only police death-squad base – the police ran similar squads from secret farms in Natal and other parts of the country – but it was the most prominent. Radebe said Vlakplaas was the 'only unit that could operate anywhere' in South Africa. Recalling his career as Vlakplaas commander, Eugene de Kock commented, 'If I may say so, I was regarded in security circles as one of the most effective [counterinsurgency] operatives in the SAP. When "dirty" work had to be done, they called for Eugene de Kock.'[38]

De Kock had joined the SAP in 1968. As Jeremy Gordin put it, 'His choice of job was analogous to opting to become a typewriter mechanic in the late 20th century; he had gone into a dying trade. Ironically, to trace his personal career path fighting "terrorism" … is to trudge the final mile of European hegemony in Africa.'[39] In 1968 the police deployed him to the counterinsurgency operation in Rhodesia after nine months at a police training college. In 1978 he moved to South West Africa to join the counterinsurgency there. In South West, in 1979, De Kock joined Koevoet, a notorious counterinsurgency unit with a reputation for taking no prisoners.

By the time De Kock came to Vlakplaas in 1983, he had been involved in more than 300 'contacts'. De Kock was so unhinged by his experience that when he was transferred to Vlakplaas, General Hans Dreyer, his commander in Koevoet, warned his superiors in Pretoria to keep De Kock away from the operational side of the Security Branch. For Dreyer, the last straw was an attempt by De Kock, supported by a band of Namibian askaris, to mount a mutiny against him. The top brass ignored Dreyer's warning. As Johan van der Merwe, head of the Security Branch and later chief of the SAP, said, De Kock was a 'hard worker'.[40] In July 1985 De Kock replaced Colonel Jack Cronje, another veteran of the Rhodesian counterinsurgency, as commander of Vlakplaas, which he then ran for eight years.

When President F.W. de Klerk disbanded the askari project in 1993 following a string of embarrassing revelations about apartheid death squads, De Kock received a pension payout of nearly R1 million. In 1995 De Kock was sentenced to two life terms and 212 years in prison for murder and assorted crimes. Later, De Kock applied to the TRC for amnesty for 70 killings. Twenty-six of these, he claimed, were committed outside South Africa; five were for the killing of askaris. Among them were Moses Nthelang, killed in 1989 for losing his firearm during a drinking spree, and Johannes Mabotha, shot twice in the heart by De Kock in 1989 for going AWOL. Mabotha's murder took place at Penge mine, the same place where Sedibe's father Ephraim had worked and about a kilometre from where Sedibe had grown up. The mine owners had given Vlakplaas permission to use the mine for training and other purposes.

Also killed were Brian Ngqulunga, shot in 1990 and buried at Vlakplaas to stop him from exposing the police death squads, and Neville Goodwill Sikhakhane, murdered in 1991 on suspicion that he was an ANC double agent. As the TRC noted in its final report, 'The threats of death used to "turn" *askaris* were not idle.'[41] Sikhakhane had become an askari in 1988 after he was recruited from Swaziland by a relative, who was already an askari, named Godfrey Radebe. Sikhakhane proved his loyalty to the Security Branch in the most lethal way possible: he betrayed a fellow ANC operative called Emmanuel Mzimela. When the Security Branch asked Sikhakhane to prove he was sincere about becoming an askari, he did so by helping them kill Mzimela, who went by the *nom de guerre* Deon Cele. Travelling in a kombi belonging to the Durban Security Branch, Sikhakhane waylaid Mzimela as he was leaving class one evening in Manzini and offered him a ride. When Mzimela got on board, he was overpowered by Colonel Hentie Botha and Warrant Officer Laurie Wasserman, who had been hiding in the back of the car. They took Mzimela to Natal and killed him the following day when he refused to turn.[42]

The Security Branch made Sikhakhane a number of promises to induce him to defect. They promised to get him a South African identity document and to have him appointed to the SAP. This would have meant a regular salary and associated benefits. When Colonel Andy Taylor, a senior Security Branch officer in Natal, failed to keep these promises, Sikhakhane took out his frustrations on his partner. He drank heavily and assaulted her each time he was drunk. Taylor confiscated Sikhakhane's firearms a few times after the partner complained to him about the abuse she was getting. It did not help.

Speaking on 20 September 1999 about Sikhakhane's poor discipline, De Kock said, 'I had the same experience at Vlakplaas with some of the askaris, the overwhelming majority, not all of them. The experience that I had built up over the years in South West or Namibia with Swapo [South West Africa People's Organisation] and the handling of defectors and traitors there and the experience here in South Africa with defectors and traitors, was that firstly these persons had been trained in the military, they were aggressive. And secondly, with regard to their defection they had developed a sense of guilt and a feeling of inferiority. And mostly they expected some form of utopia with their new master and if they did not receive that, behavioural problems would ensue and one would attempt to address such problems to the best of one's ability.'[43]

In truth, the best of De Kock's ability was devoted to prosecuting South Africa's dirty war – not to nursing the feelings of his subordinates. They knew that. As the TRC concluded in its final report, askaris were extremely effective in identifying suspected insurgents, infiltrating insurgent groups, interrogating suspects and giving evidence in court.[44] De Kock was a lethal operator, made more effective by askaris under his command. He told one interviewer, '"Turned" activists were the most effective operators because they could infiltrate the enemy. The askaris were an extremely important link in the fight against the political aspirations of the black population.'[45]

As Vlakplaas grew in the 1980s and members were divided into groups depending on their missions, each group of askaris was placed under the immediate supervision of a black member of the Security Branch, who in turn reported to a white officer. De Kock used askaris and electronic surveillance to keep tabs on his charges. The black members of the Security Branch and veteran askaris stationed at Vlakplaas were expected as a matter of course to spy on their colleagues. Each black policeman was responsible for a kombi used to car-pool to the farm and to take askaris to their various missions. One of them noted, 'If in charge of a kombi, you were in charge of about 10 or 15 guys.'[46]

Askaris were free to come and go as they pleased at Vlakplaas. But they were always expected to be available for their regular deployments.[47] They would be sent to different parts of the country, depending on the available intelligence, for three-week stretches followed by a week off work.[48] During their off-days, they could travel wherever they wanted. But they had to keep in touch via pagers, radios and telephone. They also had to inform their bosses when leaving the Transvaal. When on duty, the kombis would do the rounds of Letlhabile, a township north-west of Pretoria where most askaris lived, collecting each one from home and then driving them to Vlakplaas or wherever they were needed. Some of the askaris lived in townships near Pretoria and they, too, would car-pool.

Gregory Sibusiso Radebe, a native of Soweto who claims to have moved out of Letlhabile on the same day in 1993 that F.W. de Klerk ordered Vlakplaas to be shut down and its members paid severance packages, stated, 'Frankly, we lived freely in the township.' He said residents knew who the askaris were. 'People talked.' But what residents knew was that these were police officers – not collaborators. Radebe recalled that once, during his early days at Vlakplaas, De Kock pointed to the fence around the farm and said, 'This fence is not to keep you inside; it is to keep out the outside world.' De Kock told Radebe he could run if he wanted to, but that he would have nowhere to go. The ANC would kill him for treachery; De Kock and his men would kill him for desertion. Many askaris stayed. Radebe declared, 'In reality, we were hostages. We were captured ... In reality, these are my enemies and yet if I go back to my own ... you take each day as it comes.' He said many askaris decided to accept the police 'offer' to become collaborators in the hope that 'at the right time I will run'. Mfalapitsa claimed, 'I thought as soon as the conflict gets better, as soon as I get an opportunity, I'll try to leave Vlakplaas peacefully, without me fighting them, because I could not do that.'[49] But taking the police 'offer' to collaborate and staying until the time was right meant more than simply surviving. It also meant working for one's survival.[50]

Askaris were commonly used as bounty hunters and bait for unsuspecting insurgents. They would hang around bus stops, taxi ranks, shebeens and shops to identify people whom they knew from exile, or whose portraits they had studied in a Security Branch album that the police used extensively to track and identify insurgents. Askaris would also be deployed to army and police roadblocks. They would sit to the side in a kombi with tinted windows to observe the vehicles and individuals stopped. From there they would identify insurgents for apprehension, and the police would pounce.

Often, askaris were used to kill opponents of apartheid. In 1985 a group of student activists, acting on the orders of a man named Mike, whom they believed to be an ANC insurgent but who was in fact the askari Joe Mamasela, died in the East Rand township of Duduza. 'Mike' had given them grenades and told them to use the weapons against local councillors. The grenades were booby-trapped.[51] Their deaths led to the notorious killing of a young woman named Maki Skhosana by necklacing.[52] Skhosana's killing, which Bishop Desmond Tutu tried to stop, was televised around the world and used extensively by the South African government in a bid to embarrass the anti-apartheid movement.

In 1986 Russell Mngomezulu, Muntuwenkosi Dlamini, Russell Mthembu and Sandile Khawula, young activists from Chesterville, outside Durban, were killed in a police ambush to which they had been lured by a group of askaris including Chris Makgopa and Xolelwa Virginia Shosha, one of the few women askaris. De Kock and his fellow Vlakplaas operatives Willie Nortje and Izak Bosch were later granted amnesty by the TRC for the four murders.

On 3 March 1986 the Security Branch ambushed and killed seven activists from Gugulethu, outside Cape Town, who had been led to their deaths by the policeman Thapelo Johannes Mbelo and the askaris Gladstone Mose, Eric Shakes Maluleke and Jimmy Mbane. The operation had started with Mbelo, pretending to be a political detainee, spending the night in police cells in Cape Town, where an activist connected to the seven men had been detained by the local Security Branch. Mbelo spent his time befriending the activist and getting names of possible 'contacts' in Gugulethu.[53] He was then 'released' from detention early the next morning.

He went to Gugulethu and, using the names gleaned from the detainee, wormed his way into the local activist network. When his eagerness aroused suspicion, he pulled out. By then he had established the names of the activists. These were passed on to the three askaris involved in the mission. The askaris, pretending to be ANC cadres sent by the organisation to offer the activists military and political training, went about winning their trust. When the activists were asked to write their biographies – standard practice for people joining the ANC – these were passed on to the Security Branch. The askaris instructed the youth to attack a bus transporting police officers to the local police station. On the day of the attack, Mbane dropped the youth off at about 7:30 am at a chosen site. A police death squad, lying in wait since 5 am, mowed them down. Mbane and Maluleke were each paid R7000 for setting up the trap.[54]

Ironically, the fictions of racial solidarity that made askaris so potent as counterinsurgents under apartheid have shielded them from exposure in post-apartheid South Africa. Taking advantage of assumptions that blacks suffered similarly under apartheid, askaris have presented themselves as victims of circumstances or as 'hostages'.[55] Former ANC member Mzwakhe Ndlela has pointed out that 'even those who were apolitical or reactionary started to identify themselves with the progressive forces. And so did some of those who had openly worked for the apartheid state. Everyone seemed to have a story to tell, placing themselves on the side of those who fought for freedom.'[56]

Joe Mamasela, a self-described political serial killer recognised even by his own superiors in the Security Branch as a nasty piece of work, claimed to have been a victim of the police. 'I had no political reason to kill black people,' he said.[57] A car thief who agreed in 1979 to spy on the ANC in return for the dropping of theft charges against him, Mamasela was considered so bloodthirsty that one of his former white superiors declared that while he would take Mamasela to war with him again in the future, he would do so only with Mamasela in front of him or by his side – never behind.[58]

While black askaris traded on fictions of black solidarity to make themselves effective against their targets, their white commanders relied on their own racialised notions of solidarity to maintain secretive protection rackets. Examining the white Security Branch members who operated from Pretoria, the historian Nicky Rousseau found that, in their attempt to negotiate the tension between the illegality of their actions and the legal framework within which they operated, they turned to 'farms, abandoned police stations or mines, the roads of Bophuthatswana or rivers of the Eastern Transvaal' to create 'new terrains of terror and death', geographically separate from the 'formal physical space of security police offices'.[59] Rousseau writes, 'For the Pretoria security police, many of these [places] were drawn from the space of the everyday through an appropriation of the domestic; locations of familiarity and ties of intimacy determined involvement, sites and killing grounds.' Their strategies 'were elaborated in a manner that drew constantly on the ordinary and everyday – rugby teams, a family farm, a picnic spot – spaces and personal networks that arise in domestic rather than institutional settings.'[60]

Did these killers know that the day of reckoning would come, that they would one day have to account for their actions, necessitating the need to keep their networks tight and to limit their conspiracies to small circles? Speaking of his fellow askaris, Gregory Sibusiso Radebe commented, 'I think all of us were aware that one day the revolution would triumph. Personally, I had a feeling that when that happened, the farm would be dissolved and people would have to give account for their actions while working there. This is what made me to avoid standing out and be selected for murderous operations. I think I succeeded in doing so and, when the TRC came, I realised I had been right in my thinking. I had observed developments after independence in Zimbabwe and Namibia and I knew a similar situation would develop in South Africa as well.'[61]

Many white policemen presumably thought along similar lines. They probably believed they could rely on their networks to shield them from prosecution. For example, white officers who applied to the TRC for amnesty tended to do so in cases where askaris, De Kock (then in prison, with nothing to lose and bitter at being the only white officer left to carry the can for police atrocities) or black policemen could provide incriminating information. The rest have maintained a racial solidarity that still binds them, 20 years after the end of apartheid, as the following case demonstrates.

In 1986 Moss Morudu, a young activist from Mamelodi, outside Pretoria, joined an MK unit made up of Jabu Masina, Ting Ting Masango, Joseph Makhura, Neo Potsane, Justice Mbizana and Reginald Kekana. When the police arrested four of his comrades in September 1986, Morudu fled Mamelodi and hid out in Potchefstroom in the Western Transvaal. He sent word to the ANC that he urgently needed to get out of South Africa. The Security Branch intercepted this information. In October 1986 Smuts Mathebula, Chenny More and Jerry Matjeni, three policemen posing as MK members, took Morudu from his hiding place and delivered him to Captain Hendrik Prinsloo of the Northern Transvaal Security Branch. According to Mathebula, More and Matjeni, who were granted amnesty for Morudu's abduction, Morudu was taken to a farm named Kaallaagte, about ten kilometres east of Hammanskraal. The farm belonged to a Major Smit, a railway cop, who loaned it to the Security Branch.

Mathebula, More and Matjeni guarded Morudu for a week while he was being interrogated by Prinsloo and other white cops. Morudu disappeared a week later and Prinsloo ordered the three men to take down the army tents they had used on the farm. When Prinsloo and his fellow white colleagues appeared before the TRC, they denied all knowledge of Morudu. However, the Missing Persons Task Team of the National Prosecuting Authority, set up at the end of the TRC's life, obtained information indicating that the white officers took Morudu away from the farm about a week into his detention. They strangled him, tied his body to a telephone pole along the Saagkuildrift Road in Bophuthatswana, and blew it up with limpet mines. This was common practice among members of the Northern Transvaal Security Branch, who would dispose of the remains of victims in rural areas around Bophuthatswana. Because the white officers acted 'alone' in killing and disposing of Morudu's remains, they hid the truth. In fact, before the three black officers confessed, the white officers did apply for amnesty for killing and blowing up an unnamed activist. Thinking the truth would never come out of their network, they gave such scant details in their applications that the Amnesty Committee found them too vague for consideration.[62]

* * *

When De Kock objected to Sedibe being called an askari, he most likely had askaris as bait and bounty hunters in mind.[63] According to De Kock, Sedibe was too smart and too valuable for that. However, to believe De Kock is to accept a false distinction between the 'dirty' work of askaris and the 'intelligent' work Sedibe supposedly carried out as a collaborator. The whole business of askaris was driven by intelligence. Radebe remarked, 'People must not forget that that unit did not work in isolation. The whole conflict was based on information. That information came from the outside [i.e. exile].'[64] When I spoke to De Kock in February 2013, he repeated his by-now standard line about Sedibe: 'I never used him as an askari. I treated him like an officer.' But De Kock's claim is false. Sedibe *was* an askari. He was the same askari who identified and helped capture the ANC activist Miriam Phumla Williams outside Baragwanath Hospital, Soweto, in June 1988; who gave the Security Branch some of the information used to raid the home of senior ANC operative Paul Dikeledi in Swaziland in early 1987; and who probably gave the information used by the police to kill Dikeledi (real name Sello Motau) and Cassius Make (real name Job Tabane) in Swaziland in July 1987.

De Kock held Sedibe in high regard. According to Radebe, 'There are people whose opinions carried weight with De Kock. September's was among those.'[65] Stephen Mbanda, one of the first ANC operatives to become an askari, having joined Vlakplaas in 1980, called Sedibe one of the 'top people there'. Radebe backed up Mbanda's claim. 'I do not know what actually September gave to De Kock, but the two seemed to have a warm relationship and September was actually given a kombi and guys under his command. That was not normal at the farm because such a position was normally a preserve of black cops who'd trained at Hammanskraal and were given the task to oversee us.'[66]

One possible reason why De Kock thought Sedibe was different is that Sedibe helped recruit a senior ANC member based in Western Europe. Sometime in the late 1980s, De Kock and Sedibe travelled to Austria for this purpose. De Kock told the TRC in February 2000, 'Sedibe and I were part of this operation because Sedibe knew this member quite well and would be able to convince him to work for Military Intelligence Services. The person recruited was – to him it was only about money, it was not about moral values. We went to Germany and from there we went to Vienna where we booked into a luxurious hotel where [Sedibe] and I shared a room. This is Sedibe and I. They wanted to keep us together because we had to keep each other awake, as they could call us at any time and we had to be ready.'[67]

This relationship seems to have paid off for Sedibe. 'Judging by his lifestyle, he was the highest-paid among us,' Radebe noted. Sedibe was generous with his money and popular among his fellow askaris. 'We loved the guy,' Radebe said. 'He was friendly and kind and considerate. He would buy 15 guys liquor. He never came across as a bad person. He was a nice person, easy to go with.'[68] Bernard Malope, Sedibe's cousin and childhood friend, recalled that after his defection, Sedibe would visit their village of Matibidi in the Eastern Transvaal with lots of money. Sedibe paid for a new roof on the family house.[69]

The askari Goodman Twala claimed that Sedibe saved his life. Twala, who coped with his status as a collaborator by being constantly drunk and high on dagga, once made a drunken threat to kill De Kock, who was always humiliating him and assaulting him for indiscipline. Twala made his threat in De Kock's absence but in the presence of other askaris. One of the askaris informed on Twala. By the time De Kock confronted Twala, the latter had long forgotten about his drunken threat. Twala was with a group of fellow askaris when, seemingly out of the blue, De Kock put a gun to his temple. 'He ordered me to repeat what I said. I had no idea what he was talking about.' De Kock, placing his finger on the trigger, reminded Twala of his threat. Sedibe, who had been watching the incident from close by, asked De Kock to forgive Twala. 'That man saved my life. He intervened,' Twala recalled. De Kock put his gun down and walked away. Twala subsequently lost a leg in a car accident. He claims De Kock engineered the incident in an attempt to kill him.

How did people whose existence was based on the abuse of trust live together? Askaris say they never trusted one another. Judas Mpho Tladi stated, 'I had no friends.'[70] Tladi hated Sedibe. 'He was a terrible commander. He wanted to kill me because he did not trust me.' But askaris needed a measure of mutual trust because they hunted in packs. Sometimes, De Kock formed the packs depending on the mission at hand; often the units were based on aptitude and skills. Askaris were constantly undergoing training and De Kock put great stock in competence and expertise. For example, the askari Oscar Linda Moni, who killed Soweto youth activist Richard Ngwenya in 1989, was chosen by De Kock for that mission specifically because he was considered one of the best weapons handlers at Vlakplaas.

Askaris tended to socialise along regional and languages lines. Sedibe was close to a veteran askari named Chris Makgopa and to the policeman Johannes Koole. Makgopa and Koole were both Pedi-speakers, like Sedibe. Makgopa was a 'tall, hefty, jet-black man with squint eyes' who was nicknamed 'Russian tank' when he was in the PAC. After his defection to the SAP in 1984, his PAC colleagues changed his nickname to 'American tank'.[71] Radebe said he got along with everyone at Vlakplaas and minimised his culpability by absenting himself from certain missions. 'I made sure that if I could run away from things, I did it without raising eyebrows.' Radebe also remarked that he never trusted Sedibe, even though the two men got on well together. 'To be honest, I always thought he was working with the ANC while he was there [at Vlakplaas]. He was free; he did not appear worried.' One puzzle for Radede was that Sedibe was constantly travelling to Swaziland, his former base of operations, by himself. Sedibe would talk about his trips. 'What would a guy in his situation be doing in Swaziland?' Radebe asked.[72] He wondered if Sedibe perhaps used his visits to Swaziland to keep contact with the ANC.

Sedibe certainly seems to have moved in and out of Swaziland at will, using the name Lucky Seme, among others. In July 1987 the Swazi police arrested a man believed to be Sedibe, who the *Times of Swaziland* said was 'suspected of being a spy and hitman against ANC targets in Swaziland'. The police had followed the man to a hotel in the Ezulwini Valley 'shortly after he was seen talking to a group of white South African men outside a Mbabane restaurant'. The man was released, however, when the police discovered that 'he was not the wanted man'. The article reported, 'Police say September is wanted in Swaziland, and that they have been made to believe he may be in South Africa. However, if he were in South Africa, he would have been expected to be in jail. Fears are that he may have been a South African security agent planted into the ANC.'[73]

The Johannesburg-based *New Nation* reported in July 1987 that 'ANC activists in Swaziland claim Sidebe [*sic*] had repeatedly offered them jobs as police informants, with huge financial rewards'.[74] Could this be what Sedibe was doing in Swaziland, visiting old haunts to recruit former comrades for his new masters? Sedibe moved to Vlakplaas within four months of his defection in August 1986, pledging allegiance to the SAP in February 1987. If he was indeed travelling to Swaziland by himself, so soon after his defection, to recruit members of the ANC into the security police, what does that tell us about the speed of his 'conversion'? Barry

Gilder, an ANC intelligence operative who was part of a mission to track down Sedibe after the latter's defection, denied that Sedibe the askari worked for the ANC. Gilder said Sedibe stood out among the askaris for the passion with which he turned against former comrades. 'He was particularly active in pursuing us. He was particularly vicious in torturing some of our comrades.'[75]

The question is: why?

3

The farm

Indeed, while the notion of 'farm' perhaps conjures a picture of rural quiet, this is certainly not the case of the South African farm – or 'die plaas' – which is frequently a place of overt and underlying violence through coercive labour relations, hunting, animal slaughter, and sometimes family violence presided over by the family patriarch, 'die baas van die plaas'. Thus the zone of safety for the operation is underwritten as much by its underlying violence and death as by its seclusion.

– Nicky Rousseau[1]

Vlakplaas had been in existence for ten years before its name became publicly synonymous with apartheid death squads.[2] The farm was the brainchild of Colonel Johan Viktor, a South African veteran of the 1964–1979 independence war in Rhodesia.[3] Viktor had learned from the Rhodesians that captured combatants could be 'turned' and used to devastating effect against their former comrades.[4] Vlakplaas, which became state property in 1980, consisted of an old farmhouse, outbuildings that later functioned as barracks and detention cells, a vegetable garden as well as grazing for livestock. Viktor planned to use the farm as a base for 'rehabilitated terrorists'.[5] Among the first askaris stationed there were Jeff Bosigo, Peter Kgoadi, Thabo Makgage, Steven Mbanda, Piet Mogoai, Gladstone Mose, Joe Mamasela, Brian Ngqulunga and Ernest Ramatlala.

In August 1980 Dirk Coetzee took over from Viktor. By the time

Coetzee was demoted as Vlakplaas commander in December 1981, Vlakplaas had 17 askaris.[6] By all accounts, the first batch were a sorry lot. They smoked marijuana and drank heavily. Coetzee changed their conditions of employment. He had their salaries raised, got them clothing allowances, signed them up for the police medical aid plan and secured them firearm permits. He gave them driving lessons and helped them obtain identity documents and passports.[7] But the disciplinary problems continued. Of the 17 original askaris, two were killed, three deserted and two, Lati Ronald Ntshekang and Bobby Modiba, wound up in jail for killing their girlfriends.[8] Modiba killed two girlfriends. In fact, Coetzee was in the process of making the first murder disappear when Modiba killed the second girlfriend.[9] De Kock said discipline was so bad when he arrived at the farm in 1983 that he called it Kakplaas – Shit Farm. The askaris were supposed to help the police track down anti-apartheid insurgents but they 'failed miserably in achieving this'.[10]

Coetzee, De Kock and Viktor were among the first counterinsurgency specialists in the SAP, having learned from the Rhodesians. Until 1974, counterinsurgency was primarily a police function in South Africa. This was as much a reflection of longstanding divisions within the apartheid regime as it was of the white rulers' misreading of South Africa's fundamental political problem – the exclusion of blacks from the polity – as a law-and-order issue.[11] From 1948 to 1978 all the Nationalist prime ministers – Daniel F. Malan, Johannes G. Strijdom, Hendrik F. Verwoerd and Balthazar J. Vorster – privileged the police over the military as the state's primary instrument of violence. In fact, it was Vorster who announced in 1967 that members of the SAP had been sent north to help the Rhodesian white-minority government fight an insurgency that had started three years earlier.[12]

The Rhodesian rebellion aimed to end the system of white minority rule in which about 300,000 whites lorded it over more than four million Africans. Like many political conflicts after the Second World War, the Rhodesian war quickly assumed the divides of the Cold War, with China and the Soviet Union supporting the nationalists, and South Africa and Portugal backing the white minority regime. Rhodesia unilaterally declared its independence from Britain on 11 November 1965, following disagreement over how to proceed in the face of a rising tide of decolonisation. Thanks in part to brutal methods employed by their army and police in the 'bush war', the Rhodesians earned a reputation as being among the world's most uncompromising racists. As if to underline the point, on 20 March 1976 Prime Minister Ian Smith declared, 'I don't believe in majority rule ever in Rhodesia ... not in a thousand years.'[13] Delivered when the Second World War was still fresh in people's memory, Smith's statement smacked of Adolf Hitler's plan for a German Reich that would reign for a thousand years. It came to be read as the ravings of a 'white King Canute railing against an inevitable black tide'.[14]

Rhodesia might have been a political pariah, but for others it was a hotbed of military innovation. In the late 1960s and early 1970s, with the US on the back foot in Vietnam, southern Africa was considered by Rhodesian and South African police and military specialists to be at the forefront in developing new counterinsurgency methods. These experts were confident they were winning the war and teaching the world a thing or two in the process. In 1969 a Rhodesian officer remarked, 'When the British and the Americans talk to us again, they are going to have to rewrite all their handbooks on jungle warfare against guerrillas. We have found the answers, and they have not.'[15] Among the 'answers' was the use of askaris.

To be sure, the use of collaborators and proxies was not a Rhodesian invention. The British had used Zulu collaborators against the Zulu kingdom in the 19th century, employed Boer collaborators in the South African War, and cultivated collaborators, loyalists and 'pseudo-gangs' in British Malaya and Kenya.[16] The French had used collaborators in French Indochina and so-called Harkis in Algeria. The US had used collaborators in Vietnam. Collaboration was, if anything, the staple of counterinsurgency warfare. But the South Africans did not send their police officers north just so they could learn new ways of fighting 'jungle warfare'. There was also a strategic consideration behind the deployments: they wanted to keep ANC insurgents as far away from territorial South Africa as possible.

The ANC and the Zimbabwe African People's Union (Zapu) were working jointly between July 1967 and July 1968 on a mission to send their fighters into Rhodesia from Zambia. This became known as the Wankie and Sipolilo campaigns. The idea was that while the Zimbabwean fighters campaigned in Rhodesia, their ANC counterparts would make their way to South Africa, opening a Ho Chi Minh trail of sorts to connect the ANC's rear and front. But the mission failed. MK operatives were fed shoddy intelligence, and given inappropriate equipment and clothing. They fought creditably but proved relatively easy pickings for the Rhodesians.[17] Despite the failure of the campaigns, the South African government took them seriously. As Hendrik van den Bergh, the South African security chief at the time, remarked, 'The day we have to fight them on our soil it will be an entirely different kind of war; one where we shall have to drop the defensive and strike hard on the offensive. It will then be a total war.'[18] Van den Bergh's use of the term 'total war' is revealing because it shows that some of the key terms in theories of counterinsurgency warfare developed in Western Europe and the US in the 1960s had begun to influence Pretoria long before the beginning of what the South Africans came to call the 'total onslaught'.

The use of the Rhodesian conflict as a training ground for the SAP was so popular that at the peak of the war in the 1970s more than 4000 SAP members were fighting in Rhodesia.[19] These deployments became a rite of passage for many South African policemen, especially those who wanted to join the Security Branch. In 1977, 3383 SAP officers took courses in counterinsurgency and riot control. By 1987, the number had jumped to 12,917.[20] Among the counterinsurgency theorists favoured by the South Africans were the British Army officers Frank Kitson and Robert Thompson, the American officer J.J. McCuen, and the French general André Beaufre – although Beaufre was more popular among the military than he was among the police. South African counterinsurgents also studied literature from the 'other side'. Eugene de Kock read Sun Tzu and Mao Zedong, but said that he could not operate by the book. 'I was unconventional. I eventually had to throw the counterinsurgency manual out.'[21]

De Kock was both typical and exceptional.[22] He was typical in the sense that, raised as he was in the climate of paranoia that defined Afrikanerdom in the 1960s, he signed up for what he believed was a war for Afrikaner survival. But he was exceptional in that he was one of the few to fight in every South African conflict of the Cold War era. De Kock also personified a particular feature of the South African conflict, one noted by the TRC in its final report: 'By far the largest proportion of amnesty applicants from the security forces and, to a large extent, the leadership of the liberation movements, were children and teenagers in the 1960s.'[23] These youngsters grew up in a world dominated by racism, decolonisation and the Cold War. De Kock, 11 at the time of the Sharpeville shootings in March 1960, described the massacre as a key moment in his political development. 'I may have been 11 years old but I understood that the state mechanism had been used in the defence of a political system,' he remarked.[24]

For Pretoria's policy-makers, the insurgencies of southern Africa were Soviet-inspired conspiracies that could easily be put down. This view was summed up by Michael Morris, a South African cop who became a police propagandist after his spying career came to a quick end when he was exposed in London. Morris described the southern African insurgent as a 'living tragedy', a 'stateless and aimless fugitive wanderer'. According to him, the typical anti-apartheid combatant 'knows, too, that his very colleagues are informers, and those of the sell-your-soul-for-six-pence brigade'.

Calling apartheid South Africa a 'merciful nation, perhaps an understanding one also', Morris encouraged the 'turning' of captured insurgents. 'We must not overlook the indemnifying aspect of traitorship. If an informer becomes, irrespective of his background, of sufficient merit, information-wise, to the southern Security Officers with whom he will deal, he gains for himself a favourable image. One does not become blind to his faults or career, but one does acknowledge his worth.'[25]

The provision of information was not the only way in which askaris proved themselves to be of 'sufficient merit', as we know from the story of Goodwill Sikhakhane recounted in the previous chapter. Both Kevin O'Brien and Stephen Ellis claim, without providing evidence, that askaris were also expected to kill former comrades to prove their loyalty to their new masters. According to O'Brien, 'One of the prime techniques used to "turn" guerrillas was by forcing them to kill an ANC or Swapo member, either through capture or assassination, in order to implicate them and prevent them from returning to their comrades.'[26] There is indeed circumstantial evidence linking Glory Sedibe to the deaths of some of his former comrades. For example, as I recount in a later chapter, the former askari Judas Mpho Tladi told me about an episode during which Sedibe wanted Tladi to join him on a killing mission to Swaziland.

Gregory Sibusiso Radebe commented, 'Sometimes it is easy to say "this guy was an askari". But have you ever asked yourself: What makes an askari?'[27] What made Sedibe an askari? What twists and turns led to defection? How are we, in short, to understand his collaboration?

In their book *On complicity and compromise*, Chiara Lepora and Robert E. Goodin call collaboration a 'subtype of complicity', marked by difference and distance between collaborators and those with whom they collaborate.[28] 'In the realm of actions, a collaborator is not a co-principal. At most, the actions of the collaborator contribute causally to the principal's wrongdoing. They are not in any sense constitutive of the principal wrongdoing.'[29] For Lepora and Goodin, a collaborator is defined by the fact that he or she has no 'active role in the planning itself'.[30] They write: 'The relationship between the collaborator and the principal is purely that of follower to leader, in regard to the plan. The collaborator takes instructions from the plan and adjusts his own actions to it.'[31]

Perhaps. But let us examine how Sedibe defected and how his relationship with his principals developed.

* * *

Wednesday, 13 August 1986, was a perfect night for a death squad. It was cold, dark and rainy, and there were unlikely to be witnesses on the streets of Mankayane, a small town perched on Swaziland's south-western border with South Africa.[32] The eight Security Branch members chosen for the job had driven into Swaziland just before midnight in two Toyota SUVs with secret compartments to hide their weapons.[33] Their destination: the Mankayane police station, a squat two-storey building at the bottom of a valley surrounded by commercial pine forests. Their mission: a snatch-and-grab operation targeting Glory Sedibe.

The Swazi police had arrested Sedibe in Manzini two days earlier for being in the country illegally and, they suspected, for being in possession of what the Swazi media liked to call 'arms of war'.[34] Following a secret deal between three senior Swazi policemen and their South African counterparts, the Swazi police had moved him from the Manzini police station to Mankayane, closer to the South African border. The Swazis sold Sedibe to the South Africans for R150,000.[35] It was now time for the eight men to collect their quarry. Their orders were to make it look like a jailbreak engineered by the ANC.[36]

Swaziland was a playground for South African police and intelligence agents, despite the kingdom's reputation as a haven for insurgents and refugees from apartheid South Africa.[37] The two SUVs parked away from the station. As Almond Nofomela, Aubrey

Mngadi and Johannes Koole – the black members of the squad – approached the entrance on foot ahead of their white colleagues, they noticed that only one light was on in the building. The double glass doors leading to the charge office were locked. There was no sign of the Swazi police contact who was to lead them to the cells. Eugene de Kock, the squad leader, decided they would act without their escort. The men had carried out so many operations in Swaziland (from abductions and bombings to killings) that they regarded the border as a minor hurdle. They were under orders to bring Sedibe back to South Africa alive. As head of ANC Military Intelligence for the Transvaal, Sedibe was too valuable a target to kill. They were also not to shoot at any Swazis. Swaziland might have been the junior partner in a secret anti-ANC security pact with South Africa signed in 1982, but the South Africans did not want to alienate the Swazis.[38] The eight men were armed with mostly Eastern-bloc arms to make it look as if they were MK operatives.

The police cells were on the ground floor at the end of a short passage, to the left of the charge office. De Kock, 'the kind of commander who did not issue orders from behind an office desk', found a window that was not closed properly.[39] Armed with an AK-47 rifle and a Beretta 92 semi-automatic pistol, he forced the bayonet of his rifle through a small gap in the window, used the bayonet to lift the clasp, opened the window and climbed in. His men followed. He reminded them not to kill anyone. The deal with the Swazis was that none of the officers on duty at the station that night would be armed. It was quiet inside the station. As the men started towards the cells, De Kock heard a shuffle. A young Swazi officer appeared from around a corner. He was armed with a G3 rifle, which he aimed at De Kock. De Kock, standing about three metres from the officer, raised his Beretta and, pointing it at the officer's face, ordered him to drop his weapon.

The officer's G3 was in 'safe' mode, meaning he would not make it in a firefight with De Kock. He put down his rifle. De Kock asked who else was around. There was one other officer on duty.

He was unarmed and had the keys to the cells. De Kock instructed the officer to call his colleague. The officer did so and, as soon as the colleague appeared, he was accosted by two of De Kock's men. Paul van Dyk grabbed the keys and, with Nofomela, Mngadi, Koole, Izak Bosch, Freek Pienaar and Christo Deetlefs, went to the cells while De Kock watched over the two Swazi officers. Van Dyk opened the cells. There were three men inside: two stock thieves and Sedibe. Pienaar and Van Dyk had no trouble identifying Sedibe. They had studied his mug shot in well-thumbed police files that, as Breyten Breytenbach once said, the Security Branch 'brought up to date the way other perverts would their girly magazines'.[40] Asked to confirm his identity, Sedibe denied he was the person the squad was looking for. But Van Dyk knew he had his man. He ordered Sedibe onto his stomach on the floor. As Sedibe did so, Van Dyk hit him on the head with the butt of his rifle. Nofomela told the stock thieves to go home. The thieves were not happy about this: they preferred the warmth of the police cells.

Sedibe, who must have known that the men were South African agents, fought for his life. Six men tried to pin him to the floor. He would not lie still. Van Dyk choked him with a scarf and he passed out. They then carried him to one of the cars. Inside the vehicle he regained consciousness and put up another fight. This time, Mngadi smashed a Makarov pistol into Sedibe's face, hitting him so hard that the silencer on the gun bent almost double. This knocked Sedibe out. It also left him with a deep long gash down one side of his nose. He carried the scar from that hit 'like a medal of honour' for the rest of his life[41] – testimony to the fight he put up once he knew who his attackers were; and proof for some, including De Kock, that he was not always the traitor that he became. While the rest of the men were subduing Sedibe, De Kock ordered Nofomela to disconnect the station's phone line. De Kock shot at a heater and locked the two Swazi officers inside the cells. With Sedibe unconscious, the SUVs drove the short distance back to South Africa. They crossed through a hole, about 100 metres away from the Oshoek border post, on the 'virtually unpatrolled and badly fenced' border.[42]

The convoy drove to a farm about five kilometres outside Piet Retief. The property was a legal black hole where even the fig leaf of apartheid legality was suspended. There, Sedibe's interrogation began. De Kock and Van Dyk kicked and punched him, all the while peppering him with questions about his MK comrades and their whereabouts. Sedibe would have known what kind of torture to expect from his captors. There was an MK manual about the forms of torture favoured by South African agents.[43] As the manual had predicted, Sedibe came face-to-face with 'racist sadists who converge on the captive like vultures on carrion. They leave him in no doubt that they have the power of life and death over him and the only choice open to him is to confess or die.'

This manual, published in 1984, was based on the experiences of MK operatives. It was taken for granted by MK that people always broke under torture; that they always talked. But it was hoped that captured operatives would hold out for at least 48 hours to give their comrades two days to take cover.[44] But even that knowledge could not have prepared Sedibe for the blows and the pain, the brutality and the humiliation. He could not have prepared himself for the loss of control over bodily functions. He could not have known beforehand how long it would take to 'break'. Nofomela, who was present during Sedibe's interrogation, recalled that it was not long before he started 'telling them stories'.[45]

The anthropologist Veena Das says that 'our theoretical impulse is often to think of agency in terms of escaping the ordinary rather than as a descent into it'.[46] To resist that impulse, I suggest we accept that Sedibe's telling of stories to his captors that night was his descent into the ordinary. What, after all, could be more ordinary than telling stories? But we must also accept that Sedibe's telling rested on a stark choice: talk and live, or refuse and die. As Sedibe later mentioned to one former ANC comrade, he told stories in order to live.[47]

The Security Branch wanted Sedibe alive, but his value to them lay only in the information he could provide about his comrades and the ANC. His life was worth something to the SAP only if he talked. They let him know. And he talked. By talking under torture, Sedibe underwent changes that marked him profoundly for the rest of his life: from resister to collaborator, revolutionary to counter-revolutionary and, in the eyes of the ANC, hero to traitor. These were not straightforward changes, despite the temptation to see in Sedibe's telling the point of no return, the moment that marked his transformation from resister to collaborator.

To 'hear' in the stories Sedibe told his captors his 'betrayal' of himself and his world would be, in the words of Elaine Scarry, 'to turn the moral reality of torture upside down',[48] to blame the victim. As Scarry says, there are two primary elements to torture: the first is a physical act that consists in the infliction of pain, the second is a verbal act called the interrogation.[49] The verbal act is made up of two parts: 'the question' and 'the answer'.[50] However, the connection between the physical act and the verbal act is often 'misstated or misunderstood'.[51] Scarry comments, '"The question" is mistakenly understood to be "the motive" [for the torture]; "the answer" is mistakenly understood to be "the betrayal". The first mistake credits the torturer, providing him with a justification, his cruelty with an explanation. The second discredits the prisoner, making him rather than the torturer, his voice rather than his pain, the cause of his loss of self and world.'[52]

Sedibe was certainly not spared contempt for betraying his comrades. Archie Whitehead, an ANC operative who worked with Sedibe in Swaziland, commented later, 'My own assessment, my understanding, knowing the man ... I don't think it took too much pain to turn him.'[53] Elias Masilela, who had met him in Swaziland, claimed that Sedibe 'did not like pain and hardship'.[54] Whitehead and Masilela not only think they know what Sedibe went through; they assume they would have reacted differently under similar circumstances. Perhaps. But torture is more than the infliction of pain; it is also a 'perverse theatre in which he [the tortured] is compelled to play the lead in a drama of his own humiliation'.[55] Nothing is left to chance in this theatre, from the stage where the torture takes place to the props, the instruments, used to inflict pain.

When Sedibe entered the stage – the farm – his face was bloody, his lips parched, and he had lacerations and abrasions on his body. He was also shell-shocked. As De Kock told the TRC in February 2000 when he and eight of his colleagues applied for amnesty for Sedibe's abduction, 'He had the look of shock in his eyes, the same symptoms that I observed with my own people after a combat situation. These were also the same symptoms that I observed with Swapo members after they had been in combat with us and we had captured them, disorientation, shock, fear, fright, fear for the future, pain and so forth.'[56]

Freek Pienaar, commander of the Security Branch in Piet Retief, had rented the nondescript farm for use as what he called a 'safe house'.[57] It had a farmhouse and, about 30 metres away, a pump house that served as a detention cell.[58] This contained an army-issue steel bed-frame. Sedibe, naked, was handcuffed to the bed-frame and put in leg irons. It was here that De Kock tortured Sedibe and later attended to his wounds. De Kock said, 'We treated all the abrasions and injuries, and I can also recall that his pulse rate was something like 140, it was too fast to count. I took his pulse by means of taking it for ten seconds and multiplying that with six. I gave him four of my tablets which I used for panic attacks or if I felt that I was going to have a panic attack. The tablets went by the name Lexotan. They were very strong tablets. I gave him four because I was afraid he was going to have a heart attack. He was extremely tense, he was still suffering from shock and I would venture to say that he was wild.'[59]

Fourteen years later, Sergeant Eugene Fourie, one of the policemen who interrogated Sedibe that night, recalled that the prisoner 'had an odour about him'.[60] Fourie was a member of C-2, a Security Branch section responsible for the 'interrogation and identification of arrested terrorists and the identification of terrorists abroad by means of photo albums as well as research on terrorism'.[61] What was so exceptional about that smell? Fourie could not recall if Sedibe was naked when he interrogated him. De Kock claimed that he bought Sedibe new clothes the day after the abduction as well as toiletries.[62] How was Sedibe at this stage? 'He was afraid, he did not speak freely. I was under the impression that he was still investigating every possibility of escape, which was his job by nature of the situation. That is why I kept the leg irons on unless he went for a shower. We would take him for a shower in the house, but then I would accompany him and there would also be four or five members of my unit there as well. He considered his options and his first option was without a doubt to escape,' De Kock testified.[63]

For reasons not pursued by the TRC, the amnesty applicants went out of their way to downplay the brutality of Sedibe's interrogation on the farm. De Kock emphasised how he gave Sedibe medical attention, shared his anxiety medication with Sedibe, bought him clothes and toiletries, and allowed him regular showers. Christo Deetlefs, commander of the Security Branch in Ermelo, denied that they had assaulted Sedibe once he was on South African soil. 'We wanted him to assist us on a voluntary level. We did give him a drink. He was quite a heavy drinker and it wasn't very long thereafter that his tongue loosened and we were all getting along quite well with each other.'[64] Schalk Visser, who as divisional commander of the Eastern Transvaal division of the Security Branch was the most senior officer by rank involved in the abduction, stated to the TRC, 'I am trying to tell you that in this particular matter violence was not used in the questioning of Sedibe. That violence was used by the security police in interrogations on activists is a well-known fact, but in this particular issue violence was not used.'[65]

But there was violence. Sedibe was assaulted. None of the black policemen took part in his interrogation. As Archie Whitehead said, 'They would not have risked Nofomela interrogating September. These people [black policemen] were expendable. They were never trusted.'[66] Nofomela, Mngadi and Koole performed guard duties inside and outside the pump house. That is how Nofomela witnessed Sedibe's torture. Using his hands to demonstrate, Nofomela recounted to me, 'They would take one hand to squeeze his testicles into a bubble and then smash them with the other. There is no way he could have resisted.' Nofomela described a festive mood at the farm. De Kock's men had slaughtered a sheep and were barbecuing it on a spit outside as the white cops took turns torturing Sedibe. As Sedibe 'betrayed' his comrades and his knowledge of their plots and whereabouts, De Kock and some of his men would drive back to Swaziland and, acting on the information extracted from Sedibe, attack ANC members. Nofomela claimed that De Kock and his men went into Swaziland three times that night.[67] Siphiwe Nyanda, a senior MK operative who had worked with Sedibe, confirmed this to *City Press*, saying that the 'effects of Sedibe's abduction were felt immediately'.[68]

'He had no alternative,' Nofomela stated. 'The Boers ... those guys knew how to assault a person.' The SAP had extensive knowledge of torture, drawn from, among others, the experience of the Argentine military junta in prosecuting that country's dirty war and of the French Army's bloody but ultimately unsuccessful attempt to put down the Algerian revolution. The TRC found that torture methods favoured by members of the Argentine junta started appearing in South Africa in 1982, shortly after General Mike Geldenhuys, a veteran of the Security Branch and later head of the SAP, visited Argentina and Chile that year.[69] But the connections between these countries went back years. When the South African Defence Force invaded Angola in 1975, sparking a response that saw Cuba send thousands of troops to defend Angola, the South Africans used Chilean interpreters to monitor Cuban military communications in Angola.[70] In 1979 an Argentine general named D'Almeida took part in a conference at Fort Klapperkop, in Pretoria, called by the South African government to develop new ways to defend apartheid.[71]

The exchanges between South Africa and the dictatorships of

Latin America, especially Argentina, were so extensive that Rubén 'Dolphin' Chamorro, a vice-admiral in the Argentine Navy who had headed ESMA, the Naval School of Mechanics in Buenos Aires, 'retired' to Argentina's embassy in Pretoria when his clique within the junta lost out in an internecine struggle. The naval facility housed a notorious torture site and illegal prison. Chamorro was followed to Pretoria by his fellow naval officers Jorge Perren, Jorge Acosta and Alfredo Astiz, the 'Angel of Death'.[72] Astiz earned his nickname after infiltrating the Mothers of the Plaza de Mayo, a group founded by women whose children and grandchildren had been 'disappeared' by the junta. Pretending to be a victim looking for a 'disappeared' brother, Astiz would identify women to be 'disappeared' by his military colleagues, hiding nearby, by kissing each woman on the cheek.[73] His deployment to Pretoria came after the Mothers of the Plaza de Mayo exposed him as an agent of the junta. The posting of these torturers to South Africa as 'diplomats' caused a minor ruction. Pretoria's career diplomats opposed the postings, especially that of Chamorro, on the grounds that they would only cause South Africa further embarrassment, but they were overruled by the South African Defence Force, which dominated relations with Latin America.[74]

According to Nofomela, the information that Sedibe delivered under torture was used to kill 'many people' in the ANC. 'He betrayed them on the point of torture. There was no alternative.' Nofomela remarked that Sedibe was a smart man and that even during his torture, he was 'reasoning', trying to find a way out. 'But the pain was more than he could take.'[75]

Nofomela could only imagine: one cannot feel another person's pain. As Scarry points out, pain is incommunicable.[76] To imagine what Sedibe went through, we can consider the reports of others who underwent similar experiences. Marcia Alejandra Merino Vega, a Chilean socialist captured and tortured by Augusto Pinochet's secret police in 1974, said, 'Confronted with nudity, death rattles ... produced by electric shocks, humiliations, beatings,

I shouted out without being able to control myself, the first name: Maria Angelica Andreoli. I felt that everything had ended for me. I had betrayed what I most loved at that time. It was like going down a tunnel with no end.'[77]

There is often disdain for the kind of confession described by Merino. One can hear echoes of such disapproval in Stephen Ellis and Oyama Mabandla's description in *Comrades against apartheid* of what Sedibe's captors did to him once they had him on South African soil: the police 'got to work on him', they write.[78] The historian Kevin O'Brien claims that Sedibe was 'convinced' to collaborate.[79] Vladimir Shubin, writing about ANC reactions to Sedibe's defection, commented, 'Many believed that he had been planted by the South African security in the ANC earlier, others thought that in a cowardly act he saved his own skin by betraying his comrades.'[80] Even Ebrahim Ebrahim, who had admired Sedibe as a 'very good comrade', qualified his opinion of Sedibe the defector by saying, 'but obviously he was a coward'.[81] In these passages there is no acknowledgment of the role of torture in Sedibe's 'choice' to turn – even though it was a widely known fact (and Ebrahim himself was subjected to some of the worst torture imaginable) that the SAP were among the world's leading torturers.[82] Instead, Sedibe is 'worked on' like a broken-down car; 'convinced' like some doubtful recruit to switch sides; and, in Shubin's and Ebrahim's accounts, presented as a coward interested only in saving his skin.

Some might say that, once Sedibe 'decided' on that lonely farm to become a collaborator, it was no great leap to becoming Mr X1 and, from there, to the alleged assassin who harassed and eliminated former comrades. But history never takes such neat turns. We cannot ignore the nine years Sedibe spent working for the ANC simply because he subsequently spent eight years working for the apartheid state. Yet unlike the TRC, we cannot pretend that Sedibe was only a victim of police violence and not a perpetrator of violence himself. Each label fits, but imperfectly. This is because

Sedibe's metamorphosis from Comrade September to askari was not seamless.

* * *

According to declassified portions of a confidential government file on Sedibe called, clumsily, the Directorate Security Legislation file,[83] the Piet Retief assistant magistrate R.J. Ohlsen visited him on 21 August 1986 – seven days after his abduction.[84] Ohlsen said Sedibe '*het geen klagtes geopper nie*' (had no complaints to raise). The Piet Retief magistrate, J.J.B. Tempelhoff, visited Sedibe on 1 September 1986. Sedibe had 'no complaints to raise'. On 15 September 1986 Tempelhoff tried to visit Sedibe at the Piet Retief police cells, but he was not there. The police had taken Sedibe to the local Security Branch offices for further interrogation. The magistrate went to the offices, where he interviewed Sedibe in private. Sedibe had 'no complaints to raise'. Tempelhoff said, 'On the contrary, he [Sedibe] expressed his satisfaction with the good manner in which he was being handled.' On 30 September 1986, the assistant magistrate A.P. Marais visited Sedibe at the Piet Retief police station. Sedibe had 'no complaints to raise'.

When the inspector of detainees (a post created in 1978 in response to public outrage over the police murder of Steve Biko) visited Sedibe on 24 August 1986, he found him in 'good health' and 'happy' with his food. The inspector concluded, '*Hy word goed versorg*' (He is being well looked after). On 28 August 1986, he was told Sedibe had been taken away for investigation and was unavailable.[85] The inspector paid Sedibe another visit on 14 October 1986. Asked about his health, Sedibe answered, '*Reg*' (Right). About the food, '*Baie goed*' (Very good). About his general treatment, '*Ek het nie klagtes nie. Hulle behandel my baie goed*' (I have no complaints. They are treating me very well.) The inspector concluded, 'He is well looked after.' According to Sedibe's declassified file, all but one of these visits took place in the Piet Retief police cells. By the time the visits started, on 21 August 1986, Sedibe was already a detainee in terms of section 29 of the Internal Security Act of 1982.

We could see these visits, complete with their rituals and bureaucratese, as an illustration of apartheid's 'obsession' with due process. But, as the legal scholar Lawrence Baxter wrote, 'Of all those who fall prey to the powers exercised under the Internal Security Act 74 of 1982 surely the most wretched are those detained under section 29.'[86] In terms of section 29, a person could be arrested and detained without a warrant, and be held indefinitely, subject only to the requirement that the order for his or her detention be renewed every 30 days by the minister of law and order. No person other than the minister or an authorised state official was entitled to information about the detainee. The only officials who could visit the detainee without permission were magistrates and district surgeons, who had to visit every 14 days, and the inspector of detainees, who had to visit 'as frequently as possible'.[87] There is no indication from Sedibe's declassified file that a district surgeon or doctor ever visited him. As Baxter comments about section 29, 'In effect, the detainee languishes in solitary confinement and at the mercy of his or her gaolers, enjoying only the token protections prescribed by the Act.'[88]

Being the lead in the 'drama of his own humiliation', Sedibe could do nothing more than play his part and say 'No complaints' each time a representative of the state that had kidnapped him asked about his health and the quality of the food and care he was getting. It is curious that while everyone who met Sedibe after his abduction remarked on the big scar running down one side of his nose, none of the state officials who visited him while he was in detention mentioned it, as fresh as it must have been. Indeed, that was not the only scar Sedibe bore. According to his widow, Sedibe had scars all over his body.[89] But the one on his face was unmissable.[90]

Sedibe might have become a formal detainee a week after his

detention, but we must wonder what difference that made. Apartheid rule was a permanent state of emergency. As Sedibe's case shows here, the apartheid state ruled in two modes – the legal and the extra-legal. Despite claims to the contrary, the rule of law under apartheid was a fiction. Sure, the fiction had real material effects and occasionally resulted in anomalies. But it was still a fiction. Sedibe's story also shows the fatal intimacies that bound those, like De Kock, sworn to protect apartheid and those, like Sedibe, who fought against apartheid. What could be more personal than De Kock sharing his anxiety meds to prevent Sedibe from dying of a heart attack, or using his bare hands to beat Sedibe to within an inch of his life, almost precipitating the very heart attack he did not want to claim Sedibe?

4
The choice

Some fled the country, some were held solitary in their cells and, refusing to speak, were kept on their feet under interrogation until they collapsed. Some did speak. Max was tried and sentenced to five years' imprisonment but he was called as a State witness after serving fifteen months, and he spoke. He was beaten when he was first arrested, that we know, but what else he was confronted with later, what else they showed him in himself, we do not know – but he spoke.

– Nadine Gordimer[1]

Sedibe's interrogation lasted three months:[2] three months of being given a 'choice' that was not a choice: talk and live, or refuse and die. How soon did Sedibe agree to cross over? Nofomela said Sedibe started talking within hours of his capture. A day after Sedibe's kidnapping, Assen Jeremiah Thimula (MK name Tallman) and Mbongeni Kone (MK name Bernard Shange), two operatives whose mission to infiltrate South Africa from Swaziland Sedibe knew about, were killed in an ambush by De Kock and his men. Sedibe later claimed credit for giving them up.[3] Sedibe's family suspect that he might have been led by his captors to believe that he had betrayed Thimula and Kone, thereby making it seem as if there was no turning back.[4]

By early November 1986, Sedibe had called his brother Kaborone and an aunt, whom he had not seen in nine years. During an emotional meeting at a small Johannesburg hotel, he informed his brother that he had been captured and was now working for the police.[5] He told them that he had been betrayed by his own comrades and tortured by the men from Vlakplaas. Recalling the meeting and his brother's demeanour, Kaborone stated, 'He looked relieved to see us. I think they [the police] were trying also to break him down, thinking that seeing his family would make him relax.'[6]

The ANC, still uncertain of what had happened to Sedibe, began to suspect that he had gone over to the other side. In a secret report dated 10 November 1986 and sent from Swaziland to ANC headquarters in Zambia, Ebrahim Ebrahim, using the codename Mzwandile, wrote, 'It seems that September is working with enemy. All his local contacts have been harressed [*sic*]. His wife came down from H [Maputo] after getting a phone call in H. We suspect the call was from September. She came to Bay [Swaziland] on pretext of collecting his belongings in Bay. On arrival here she just disappeared. We think she has joined him.'[7] She had.

Sedibe had called Ção at their Maputo flat sometime in October and, as Ção later told Nadja Manghezi, she 'nearly got a shock because she already thought he was dead'.[8] Sedibe instructed her to travel to Swaziland. Ção gave up her job at a mapping agency in Maputo. 'She didn't say goodbye to anybody, and didn't even tell her mother. She found some excuse that she had to take the child to see some of September's family in Swaziland and therefore had to take the child with her, otherwise she had never been allowed to go.'[9] Ção and her three-year-old toddler spent the first night in Swaziland. The following day they went to the Oshoek border post, where they were met by De Kock's men and driven to Piet Retief. 'To her surprise she didn't get a stamp in her passport, and they [De Kock's men] said she wouldn't need it.'[10]

Ção was born on 14 September 1963 in Mozambique. An orphan, she grew up in a Catholic boarding school and was later adopted by a woman named Bea, who worked at the school. As the school only went up to sixth grade, Ção had to transfer to a high school and moved in with Bea in Maputo. Bea was in a relationship with a South African exile and MK veteran named Julius Maliba, also known as Manchecker. Maliba, like Sedibe a Pedi-speaker, who also struggled with diabetes and high blood pressure, was one of Sedibe's MK commanders.[11] Both men were attached to the Transvaal rural machinery, responsible for MK's insurgency in the province's rural areas. Sedibe would visit Maliba at home for work and leisure. That is how he met Ção, who was ten years his junior. Sedibe moved in with Bea and Maliba in 1982.[12] De Kock told me Ção was so beautiful that he had trouble 'protecting' her from some of the white members of Vlakplaas.[13]

Sedibe paid lobola for Ção in 1983 and they had their first child that same year. But their life together was disrupted by the Nkomati Accord in March 1984, which forced Sedibe to live as a fugitive between Mozambique and Swaziland. Life with Sedibe became a 'hide-and-seek game', with Sedibe constantly moving house and squatting with comrades.[14] Ção and Sedibe's association with Maliba did not help Sedibe when the older man later came under suspicion by the ANC for being a traitor. Given their association, questions would be asked whether Sedibe was turned through torture or if he had always been an apartheid agent within the ANC. Maliba, who moved to Zimbabwe after the Nkomati Accord, was 'accused of giving information to the enemy', but he was never arrested, charged or expelled by the ANC.[15] The askari Gregory Sibusiso Radebe claimed to have seen Maliba once arrive by an SAP helicopter at a secret police farm.[16] Maliba had allegedly come to the farm to meet his South African handlers.

* * *

According to the policeman Freek Pienaar, Sedibe was reunited with his wife and daughter two or three weeks after his abduction.[17] Ção said that they only met nearly two months after Sedibe's capture.[18] In any event, as De Kock told the TRC, being reunited with his wife and their daughter was one of the conditions on which Sedibe agreed to switch sides.[19] It was still the height of petty apartheid in South Africa, and De Kock said he had to fight to have the Moolman Hotel, a 'whites-only' establishment in Piet Retief, set aside a room for Ção and her daughter.[20] Even then, the family were kept away from the main area and had to take their meals in their room – away from the white guests. Ção asked Sedibe why she could not stay with him. 'He gave some explanation that his hostel was only for men. And they couldn't stay in her hotel because he was black. She was not White either, but was told that they were kind enough to let her stay since she was not a South African.'[21]

Ção most likely did not know that Sedibe was formally a detainee and that he was still being debriefed, interrogated and turned. By 'hostel' Sedibe probably meant the cells at the Piet Retief police station and the pump house on the farm where he had been held. We know Sedibe was still a detainee because Pienaar, who became Sedibe's handler after his turning, bought Sedibe's daughter a tricycle, which she would ride around their hotel room and the police offices while Sedibe was being interrogated and debriefed.[22] The money for the tricycle and for the stay at the Moolman Hotel came from a Security Branch slush fund controlled by De Kock.[23]

By late November 1986, the ANC knew that Sedibe had turned. Sidney Msibi, a senior ANC intelligence officer abducted from Swaziland on 26 June 1986, was asked by one police brigadier during interrogation why Sedibe hated him. 'I said I wasn't aware that he hates me,' Msibi told an ANC comrade codenamed Stevens, who then wrote a report for the ANC.[24] Msibi, referred to by the *nom de guerre* Bongani in the report, said that once, during a police investigative outing to a spot near the Piggs Peak border post between Swaziland and South Africa, he saw Sedibe in the company of South African security policemen. 'When I got there I was photographed pointing at the area. There were two cars parked in the area when I got there. In one of the cars there was September drinking cold drinks and chatting with the Boers. After this I became suspicious of this fellow. Again on the second time I saw him in a happy mood with the Boers. It is then that I became convinced that he was collaborating with the enemy.'[25] Msibi was shot dead by an unidentified gunman in Soweto on 5 July 1988.

Additional confirmation of Sedibe's collaboration came in December 1986 following the abduction, also from Swaziland, of Ebrahim, who had previously spent 15 years on Robben Island for sabotage. When he was taken on 15 December 1986, Ebrahim was subjected to such mental torture by his captors that he told his lawyer, Priscilla Jana, in a note smuggled out of detention that 'if I survive it I would not be a human being'.[26] Ebrahim stated that by the fourth day of his detention he was a 'mental and nervous wreck'. His torture included exposure to sharp piercing noise and confinement in a special cell with little air. 'I felt I was going off my head. It was like being in a "hell". It completely wrecked my nervous system. I couldn't sit or sleep.' Among his interrogators was Sedibe, who had been a close comrade only four months earlier. As with almost all captured insurgents, Ebrahim was given the choice to switch sides. He refused. 'I'd rather go to my grave than betray one single person or organisation.' During his testimony as Mr X1 against Ebrahim, Sedibe denied taking part in Ebrahim's interrogation. He stated that he was there merely to confirm Ebrahim's identity to the police.[27]

The story of how Ebrahim was able to smuggle out his note is itself telling of the contradictions of apartheid (simultaneously legal and extra-legal) as well as the resourcefulness of those who fought against it. Ebrahim was kidnapped on a Monday evening from his house in Mbabane by two black men. The men had knocked on his door and asked for a wheel spanner, saying their car had broken down. Ebrahim was about to give the men a spanner when they produced firearms and threatened to kill him and his domestic worker, Dumisane Zwane. The two kidnappers identified themselves as members of the SAP. They bundled Ebrahim into a car and drove him to South Africa, crossing three or four border fences along the way. Ebrahim remarked later, 'When they abducted me, they did not know what to do with me.'[28]

The previous weekend had been murderous for the ANC. The Friday before Ebrahim's abduction, a 16-strong South African Special Forces team had killed Msizeni Shadrack Maphumulo, an MK operative and former Robben Islander, during a botched abduction. South African security agents had also kidnapped the Swiss couple Corrine Bischoff and Daniel Schneider, and Grace Cele, a Swazi citizen who headed a Canadian non-governmental organisation in Swaziland. The kidnappers suspected the three of working with the ANC. Bischoff and Schneider were released that same weekend after the Swiss government protested. Cele spent two months in detention, despite protests by the Swazi government.[29] But Ebrahim was too big a catch to kill, so the two agents took him to Pretoria. Ebrahim remarked, 'I knew they were getting rid of people. So when they said they were detaining me under section 29, I knew there would be a paper trail.'

Led by Christo Deetlefs, who had also participated in Sedibe's abduction, Ebrahim's interrogators subjected him to the kinds of psychological torture detailed in the US Central Intelligence Agency's infamous KUBARK torture manuals. One must wonder why Ebrahim was subjected to psychological torture only, while Sedibe was treated to savage physical brutality. This is not to say that one was better than the other: torture is torture. Did race have anything to do with the type of torture used in each case, or was the choice determined by what the police already knew about each man? As the CIA asserted in its manual, 'Persons of considerable moral or intellectual stature often find in pain inflicted by others confirmation of the belief that they are in the hands of inferiors, and their resolve not to submit is strengthened.'[30]

This being South Africa, and Ebrahim's abductors being men of the 'law', they had to accord him his 'rights'. These included the right to be seen by a magistrate. Fortunately for Ebrahim, who was held at the notorious John Vorster police station in Johannesburg, the judge assigned to him was Johann Kriegler, a well-known liberal jurist. 'He ordered that I should not be interrogated at all. They should take a statement only,' Ebrahim recalled.[31] As Deetlefs and his men did not want to defy the judge, they transferred Ebrahim to Pretoria Prison. There, he was put in a cell on a floor by himself. A group of detainees from Qibla, a Muslim group affiliated to the PAC, who were on trial for terrorism, occupied cells on the floor below Ebrahim's.

Among the detainees was Achmat Cassiem, who had been on Robben Island with Ebrahim in the 1960s. Cassiem had been sentenced, at 17, to five years in 1963, making him one of the youngest political prisoners on the island. Cassiem, who founded Qibla in 1980, had been arrested in the current case after his telephone number was found on one of ten PAC guerrillas arrested at the airport in Athens, Greece, while en route from Libya to Zimbabwe. The group had been intercepted by the Greek police following a tip-off from either the South Africans or, more likely, their allies in the West.

Ebrahim recalled that by shouting at the prisoners below, he was able to establish who they were and to know that his old prison comrade Cassiem was among them. He asked the men for pen and paper. 'I had a plastic bag with my clothes in it. I tore the plastic bag and made a string out of it. I sent it down to the floor below. The guys attached a pen and paper to the plastic string and I pulled it up. That's how I was able to write my story.'[32] Using the same string, Ebrahim sent the note down to Cassiem and his comrades. The men then passed the note on to Jana when they appeared in court the following day.

Sheila Nyanda was another ANC operative who encountered Sedibe the collaborator.[33] Nyanda, whose then-husband, Siphiwe Nyanda, was a colleague of Sedibe's in MK, was kidnapped from her home in Swaziland on 24 May 1987 and taken to South Africa. Her kidnappers, Warrant Officer Lappies Labuschagne and Colonel Johan Botha, both of the Security Branch in Middelburg, had moved into a flat next to hers, pretending to be South African university students on a break in Swaziland. Labuschagne called himself André. He befriended Nyanda and so she was not surprised when 'André' knocked on her door one day. She opened the door to find him pointing a gun at her. Labuschagne and Botha threw Nyanda into her car, a white BMW, and took her to South Africa.[34] The two kept the BMW, which was used on 9 July 1987 to ambush and kill Cassius Make, Paul Dikeledi and a woman named Elisa Tsineni Augusto.

Nyanda was tortured. The police slapped her and punched her in the face; burned her left ankle, right calf and the soles of her feet with a cigarette lighter; and blindfolded her and whipped her. Her kidnappers called themselves the 'suicide squad'. When they invited her to collaborate with the police, she refused. She was then placed in solitary confinement for six months. Here we notice, too, the physical dimension of Nyanda's torture. We notice especially the physical mutilation of her body. Pictures of her taken after her release show deep burn wounds above her ankles. Was there a racial dimension to the choice of torture method adopted by Labuschagne and Botha? A doctor from the University of Natal who examined Nyanda after her release said she was depressed, had difficulty in socialising, was constantly daydreaming, could not tolerate the company of others and had erratic sleep patterns. He also found that chance remarks brought about a recall of her torture, that she had frequent headaches, and experienced excessive perspiration and poor concentration. She was tense and irritable, was startled easily and had lower abdominal pain.

In an affidavit she filed against the South African government for her kidnapping, arrest and torture, Sheila Nyanda testified that Sedibe visited her while she was in detention. He asked if she had also been kidnapped from Swaziland and tortured. He told her that some people could withstand torture better than others. But when asked about it during Ebrahim's trial, Sedibe denied having this conversation with Sheila Nyanda. He repeated the denial when asked again about Sheila Nyanda during his appearance in 1990 before the Harms Commission of Inquiry into 'certain murders'. Sedibe declared that while he knew her as Siphiwe Nyanda's wife, he did not see her or talk to her while she was in detention in South Africa.[35]

* * *

Whatever the reasons for his collaboration, Sedibe hurt the ANC and helped drive it out of Swaziland. Even before his defection was confirmed, ANC members in Swaziland were in despair. Shortly before he was captured, Ebrahim wrote to Conny Braam, leader of the Anti-Apartheid Movement in Holland, asking her to publicise the news of Sedibe's abduction. Ebrahim urged, 'Try and make sure it gets some publicity. I don't know how long we can hold out here. A few days ago the Boers attacked the house of some comrades; luckily they weren't at home, but half the house is in ruins. The international press really must give it some coverage. A lot of the comrades have already had to leave the country, and I'm holding the fort with a few others. We can't give up this post, but we won't last long if things go on like this.'[36]

A secret ANC report dated 10 November 1986 noted, 'Nearly all the internal combat units have been wiped out.'[37] The report, most likely written by Ebrahim himself, stated, 'September, fortunately, did not know the real identity of many of our political units and those handled by Mzwandile directly.' Archie Whitehead remarked, 'September literally dismantled all the structures of the ANC in the Northern Transvaal' and the effect 'was quite devastating on the Transvaal military structures'. Whitehead insisted that Sedibe even 'had a hand' in the deaths of Make and Dikeledi.[38] This was echoed by Siphiwe Nyanda, who claimed that, within hours of Sedibe's abduction, South African agents attacked the homes of ANC members in Swaziland.[39]

Ronnie Kasrils, former head of MK's Military Intelligence,

reported that three MK members were killed within days of Sedibe's capture.[40] Kasrils called December 1986 a 'particularly tragic month' for the ANC in Swaziland. Elias Masilela remarked that Sedibe's 'defection goes down as the biggest in the history of the ANC'.[41] According to him, the information that Sedibe gave to the Security Branch 'inflicted untold emotional, psychological and physical havoc on many people and sent shock waves across not only Swaziland but also the region'.[42] Sedibe was so central to the ANC's underground activities that 'no amount of change to the underlying structure of the organisation in Swaziland would have been enough to eliminate the risk. The risk was just too deep to fathom.'[43] Barry Gilder, a former ANC intelligence officer, took a similar view. There was 'no hard-drive, no back-up computer, with everything September knew'.[44] The damage of his collaboration could not be contained.

The Security Branch celebrated their prize catch. They used Sedibe 'formally' to testify against former comrades in court and covertly to hunt down ANC operatives on the ground. Police Commissioner Johan van der Merwe praised Sedibe for his fluency in English and for being a good speaker – two important skills for propaganda purposes.[45] Sedibe *'het waardevolle diens gelewer'* (gave valuable service), said Van der Merwe.[46] In 1987 Sedibe even starred in a South African Broadcasting Corporation propaganda documentary shot at Vlakplaas (described as an unnamed secret location in the film) for South African and American television audiences. In the documentary, Sedibe and another askari, their faces hidden behind balaclavas, claim they were trained by the 'Russians' to sow chaos in southern Africa. The documentary sought to undermine the ANC's growing diplomatic success in its quest to isolate Pretoria. It followed ANC president Oliver Tambo's meeting with US Secretary of State George Schultz in Washington DC in January 1987. This was Tambo's second high-profile meeting with senior officials from a Western government. In June 1986 he met with Lynda Chalker, a minister in British Prime Minister Margaret Thatcher's government.

Thatcher and US President Ronald Reagan were staunch allies of the apartheid government.

De Kock told the TRC's amnesty hearing into Sedibe's abduction, 'In my mind he never turned out to be an *impimpi*. He was an intelligent man, he gave them [the police] just enough to satisfy them and to keep them happy, but it was about his survival.'[47] De Kock claimed that Sedibe only gave about ten per cent of the information he had on the ANC and its activities. 'Mr Sedibe was a blue-blooded ANC member, he was a blue-blooded member of MK, he was a blue-blooded son of Africa. He was my equal on the other side.'[48]

Some commentators have challenged claims that Sedibe helped to destroy the ANC's military networks in Swaziland and the Transvaal, despite the ANC's own such conclusions. The historian Hugh Macmillan, for example, believes that the ANC was too compartmentalised for Sedibe to have known as much as he claimed to know.[49] This is a fair comment but it puts too much faith in the ability of ANC members to keep discipline.

Sedibe and some of his former comrades were notoriously lax. Archie Whitehead has remarked that Sedibe and his unit were so undisciplined that he eventually refused to work with them. 'It came to a point where I was refusing to cooperate with them because they were so weak. There was essentially one point where we fought bitterly over discipline.'[50] Whitehead said Sedibe would sometimes poach Whitehead's operatives, in breach of ANC discipline.[51]

Ivan Pillay, one of the key ANC operatives in Swaziland, recalled how he was horrified to discover that Sedibe knew where he lived.[52] Operatives worked on a need-to-know basis. They were not supposed to make it a point to learn where others lived – unless it was necessary. As for where Pillay lived, it was not for Sedibe to know.

Stephen Ellis and Oyama Mabandla confirm that Sedibe hurt the ANC. 'Sedibe gave the Security Police information enabling them virtually to wipe out MK in Swaziland.'[53] They point out, however, that Sedibe was the least of the ANC's problems. 'It gradually appeared to ANC Intelligence operatives that, even before Sedibe's treachery, their network in Swaziland had been riddled with spies.'[54] Among the apartheid agents in the ANC in Swaziland was Edward Lawrence, whose MK names were Cyril Raymonds, Ralph Mgcina and Comrade Fear.

Comrade Fear, who died under mysterious circumstances in ANC detention in Zambia in 1988, had infiltrated the ANC through university student politics.[55] He had been recruited to the Security Branch through a relative in the SAP. When Comrade Fear was unmasked by the ANC, he was about to be promoted as MK's head of operations.[56] This would have placed him in command of every MK plot.

Archie Whitehead, who went to high school with him, claimed that Comrade Fear rose through the ranks of MK because he knew how 'to arselick in order to ingratiate' himself with his superiors.[57] Ray Lalla, who knew both Sedibe and Comrade Fear, commented, 'Fear had a very cynical way of giving people names.'[58] Comrade Fear's nickname for Sedibe was Dois M, from the Mozambican beer that Sedibe liked. One former MK operative told me that he narrowly avoided capture by South African agents after arriving late for a meeting that only Comrade Fear knew about. The operative's car had broken down on the way.

In 1984 Thabo Mahlopo, working for the ANC underground in Natal, was arrested by the Security Branch shortly after his return from Swaziland. Mahlopo had been instructed by the ANC in Swaziland to reconnoitre possible targets in South Africa. Mahlopo did as instructed. 'On his return [to South Africa] he was immediately arrested and he was confronted with the full report that he had submitted in Swaziland,' stated an ANC intelligence report dated September 1985.[59] Mahlopo was sentenced to 20 years in jail. Phila Ngqumea, an ANC operative based in East London, was another person to fall to apartheid agents in the ANC. 'When he was arrested he was shown a statement that he had made to our comrades in Lesotho,'[60] said an ANC report. De Kock once remarked that South Africa's spy network in the ANC was so extensive that the police would often get copies of secret ANC and MK decisions on the same day those were taken.[61]

This was confirmed in the trial against Dladla, Ebrahim and Maseko. The state wanted to make this a case against the ANC's landmine campaign in the rural areas. Dladla and Maseko, who belonged to MK, had been caught at a roadblock in June 1986. The police had evidence linking them to the planting of landmines in the border areas. The prosecutors used Sedibe's testimony to try to nail Ebrahim, who worked for the political side of the ANC. Ebrahim commented, 'He fabricated evidence against me. They were scraping the barrel to find evidence against me. So he [Sedibe] said I instructed him to plant landmines. Of course, that was a complete lie. I had absolutely nothing to do with landmines. I did not even know what they looked like.'[62]

It turned out that the National Intelligence Service (NIS) had information linking Ebrahim to ANC headquarters in Lusaka, which they had not shared with the Security Branch and the prosecutors. 'They had documents in my own handwriting sent to ANC headquarters. So somewhere they must have intercepted the documents.'[63] The spies had not passed this information on because they did not want to share knowledge of their agents in the ANC with their police rivals. It was only when the prosecutors started 'scraping the barrel' to find evidence against Ebrahim that they divulged the information.

Describing the ANC's communications network between Swaziland, Mozambique and Zambia, Ebrahim explained, 'I would get reports from home, compile them. Maputo would send people to Swaziland, foreigners we trusted. I would seal the report nicely and then send it with them. From Maputo, it would go to Lusaka.'[64] The raw material for Ebrahim's reports came from underground activists such as Ismail Mohamed, the first black professor of mathematics at Wits University in Johannesburg. Mohamed, who had taught in Swaziland and had children in exile in the ANC and at home active in the anti-apartheid movement, would travel to Swaziland for 'work' or holiday. There he would meet discreetly with Ebrahim to talk about political developments inside South Africa. This was something which Mohamed was eminently qualified to do: he was exposed to student and youth activism at Wits and was active in the United Democratic Front.

Sometimes Ebrahim's reports to Lusaka would be straightforward; at other times they would be in code. Among the documents confiscated from Ebrahim's house when he was abducted in December 1986 and entered as an exhibit in his trial was a coded message drawn up using a page from Nathaniel Hawthorne's Gothic novel *The house of the seven gables*. The coded message, based on page 81 and line seven of a chapter titled 'Maule's well', informed the ANC in Lusaka that two people named Zak (probably the lawyer and activist Zak Yacoob) and Y. Mahomed were travelling to London for two days and that someone from the ANC head office must see them. Yacoob and Mahomed were lawyers active in the UDF. Judging by the copy of the exhibit in the trial records, the police had broken the code. But it is doubtful they would have used Sedibe for that particular purpose. He was too undisciplined and, according to Ray Lalla, not much of a strategic thinker. He also lacked the patience necessary for the kind of tedium needed to decode a document. But that did not make Sedibe any less effective as a collaborator.

According to Jacques Pauw, Sedibe was arguably the most effective ANC defector to work for the Security Branch. 'He was probably the most useful askari in the history of the unit and gave unit members sufficient information to enable them to virtually wipe out Umkhonto we Sizwe in Swaziland,' Pauw wrote.[65] There is perhaps no greater proof of Sedibe's value to the apartheid government than the fact that even before the Vlakplaas death squad was disbanded in 1993, its members paid off or transferred to 'regular' police divisions, Sedibe and another askari named Chris

Mosiane were the only ones to be transferred to the Directorate of Covert Collection (DCC),[66] a secret unit within Military Intelligence charged with the penetration and destruction of the ANC. When Sedibe died in March 1994 he was working for the directorate, and the man who allegedly poisoned him was a senior officer there.

To hear some people tell it, the story of Sedibe is a straightforward tale of a hero-turned-villain. Siphiwe Nyanda and Solly Shoke, another MK operative who worked with Sedibe in Swaziland, refused to be interviewed for this book on the ground that to write about Sedibe would be to glorify a traitor.[67] Some people in the ANC even go so far as to claim that, far from having been turned through torture, Sedibe was always an apartheid agent.[68] *New Nation*, a newspaper aligned to the ANC, published a story about Sedibe in July 1987 titled 'Unmasked: South Africa's ANC spy'.[69] The paper alleged that Sedibe had infiltrated the ANC in the early 1970s. 'In that period, the entire ANC RPMC [Regional Politico-Military Council] in Swaziland has been wiped out,' declared the newspaper.

The report was filled with inaccuracies, starting with the date when Sedibe joined the ANC. But the report did warn, correctly, that Sedibe 'could turn out to be a star witness in at least 10 pending trials'. *New Nation* was popular with anti-apartheid activists and its report about Sedibe, whom it denounced as a 'pompous spy, who is described as being very sure of himself but not a very quick thinker', might have been intended as a warning to operatives in the ANC underground unaware that Sedibe had switched sides.

By June–July 1988, when *Work in Progress* was reporting on 'The strange saga of Mr X1', Sedibe's shift from resister to collaborator seemed complete. Mr Justice Daniels, the judge presiding over the trial of Dladla, Ebrahim and Maseko, had ruled on 17 February 1988 that 'The witness is exempted from the duty to disclose his real name to the court and he is authorised to adopt the pseudonym X1 for the purposes of this trial'.[70] The use of pseudonyms by state witnesses was common in South African political trials, despite the objections of defence lawyers. Prosecutors always claimed that the idea was to protect state witnesses from possible reprisals. This was a futile exercise in this case, as *New Nation* had already unmasked Sedibe.

But Sedibe was not the only witness to enjoy state-sanctioned anonymity. As Glenn Moss reported in *Work in Progress*, 'X1 is not unique. Indeed, already the state has produced three further alleged ANC defectors – X2, X3 and X4.'[71] In the course of researching this book, I established the real identities of X2, X3 and X4. In January 2014, I met X2 for a chat. He did not know that I knew he had been Mr X2: I kept my knowledge to myself.

X2 is the man I have named here Judas Mpho Tladi. X3 was Chris Mosiane, Sedibe's colleague at Vlakplaas and later in Military Intelligence. Mosiane's MK name was Ezekiel More. X4 was Oscar Linda Moni, whom we have already met. Moni's MK name was Stanley Gweje. Incidentally, only seven askaris applied to the TRC for amnesty. Among the seven were Mosiane, Moni and Mfalapitsa.

Many of those who were willing to discuss Sedibe for this book commented on his lack of bravery. Sedibe was a 'big coward', according to Archie Whitehead.[72] 'Because he was a coward, the minute he was in the hands of the Boers he turned a 180 [degrees].' Whitehead told me that it would not have taken much to break Sedibe. 'I think he essentially broke without much pain.'[73] Even Elias Masilela, who was otherwise sympathetic, accepted claims by some of Sedibe's comrades that he broke because 'he did not like pain and hardship. He naturally sought an easy life.'[74] This is a strange claim because Sedibe had devoted nine years to the ANC by the time of his capture.

One of the harshest judgements against Sedibe came from Ronnie Kasrils. 'I had known him [Sedibe] for some time but was never too sure of him, owing to his suspect nature. Some comrades thought he was a coward ... Physically, he reminded me of Bruno Mtolo, the traitor from the Durban sabotage days, and it gave me an uneasy feeling about him.'[75]

Kasrils said there were even claims by some in the ANC that a thigh wound Sedibe received in Mozambique in 1981 during a raid by South African Special Forces might have been self-inflicted.[76] Sedibe's first and only MK mission to South Africa, undertaken in 1977 following the completion of his military training in Angola and East Germany, had ended in disaster when one comrade was killed and another injured. Sedibe retreated to Mozambique. The mission had been betrayed and Sedibe lived under a cloud of suspicion for a while. 'It was my feeling that I was being watched,' Sedibe told the court during his testimony against Dladla, Ebrahim and Maseko.[77]

Recalling the failure of Sedibe's mission, Archie Whitehead remarked, 'He once went into an operation in Sekhukhune[land]. He came out running like nobody's business.'[78] Whitehead took this as proof of Sedibe's cowardice. Whitehead found Sedibe to be a man of contradictions. 'One thing that came out during training is that he was a big coward. At the same time, what was a contradiction is that he was a marksman. He would hit bullseye every time that he shot.'[79]

We cannot discount the fact that such judgements come in the wake of Sedibe's collaboration. Gabriella Turnaturi writes that betrayal affects not only relations between individuals but also the individuals' sense of a shared space and time.[80] 'Once the betrayal has occurred, everything seems clear and simple, and the complex personality of the betrayer is reinterpreted and explained by betrayal – as if a definition on the basis of that negative sign could embrace the entire individual.'[81] Sedibe's defection destroyed his comrades' shared sense of struggle. The defection became a gulf between two extremes: a 'before' and an 'after' in their shared life of struggle and hardship.[82] This does not mean that their judgements against Sedibe are of no use to us, but they need to be seen in context. They help us understand how Sedibe's former comrades thought about him and about his treachery. But they do not help us understand the phenomenon of collaboration.

There is no dispute over Sedibe's collaboration. But there is a dispute over *why* he collaborated. 'When he turned, he turned with a passion,' said Barry Gilder. 'He would go out of his way to find us and hurt us.'[83]

5
The inferno

War might be a science, and it might rest on grand strategy, but war is made by people.

– Hein Grosskopf[1]

It would be easy to take Sedibe the askari and freeze him proverbially in the ninth and last circle of the inferno, which Dante reserved specially for traitors, the 'misbegotten rabble of all rabble'.[2] But condemning Sedibe to hell would offer no insight; seeing him in only one guise as a traitor would leave us with a warped view of the man. This is because Sedibe was more than the sum of his treachery. He was also a tragic figure in the world of 20th-century counterinsurgency, one whose story is all too familiar on several continents.

If Argentinians see a familiar face in the portrait of Sedibe in this book, it might be because he reminds them of Munu Actis, Cristina Aldini, Liliana Gardella, Miriam Lewin and Elisa Tokar, Argentine activists captured by that country's military junta in the 1970s, tortured and turned into collaborators.[3] Sedibe's portrait might also remind Argentinians of Mario Firmenich, a leader of the Montoneros guerrilla group who was in fact an agent of the junta. Firmenich used the Montoneros to carry out 'terrorist acts' that were then seized upon by the generals to justify their murderous reign, which claimed more than 30,000 lives between 1976 and 1983.[4] Hebe de Bonafini, president of the Mothers of the Plaza de Mayo in Argentina, called Firmenich 'a traitor, a cadaver ... a despicable human being in every sense of the word'.[5] Gabriel Garcia Marquez, who interviewed Firmenich in 1977, described him as the 'strangest man I've ever met'.[6]

If Brazilians find Sedibe's tale familiar, that might be because the story reminds them of José Anselmo dos Santos, also known as Cabo Anselmo, an 'activist' whose collaboration with the Brazilian dictatorship in the 1960s and 1970s claimed between 100 and 200 lives, including that of Anselmo's Paraguayan wife, Soledad Viedma.[7] For Chileans, Sedibe's story might sound familiar because it is, in a sense, the story of Luz Arce Sandoval, Marcia Alejandra Merino Vega and Maria Alicia Uribe Gómez, Chilean militants who, after capture by Augusto Pinochet's secret police, were tortured and turned. They were then employed to ensnare former comrades and members of the anti-Pinochet underground, by means of tactics similar to those used by askaris.[8]

Sedibe's story might also remind Chileans of Miguel Estay Reyno and Osvaldo Romo Mena, left-wing activists who, after their capture by Pinochet's agents, turned into unapologetic collaborators. Estay, a member of the Chilean Communist Party, became one of Pinochet's loyal functionaries after his capture in 1974. In 1985 he participated in the beheading of three Communist Party leaders. Called in 1993 to account for his crimes, Estay said, 'My involvement with the PC [Communist Party] was so great that I had no alternative, I felt that it was my obligation to work against what I myself had helped to create.'[9]

Germans might hear in Sedibe's experiences the stories of the Stasi collaborators who fed the East German bureaucratic machine details about people's lives. If Germans cast their minds further back to the Holocaust, they might even recall the story of Stella Goldschlag, a German Jewish woman who, after having been captured and tortured by the Gestapo, agreed to collaborate with the Nazis, working as a *greifer*, a 'catcher', to identify and nab Jews hiding as non-Jews, in return for the lives of her parents. The Nazis killed her parents anyway.[10]

Sedibe's tale might remind Guatemalans of Emeterio Toj Medrano, a Mayan activist and insurgent who was captured by agents of the military dictatorship on 4 July 1981, tortured and then turned against his former comrades. As Betsy Konefal tells Toj's story, 'The army recognised what they had in their hands. Rather than kill their captive, they saw potential value in keeping Toj alive, and he became their weapon in a round of psychological warfare aiming to divide Mayans in opposition groups from their Ladino counterparts.'[11] Toj escaped from his military captors four months after his capture. But the damage had been done.

Sedibe's story could be told in a number of languages, including the Afrikaans of the *hensoppers* and *joiners* who worked with the British against their fellow Afrikaners in the South African War; the Arabic of the Harkis who fought with the French against Algerian independence; the Umbundu and Ukwanyama (to mention just two languages) of the Africans who fought for Portugal against the liberation of Angola; the Kikuyu of Kenya's pseudo-gangs who, working with the British, helped destroy the Mau Mau; and the Shangaan (to mention just one group) of the Africans who fought for the Portuguese in Mozambique, in an independence war in which more locals fought on the Portuguese side than on the side of Frelimo.[12]

In political terms, counterinsurgency was broadly discredited by Europe's colonial experience in Africa and Asia, as well as Washington's war against Vietnam and its adventures in Latin America and the Caribbean during the second half of the 20th century. But with the advent of the so-called war on terror in the last decade of the 20th century, counterinsurgency has come back into fashion. Inevitably, however, the clean-shaven and well-turned-out politicians and generals behind its resurgence speak of the doctrine only in terms of surges and strategy, and never of the brutality, corruption and mangled bodies that are the end result.

The historian Caroline Elkins argues that contemporary proponents of the doctrine of counterinsurgency draw the wrong lessons from the history of the British empire, taken by some commentators to have been good at administering the colonies and fighting so-called irregular wars.[13] The British used collective punishment, curfews, detention without trial and a range of other repressive laws to mount counterinsurgencies. 'In the final accounting, repressive laws and undemocratic institutions, not peace and progress, are the primary bequest of the British to their onetime empire,' Elkins writes.[14]

Laleh Khalili argues that counterinsurgency 'refuses politics'.[15] Proponents of the doctrine refuse to see the subjects of their doctrine as political agents in their own right, and reduce political contestation to 'technical problems to be solved'.[16] Stathis Kalyvas points to a similar conceptual problem in his review of *The US Army and Marine Corps counterinsurgency field manual*, which was published to much fanfare in 2007 with a foreword by General David H. Petraeus, at the time the poster boy of 'the surge', America's counterinsurgency strategy in Iraq.[17] According to Kalyvas, the manual broke 'little new ground' and was a reformulation of strategies developed in the 1960s, 'primarily in response to anticolonial or communist insurgencies in such places as colonial Algeria or Malaya'.[18] As Kalyvas points out, even Petraeus's 'surge' in Iraq worked because some former Sunni agents 'switched sides' and collaborated with the US after their elites negotiated deals with the American military.

One reason why some refuse to accept that the doctrine of counterinsurgency is by definition brutal, corrupt and corrupting is that, as Hans Joas and Wolfgang Knobl comment, 'A substantial number of social scientists are still caught up in the peaceful-utopian world of the European Enlightenment and continue to dream the "dream of non-violent modernity".'[19] Joas and Knobl argue that violence is key to the constitution of the modern world. Anthony Giddens makes a similar point, pointing out for example that 'British armies were involved in 50 major colonial wars between 1803 and 1901'.[20] Giddens calls violence the 'very medium of government'.[21]

* * *

Sedibe's abduction in August 1986 was not a random incident carried out by apartheid agents working freelance. It was a calculated counterinsurgency operation put into action two months after President P.W. Botha declared a state of emergency. Botha issued his declaration on 12 June 1986, four days before the tenth anniversary of the 1976 students' uprising. The declaration was part of a government strategy premised on two pillars: reform and repression. The strategy sought to deal with 'both black hopes and white fears'.[22] In effect, Botha, whose commitment to white domination never wavered, sought to reform apartheid in ways that would allow his government to co-opt sections of the black community while repressing anti-apartheid organisations fighting for a nonracial democracy.

The reforms pursued by Botha's government included the granting in 1984 of limited self-government to blacks resident in 'white' South Africa; the institution, also in 1984, of a tricameral parliament made up of coloured, Indian and white chambers, with whites retaining a veto over all major legislation; the repeal, on 23 July 1986, of laws requiring blacks in 'white' South Africa to carry passes; as well as the elimination of petty apartheid. The reforms were accompanied by infrastructure developments in South Africa's black areas, especially those considered hotbeds of resistance. The repressive measures adopted by Botha's government, on the other hand, consisted of abductions, assassinations, detentions, and the fomenting of vigilante violence to undermine community struggles against apartheid.

The mix of reform and repression had been urged on Botha by a number of advisers, including Samuel P. Huntington, a conservative Harvard University political scientist who from time to time also served as a policy adviser to the US government. Huntington warned in 1981 of a looming catastrophe over the next two decades in the 'South African political system that will only be resolved by fundamental change of that system'.[23] He rejected the idea of a nonracial liberal democracy on the grounds that it was incongruent with South African traditions and irrelevant to the country's needs. 'The key issue here is whether South Africa is a society of individuals or a society of racial communities. The record would suggest that it is far more the latter than the former.'[24] Huntington called for a political system in which 'all four racial communities would play appropriate roles'.[25] This would allow for the 'sharing' of political power without altering the racial composition of South African society.[26] He said violence was a necessary accompaniment to reform and that the reformer 'must be ready to welcome and use violence when it serves his purpose'.[27]

Huntington was not the only prominent American to take an active interest in the reform (or perpetuation) of apartheid. In fact, the doctrine of counterinsurgency in South Africa cannot be understood in isolation from South Africa–US relations. Starting in 1962, when President John F. Kennedy set up a Special Group on Counter-Insurgency to confront challenges to the post-war order, especially in Southeast Asia, Pretoria and Washington developed complicated but close military ties.[28] The South African government had already aligned itself with the US government in the Korean War in 1950, but Kennedy's initiative allowed the South Africans to use US interest in the doctrine of counterinsurgency to push for closer ties. Kennedy founded his special group partly in response to a speech delivered by Nikita Khrushchev, leader of the Soviet Union, on 6 January 1961, in which Khrushchev expressed Soviet support for national liberation wars.

In 1961 the US government advertised 'spaces for foreign military officers in US training courses'.[29] South Africa asked to send three officers, one each for courses entitled Special Forces Officer, Counter-Insurgency Operations and Psychological Operations. 'The US turned down the first two spaces and allowed the third. Subsequently, we reserved one space for a South African officer in both the Infantry Officer Career and Command and General Staff

Officer courses in 1962.'[30] The South African officer selected for the two courses was Magnus Malan, who spent 1962–1963 at the US Army Command and General Staff College in Fort Leavenworth, Kansas. There Malan 'imbibed the latest US theories of counter-insurgency'.[31] Malan – first as chief of the South African Army, then as chief of the South African Defence Force and subsequently for 11 years as minister of defence – was one of the key architects of the apartheid worldview. He was also a proponent of what he and his colleagues called 'total strategy' – in terms of which Sedibe's abduction was later carried out.[32]

The strategy was 'often neither total nor strategic', but it scarred southern Africa for the last three decades of the 20th century.[33] In the view of Malan and P.W. Botha – who, as South Africa's defence minister (1966–1980), prime minister (1978–1984) and then president (1984–1989), was Malan's political benefactor – South Africa was confronted with a total onslaught inspired by the Soviet Union and had to respond with a total strategy. The idea of a total strategy was the brainchild of André Beaufre, the French general and military strategist who had fought in the Second World War, Indochina and Algeria, and commanded French forces during the 1956 Suez crisis.[34]

Beaufre's idea, simply put, was that militaries needed to think of their battlefronts in total terms, meaning there should be no distinction between the civil and the military spheres. In other words, the military's ambit must extend beyond the traditional battlefront to all aspects of society: hence the need for a total strategy.

Beaufre was popular with Botha and the strategists in the South African Defence Force. In addition to his American training, Malan had been sent by the South African Defence Force to Algeria 'to gain experience under Gen. Beaufre's tutelage'.[35] Maritz Spaarwater, an officer in South Africa's Military Intelligence and National Intelligence Service, visited Beaufre in Paris sometime between 1970 and 1972 while he was on study leave from the South

African military and pursuing a master's degree in international law at the University of Cambridge. In his memoirs Spaarwater called Beaufre a 'renowned military commander and strategist',[36] whose 'ideas have infused and enriched training and theorising in military establishments the world over, including the SADF'.[37] Beaufre was of course not the only strategist the South Africans turned to. They drew heavily on American and British military theorists.

As set out by such strategists as J.J. McCuen, an American Army officer who fought in Vietnam, and Frank Kitson, a British officer who served in Malaya, Kenya and Northern Ireland, a successful counterinsurgency strategy depended on control over populations.[38] That is why confinement and the idea of 'winning hearts and minds' (Wham) were so central to the doctrine of counterinsurgency.[39] It rarely worked this way in practice.

Laleh Khalili writes that 'even as the theoreticians and practitioners of counterinsurgency speak of Clausewitz's truism that war is the continuation of politics, in practice counterinsurgency refuses politics, or at least transforms political conflicts and contestations, revolts and insurgencies, into technical problems to be solved. This inability to recognise the politics that defines and structures revolt means that counterinsurgency simply becomes another way to better fight a war. Yet in simply tinkering with the tactics, counterinsurgency produces its own defeat again and again, with no memory of prior losses, thus repeating the same fundamental mistakes.'[40]

We find the same mistakes in the ways in which people like Malan and Spaarwater thought about South Africa's political problems. Malan once told the journalist Hilton Hamann: 'If I can be frank, I doubt if the police understood the onslaught. They didn't understand what the conflict was about. They were never trained in it. They weren't addressing the cause of the problem, because they didn't understand it. They were referring back to previous experiences of an uprising without a political cause behind it. This was something totally different.'[41] For Malan, of course, the 'political cause' was the Soviet Union's expansionist designs on southern Africa, especially South Africa and its minerals. Not once during his interview with Hamann did Malan give any indication that he understood that South Africa's fundamental problem was the denial of citizenship and basic human rights to the majority of its inhabitants. Spaarwater, writing with the benefit of hindsight, said he was always 'fully conscious of the incomplete nature of our "democracy", but was confident that government policy was heading toward the eradication of its many anomalies and shortcomings'.[42] What were these shortcomings and how could a total strategy overcome them? According to Spaarwater, 'Beaufre emphasised the necessity of the involvement of the total capacity of the state in waging war.'[43]

How did the South Africans apply Beaufre's teachings? Part of the answer can be gleaned from Georg Meiring, one of the generals in the South African Defence Force and another keen adherent of Beaufre's total strategy. Meiring told Hamann: 'We [the defence force] got involved in everything. For example, we had veterinarians and doctors all over the show. We had teachers, we repaired windmills and waterholes. We looked after sick cattle and we built roads; you name it, we did it.'[44]

Meiring's comments are revealing for what they say about his government's worldview. Apartheid did not represent the failure of a particular model of 'development'. Apartheid failed, ultimately, because it rested on a fundamental denial of reality: South Africa was a multiracial country that could only work if all who lived in it enjoyed the same freedoms, rather than relegating the black population to serve as a source of cheap labour. Total strategy denied that reality.[45] Instead, apartheid strategists sought to reduce South Africa's problems to outside agitation by the Soviets and their fellow travellers, as well as to inadequate welfare provisions for black South Africans.[46]

Apartheid's military and political strategists thought they could manage South Africa's 'incomplete democracy' through what has been called 'comprehensive social engineering'.[47] This depended on the establishment of a massive bureaucracy, with military, police and spy agencies at its centre. The bureaucracy was called the National Security Management System (NSMS). This bureaucratic manifestation of total strategy has been described as a 'fairly sophisticated authoritarian response to the dilemmas faced by the government of a country deeply divided on race and economic lines'.[48]

Magnus Malan believed that the NSMS 'must be given credit for stabilising internal unrest' in black townships in the mid-1980s.[49] The system sought to harness the total capacity of the state to effect reform and repression simultaneously. But, as the political scientist Annette Seegers argues, the system was founded on the myth of military efficiency.[50] It began from the assumption that, unlike regular bureaucrats, the military could get things done efficiently. This myth was central to the organisation of the system because, as Seegers says, the formal intent was to make government more efficient by coordination and by the raising of bureaucrats' consciousness.[51]

In real life, the NSMS was far from the efficient, well-coordinated and sophisticated bureaucracy envisioned by the military and others. F.W. de Klerk, who dismantled the NSMS shortly after taking over from P.W. Botha in 1989, called it an 'intrusive bureaucratic system'.[52] He remarked: 'Its influence was quietly resented, not only by the broad public service, but also by cabinet ministers with non-security portfolios.'[53] De Klerk said the system and the bureaucratic tentacles it spawned undermined the 'sound principle of full collective responsibility within the cabinet'.[54] Botha and De Klerk were political rivals, and so it should not surprise us that De Klerk should have been so hostile to Botha's ideas. But implicit in De Klerk's reflections on the NSMS is an attempt to say that, but for Botha's authoritarian streak and the meddlesome ways of his securocrats, the apartheid bureaucracy was on the whole a fine system. De Klerk, of course, is not alone in presenting political violence as exceptional rather than central to apartheid itself.

The NSMS was not simply about the provision of welfare and better services to black South Africans. Botha's government used it to eliminate anti-apartheid activists while pouring money into black areas. Employing language derived straight from McCuen's counterinsurgency manual, the NSMS in the mid-1980s designated 34 townships around South Africa as 'oilspots'.[55] The term referred to the 'establishment of "strategic bases" from which the security forces believe they can "regain control" over the black population'.[56] Among the townships identified as an oilspot was Katlehong, my hometown. Here, state-driven development projects, such as the construction of new middle-class neighbourhoods and the provision of electricity, went hand in hand with mass arrests.

Apartheid's development projects cannot be divorced from government repression. In his memoirs De Klerk glosses over this fact. He frames state violence as an exception to the rule, saying only that the security services adopted 'some unconventional methods to combat the revolutionary threat'.[57] De Klerk writes that askaris were there 'ostensibly combating the revolutionary threat by legal means under the leadership of white police officers'.[58] The use of 'ostensible' is meant to suggest that whatever excesses the askaris committed were done on a freelance basis.[59]

The problem is not what De Klerk (and Botha before him) knew personally about South Africa's counterinsurgency, though it is reasonable to suggest that they knew more than they have told. Rather, the problem is with the doctrine of counterinsurgency itself. By definition, counterinsurgency is a dirty business. It is violent and depends on corruption to achieve its aims. As Annette Seegers points out, "COIN's [Counterinsurgency strategy's] moral challenges do not come from the proverbial few "bad apples"; the very nature of COIN tests all who participate in it.'[60] Not only does the doctrine lead to moral compromises but, Seegers says, 'Authoritarian regimes are also likely to dip into the lethal cupboard of COIN: murder and torture.'[61] This is what happened in South Africa. The

Security Branch began to apply torture systematically in the 1960s and assassination in the early 1970s.[62] Anita Gossman comments: 'COIN is rarely if ever clean.'[63] In fact, she adds, 'Winning the will of the people remains elusive when COIN actions are inherently counter to the political desires of the people.'[64]

Seegers argues that counterinsurgency is not only abusive, but it also tends to attract certain personalities. 'In addition, participants in covert operations are often people who first fought on the opposing side but then, upon capture, are given the "choice" to change sides. The choice of course is not authentic, as refusal will most likely result in death, especially when political opposition has been criminalised. The then "turned" fighters distinguish themselves by actions euphemistically described as being "beyond the call of duty". Such extremist behaviour thus does not always flow from fanatical devotion to a cause; in fact, the opposite is true. "Turned" fighters struggle to prove their loyalty to new masters as they, after all, have already switched sides once.'[65]

Askaris, Seegers writes, follow a simple declaration: 'By the extent of my cruelty you will know the depth of my loyalty.'[66] As we read in the work of Vincent Crapanzano on the Harkis, the Algerians who fought with the French during the independence war, there was a special group of Algerian collaborators known as the *rallies*. They were made up of 'turned' insurgents. Crapanzano says: 'These *rallies* were rumoured to be more ferocious than other Harkis since they had the most to lose if they were ever captured by the ALN [the National Liberation Army]. To ensure their loyalty, the *rallies* were sometimes photographed in the midst of French officers drinking to France or as they were interrogating prisoners; they were told that, were they to desert, their photographs would be sent to the ALN.'[67] According to Crapanzano, such was the reputation of the *rallies* that captured insurgents would ask that French officers interrogate them instead. 'The *rallies* were said to be the cruelest and most efficacious of interrogators.'[68] The French, of course, used this to their advantage to make insurgents talk.

We might think that, more than 20 years after the collapse of apartheid, the associated worldview no longer has any adherents. We would be wrong. Maritz Spaarwater, for example, claims that, far from having been a set of ideas inspired by the Cold War and South Africa's self-positioning in that war, total strategy was actually a logical response to the ANC's campaign of violence against apartheid. So, instead of the notion of the 'total onslaught' being a bogey conjured up by apartheid ideologues to justify their need for a total strategy, Spaarwater claims, it was in fact a real threat to which the South Africans had to respond. 'Even today, few people are aware that the concept of total onslaught originated with the ANC at Morogoro.'[69]

Spaarwater is referring to a consultative conference held by the ANC in Morogoro, Tanzania, in 1969. The conference, attended by about 60 delegates, followed the failure of the ANC's Wankie and Sipolilo campaigns in 1967–1968.[70] The Morogoro meeting was an attempt by the ANC to address the grievances of its members, take stock of its failures and develop new strategies. Anyone looking for evidence to back up Spaarwater's claim that the gathering developed the concept of a total onslaught will search in vain.[71] But the search will show the ANC's affirmation of the principle that the struggle against apartheid was, above all, a political struggle and that its military campaign must at all times be subordinate to its political objectives. The conference reduced the size of the ANC's national executive committee to improve coordination and management. It set up a revolutionary council to manage the day-to-day prosecution of the struggle against apartheid. The ANC also clarified its strategic direction by declaring that the struggle against apartheid rested on four pillars: mass mobilisation; the armed struggle; the development of an effective political underground in South Africa; and a concerted and systematic push for the international isolation of apartheid South Africa.[72]

This, for Spaarwater, constituted the total onslaught. 'When the government took the self-evident, logical decision to develop a "total strategy" to counter every facet of this total onslaught by our enemies – they would have been culpably derelict in their duty if they hadn't done so – their communication on the issue was so ham-handed that the message that it had originated as a response to the ANC simply never got through.'[73] It is startling to hear one of the key apartheid ideologues lament that the failure of total strategy was the result of bad public relations. Spaarwater's argument merely confirms that the apartheid rulers were politically blind and mistook the echo of their own delusions for a real threat, particularly when one considers how ineffectual MK was at this time.[74]

The worldview of the white-minority regime is captured in a series of draft defence strategies from 1973 onwards. P.W. Botha's preface to the 1973 White Paper on Defence and Armaments Procurement stated, for example, that South Africa was a target of international communism and its cohort of 'leftist activists, exaggerated humanism, permissiveness, materialism and related ideologies'.[75] It was also, in his words, a special target of 'black radicalism, exaggerated individual freedom, one man-one vote, and a host of other slogans employed against us on a basis of double standards'. This is the type of thinking that informed those who abducted Glory Sedibe. As far as apartheid's foot soldiers were concerned, they were fighting a total war against a total onslaught. Sedibe, in his role as an MK operative, was part of that onslaught. By turning him, the Security Branch sought not only to smash the ANC in Swaziland but also to wage psychological warfare against the liberation movement, showing that no ANC member was immune to capture, conversion and 'rehabilitation'.

How, then, did Sedibe's conversion manifest itself? To answer this question, we have to look at the ways in which Sedibe the askari straddled the divide between apartheid's legality and illegality. We have to look at both the formal and overt aspects of his work as an askari, and the covert dimensions of his actions as a collaborator.

6
The file

Pornography is an appropriate genre for police reports.
– Istvan Rev[1]

In July 1996 the novelist Mark Behr, about to be unmasked as an apartheid spy, confessed to having been an 'agent of the South African security establishment' for four years while a student at the University of Stellenbosch.[2] Behr said a 'probably well-meaning relative who was a high-ranking officer in the South African Police' had recruited him in 1986 to spy on anti-apartheid activists on campus. He agreed to join up for mercenary and ideological reasons: the secret police paid for his studies while he, having served proudly as an officer in the South African Defence Force before, had identified politically with apartheid at first.

Behr declared that he knew from the moment he signed on to work for the Security Branch that what he had agreed to was wrong. 'One had to be either an idiot or a psychopath not to be aware of that.' Behr did not mention the impetus behind his confession, delivered as a keynote address at a conference in Cape Town on the TRC. He said it was with the 'profoundest imaginable regret' that he was acknowledging his past. He declared he had lacked the 'moral courage' to stop his spying and to speak out earlier about his actions – even though he had realised the 'moral decrepitude of working for the state' right from the beginning of his career as a spy.

Behr said he accepted full responsibility for his support for a 'system that not only denied people's most basic rights and freedoms, but a system which divided, tortured, murdered and assassinated human beings, backed by precisely the security system I was involved in'. He acknowledged that the system he had served had also gagged the media and lied to the public in order to hide its activities. 'While I have not murdered or tortured, and while it is unlikely that my activities on a campus like Stellenbosch led directly to any such atrocities, I must and do take responsibility for my contribution to making "the system" work. There cannot be, and will not be any justification for this.'

Behr's confession, in which he did not once refer to any of his targets by name, sought to minimise the extent of his collaboration. He drew a line between his spying and the brutality that – as even he acknowledged – defined apartheid. He remarked that while he had willingly served a violent system, he himself had not committed any violence.

Behr's remarks enraged some commentators, including Guillermo O'Donnell, the Argentine political scientist well known for his studies of authoritarian rule in Latin America. O'Donnell, who had taught Behr at the University of Notre Dame in the US while he was a graduate student there, said Behr's confession was less than candid and that his efforts to downplay the extent of his collaboration nullified his apology. According to O'Donnell, Behr refused to come to terms with his 'deeper responsibility' to his victims. 'I say this because you and I know that informers of cruel regimes do not "directly" torture and kill; this particularly dirty part of the work of the "security establishment" is done by others. We know, too, that informers, torturers, murderers, and their bosses (who, like informers, do not "directly" torture and murder) are all integral parts of a cruel chain of events [in which] those who did not touch the bodies of the victims are no less responsible than those who did.' Regarding Behr's claim that one reason he accepted the spying job was to have his studies paid for, O'Donnell said the baseness of Behr's motives called to mind Hannah Arendt's claim about the banality of evil – 'so much infamy for so little!' declared O'Donnell.[3]

By telling his audience that he had only spied, and not killed or tortured, Behr was using one of the oldest tricks in the betrayal business. It is revealing, for example, that not once in his confession did Behr confess to what exactly he did. Nor did he say what he did to whom, when and how. But he wanted his audience to believe that it was 'unlikely' that his targets came to harm because of him. As O'Donnell asked, 'Have you tried to find out what happened to the individuals on whom you reported? Why do you not tell us about this, in a text in which you – just you – are the only human being who apparently matters?'[4]

Collaborators often suggest that their betrayal did not cause direct harm to their targets. Some claim that they only shared gossip with their handlers, nothing that could hurt those on whom they informed. Others offer different justifications for their actions. Luz Arce, a socialist who worked for Augusto Pinochet's secret police after she was turned through torture, claimed that she always tried to protect the leaders of the underground opposition. Arce said she only gave up low-level activists, prompting the relatives of some of those killed on account of her betrayal to question how exactly she had measured the worth of the lives of those she betrayed.[5]

Barbara Miller writes that in the former East Germany, 'Stasi informers were primarily engaged in the amassing of vast amounts of seemingly trivial pieces of information which could potentially be used to demobilise the enemy'.[6] She disputes claims by informers that their work did not amount to much. The Stasi – whose 62,500 tonnes of files would stand 200 kilometres high if stacked up – 'could never have functioned as it did if it had been constantly fed erroneous and fabricated information'.[7] Informers might have persuaded themselves that their work did not matter in the greater scheme of things. It did. The trivia about people's affairs, drinking problems and other minutiae that informers fed into the Stasi system mattered. 'It was ... precisely this sort of seemingly trivial and banal personal information which could be extremely useful to the Stasi. Such information could potentially be used to blackmail others, and it also helped construct a comprehensive personality profile of designated state enemies, which would facilitate the creation of plans to dispose of them.'[8]

The Stasi files, of course, did not prevent the collapse of the East German regime. One reason for this is that their very exhaustiveness 'stripped them of meaning'.[9] With files on six million of East Germany's 17 million citizens, the secret police could not avoid getting buried in all sorts of trivial details about the messiness of people's lives.

It is easy to see, when reading Glory Sedibe's Security Branch file, why informers would consider their work less harmful than it actually was. His 152-page file is full of personal details about his former comrades: so-and-so is missing two front teeth, so-and-so walks with a limp, so-and-so plays for this soccer club, so-and-so likes his drink a bit too much, so-and-so had an affair with so-and-so. Such details make it hard to believe that this trade in salaciousness was in fact the substance of secret police work.[10]

* * *

According to Hugh Trevor-Roper, whose reputation suffered in 1983 after he wrongly authenticated a set of forged Nazi documents, there are three questions to be asked of any document. Is it genuine? Did someone knowledgeable write it? Why does it exist?[11] To answer the first of Trevor-Roper's questions: it is safe to assume that Sedibe's file is indeed genuine and that its contents came from Sedibe's interrogation and 'debriefing' by the security police following his abduction from Swaziland in August 1986. The security police intended the file for internal use, making it unlikely they would have stuffed it with inaccuracies. To answer the second question: Sergeant Eugene Fourie, based in C-Section in the Security Branch headquarters in Pretoria, compiled the file. His job included the maintenance of files on known and suspected insurgents. He was knowledgeable about his job.[12]

Why does Sedibe's file exist? The answer comes in two parts. First, the file exists because the Security Branch compiled it using the information Sedibe gave them, voluntarily and through torture during his interrogation and debriefing. Second, it exists (or, rather, survived the end of apartheid) because of the TRC. The commission noted in its final report that when it came to gaining access to the surviving portions of the apartheid security archive, the renamed South African Police Service was 'more helpful' – in contrast to the (also renamed) South African National Defence Force. The TRC said the Defence Force was 'reticent' about giving it access to its archive.[13] In truth, the police were 'more helpful' to the TRC because their new bosses (drawn from the ranks of the ANC) had the political will to open up the Security Branch archives. In contrast, the Defence Force, although also led by former ANC insurgents, showed no similar inclination. This reticence may have stemmed from the fact that the Defence Force committed most of its crimes during apartheid outside the country, which meant that those responsible could not enjoy the protection of a TRC amnesty. They were still liable for prosecution in other jurisdictions.

Yet the reason Sedibe's file survived may be more prosaic: that it was simply missed. For about six months in 1993, the National Intelligence Service alone destroyed about 44 tonnes of files, microfilm, audiotapes and computer disks. The archival purge took place at an industrial furnace in Pretoria belonging to the steelmaker Iscor and at a facility in Johannesburg.[14] The destruction sought, in the words of Bell and Ntsebeza, to 'eradicate all evidence of the nightmare memories of the tortured and the living dead, to obliterate all trace of those victims whose physical remains lay scattered countrywide in unmarked graves'.[15] But that was not the only reason. 'Into the flames too went the files of the frightened ones, their craven acceptances of compromise and collaboration etched in dry officialese, but still sweating fear from every syllable. There were also the records of the venal individuals whose greed had driven them to verbal betrayal and beyond. The pasts of thousands of part-time whisperers of secrets and betrayers were turned to ashes.'[16] The National Intelligence Service was not the only outfit to destroy its archive. So too did the military and the Security Branch, starting in 1989. The archivist Verne Harris comments, 'It is far too early to come to any conclusions about the impact of the 1990–94 purge on social memory in South Africa.'[17]

By the time Vlakplaas was disbanded in April 1993 following public revelations of its activities, Sedibe had been working with the DCC of the SADF's Military Intelligence since mid-1990. We know this because the last entry of Sedibe's name in a Vlakplaas personnel logbook is for the month of June 1990. It lists Sedibe as being on leave from 29 May 1990 to 2 July 1990. Thereafter Sedibe's name does not show up again.[18] This is likely to have been the time when he began working for the directorate. Recalling Sedibe's transfer, his widow, Ção, said, 'With the move his salary went up and his timetable changed. He used to work normal hours when he was with the police [at Vlakplaas], but now he would be away from the place for two weeks, then one week normal working hours and then one week off.'[19]

Sedibe's new employer, the DCC, was responsible for apartheid's dirty tricks. The directorate employed criminals and used front companies for its activities. It operated out of secret locations and safe houses. But its main base of operations was a large open-plan office in the Momentum Mews Building in the Pretoria suburb of Lynnwood Ridge.[20] The directorate had worked in tandem with police death squads. In fact, it would have continued its operations but for a raid on its headquarters in November 1992 by Judge Richard Goldstone, head of a government-appointed body set up to probe state violence. Before the raid, the directorate was complacent. Bell and Ntsebeza write, 'Secure in its secrecy, the DCC had not apparently destroyed the records of deeds done, operations running, authorisations given and payments made, or the lists of named assassins, blackmailers, collaborators and targets.'[21]

It is possible that Sedibe's file moved with him to the directorate.

It is also possible that someone held it as insurance – something with which to keep Sedibe from revealing what he knew. The ANC 're-turned' some of Sedibe's fellow collaborators. But such efforts did not always succeed. On 21 November 1991 Lieutenant W. Riaan Bellingan, a senior member of Vlakplaas, sent a confidential report to Major-General J.L. Griebenauw, head of the Crime Information Service, informing him about an ANC attempt to 're-turn' Chris Mosiane, Michael Matikinca, Ernest Nonjwangu and Collin Khumalo. The four were members of an MK Special Operations unit when they were arrested in Swaziland on 14 April 1984 by the Royal Swazi Police. The arrests were part of an anti-ANC clampdown by the government of Swaziland following the signing of the Nkomati Accord. Instead of deporting the four to Zambia, as was often the case with arrested ANC members, the Swazi police took them to a police station in a small town called Bhunya. Like Mankayane, Bhunya was conveniently close to the border with South Africa. The Security Branch kidnapped the four and took them to South Africa, where they were tortured. All four became askaris.

Now in 1991 the ANC was trying to win them back. According to Bellingan, an MK member, Pat Moloi, acting for the MK leader Siphiwe Nyanda, who had worked with the men in Swaziland, had met Mosiane in Soweto and proposed that the four appear before an international media conference to tell the world the truth about what had happened to them. 'By so doing, they would embarrass the Government and the National Party,' Bellingan wrote. The ANC offered to take the four and their families to places of safety outside South Africa. Moloi, who had met Mosiane in Soweto in October 1991 and spoken to him by phone in November 1991, asked Mosiane to compile a list of all askaris from the ANC and PAC and to detail the conditions under which each person had been turned. 'This tactic by the ANC could cause the Government embarrassment if not handled well,' wrote Bellingan, who called on his superiors to determine the 'loyalty' of the other three askaris. In the end, the four askaris did not turn.[22]

According to Barry Gilder, 'There were askaris that we turned back. There were a couple that we eliminated, executed inside the country. And he [Sedibe] was a target for that. But it was very difficult as he was moving around all the time. It was very difficult to watch him.'[23] This did not mean the ANC was averse to winning Sedibe back. As mentioned earlier, when Sedibe died in March 1994, he was talking to the ANC about returning to the fold.[24]

* * *

Sedibe's Security Branch file is a debriefing report compiled on 19 February 1987 by Fourie in Pretoria. The file is divided into six sections.[25] The first gives a brief description of his arrest; the second provides a biographical sketch; the third lists Sedibe's *noms de guerre*; the fourth talks about when and how he went into exile; the fifth (the timeline mentioned previously) gives a breakdown of where he lived and the countries he visited while in exile. The sixth and final section is titled *uitkennings* – Afrikaans for identifications – referring to Sedibe's identification of some of the estimated 7000 portraits of known and suspected activists in exile that were pasted in an album held by every Security Branch unit in South Africa.[26] The album, in which a suspect's race was marked by number – with 1 for whites, 2 for Indians, 3 for coloureds and 4 for blacks – was made up of photographs taken from various sources. These included family albums, the Bantu Identification Bureau, school yearbooks, sports clubs and informers.

Breyten Breytenbach, who spent seven years in prison for anti-apartheid activity, noted that the album and its accompanying manuals contained 'photos and curricula vitae of the South African "terrorists" and "trainee terrorists" abroad'.[27] Speaking of the Security Branch, Breytenbach said, 'their knowledge of "the enemy" was quite astounding.'[28] Even the ANC was aware of the album and warned its members about it in 1984.[29] Breytenbach and the ANC knew about the album because, after an insurgent's capture and the inevitable torture, the album was one of the first things the police brought out. In fact, for many captives, the album initiated their first act of collaboration. Having told their captive everything they knew about him or her, which was usually extensive, the police would order the prisoner to identify people in the album. The captive would have to tell the police what he or she knew about those who were pictured: who they were, how the captive knew them, where they lived, what sort of training they had received and where, who they were sleeping with, their quirks and weaknesses, and so on. Captives talked. It was often the only way to gain some respite from torture or to save oneself.

Gathering such mundane details about people's lives enhanced the police's sense of omnipotence. It allowed them to pretend that they knew their enemies better than the enemies knew themselves. Breytenbach, for example, was astonished by what the police knew about him.[30] Mwezi Twala, an ANC member who defected to the Security Branch in the late 1980s, was also astounded by the breadth of knowledge displayed by the officials who debriefed him after his defection. 'It was mindboggling to listen to their exposition. They knew more about me than I did.'[31]

Hugh Lewin, who spent seven years in prison for sabotage, writes this about his police interrogators and torturers: 'And they began telling me *all* [his emphasis] about myself, precisely so. It was eerie.'[32] That was exactly the desired effect. The police wanted their captives to believe that they were in the clutches of an all-knowing power. They wanted to make their captives feel helpless, powerless and small, and did so by drawing on the knowledge bank built with scraps of information such as those offered by Sedibe.

As the historian Istvan Rev comments, 'The secret police archives are gold mines for the historian who, nevertheless, cannot be unambiguously grateful for the help provided by the informer.'[33] Rev's warning is important for thinking about how we approach the contents of Sedibe's file. First of all, there is the question of ethics. How should we deal with the fact that many people that

Sedibe named in his file are still alive and likely to be hurt should his claims about them – true or false – be exposed?[34] Rev says historians are often accused of 'illegitimate moralising' when it comes to their handling of controversial archives.[35] My attempt to deal with the ethical implications of this book without 'illegitimate moralising' included asking a few of those named in Sedibe's file for permission to quote his claims about them. In most cases, I have simply given the named individuals pseudonyms to protect their privacy. But there are also instances where the individuals named by Sedibe are dead or so well known and the information about them so banal as to obviate the need for privacy.

The entries in the identifications section of Sedibe's file follow a certain format.[36] The file is arranged in alphabetical order. There are, first, two numbers: one is a security police number for the subject; the other refers to the subject's picture. Then comes the subject's name and, next to it, an indication of where they came from. A line indicating which organisation the subject belonged to follows. Then comes a section titled *opmerkings* – Afrikaans for comments or observations – that contains seemingly trivial details about people's lives.

Take, for example, the entry on a man we shall call Andrew Anderson. After listing his political career, the places where Sedibe knew him from, and Anderson's activities in exile, the entry gives the following details: Andrew Anderson was involved in a car accident in a southern African country sometime in the 1980s and lost two front teeth. His wife works for a financial institution in a southern African country. He is a heavy drinker and lacks discipline. Another man, let us call him Hunter Bernard, is nicknamed after a waterbird because he once killed such a bird in an ANC camp for its administrators to feast on. Bavumile Malan (not his real name) is a married trade unionist but is in love with his secretary. Malan is a tribalist who favours recruits from his home province, the Eastern Cape. He always steers recruits from his province away from MK and towards study opportunities. Mandla Tshabalala (not his real name) is a heavy dagga smoker. Dambo Sgebengu (not his real name) once stabbed his wife with a knife. She went to hospital; he went to jail in an East African country. Dibi Tsempe (not his real name) is from Soweto and was once held in an ANC detention facility in southern Africa following suspicion that he was an apartheid agent. David de Jong (not his real name) is a white member of MK who keeps his hair short and wears an earring. He speaks a smattering of an African language and has the demeanour of a *skollie* – Afrikaans for hooligan. Brian Gibson (not his real name) is also a white member of MK. He once had an affair with the wife of a colleague. Tshontsha Dikoloi (not his real name) is part of a two-man car-thief racket, and he and his partner-in-crime are known as Rum and Maple. Thuto Sfundiswa (not his real name) is a mathematics and English teacher. He is haughty and speaks such *hoë Engels* – posh English – that people often cannot understand what he is saying.

In a case of history repeating itself, except both times as tragedy, Sedibe observes the following about Ebrahim Ebrahim: he will read any book he can lay his hands on. This is similar to an observation made in 1966 about Ebrahim by Bruno Mtolo, one of the first ANC insurgents to defect to the police. Mtolo, whose state witness testimony helped send Ebrahim to Robben Island for 15 years in the 1960s, accused Ebrahim of being a 'lazy chap' who 'wanted to lie on his back, reading novels and selected works of Lenin without doing anything'.[37] Another of those identified by Sedibe was Jonas Gwangwa, the famous trombonist and a member of the ANC in exile. According to Sedibe's file, Gwangwa was involved in a car accident in a southern African country in 1981 and had one stiff leg as a result of a steel implant.

Not all entries are as detailed as Gwangwa's. There is, for example, little personal information in the entry on Joe Modise, the commander of MK and Sedibe's relative by marriage, other than that he lived with his wife, Jacqueline Sedibe, in a house in Lusaka. The file notes that one E.S. Zikalala was arrested by the ANC in

1981 on suspicion of being an apartheid agent but was cleared and released.[38] Jacob Zuma lived on Julius Nigere [*sic*] Avenue in Maputo, with a wife whom he married in 1985. The wife worked as a hostess at the airport in Maputo. Zuma was also married to a medical doctor named Nkosazana Zuma, who lived in Swaziland.[39]

The file's attempt at exhaustiveness means that no detail is too insignificant, no biography too small. Together with the foot soldiers are leaders of the revolution: people like the ANC president, Oliver Tambo, and Communist Party bosses Moses Mabhida and Yusuf Dadoo. Sedibe's file records that Tambo was the president of the ANC and Sedibe had seen him in Angola and Maputo on numerous occasions. The file says that Dadoo visited the Teterow military training camp in East Germany in 1977. Sedibe 'believes he is dead'. Albie Sachs, an ANC lawyer, had a house on Julius Ngere [*sic*] Avenue in Maputo, which the ANC used to lodge its leaders for a day or two. Edward Joseph (not his real name) was separated from his wife after she had an affair with Jonathan Solomon, a senior member of the organisation. The wife moved to Europe.

Ivan Pillay, a senior member of the ANC underground, lived with his wife in Swaziland, and drove a white Ford Escort. Nomvula Madikizela (not her real name) received military training in East Germany, where she was a section leader. She moved to a southern African country after her training. She had a relationship with a senior MK member, Simphiwe Nzama (not his real name), in 1979. When she fell pregnant with his baby, she went to an East African country to deliver the child. She suffered a nervous breakdown in 1980 when she found out that Nzama had married another woman in the meantime.[40]

Reading Sedibe's file more than 20 years after the end of apartheid and the Cold War means appreciating what Kirsten Weld calls the 'distinct archival logics' behind the creation and existence of such files. By this, Weld means the 'two organising principles, or two reasons for being' of files such as Sedibe's. The first logic, the reason why the file exists in the first place, is one of apartheid surveillance and social control. The second logic, one of 'democratic opening, historical memory' and the pursuit of justice, governs our attempt to read Sedibe's file against the apartheid archival grain. By employing the second logic, we can mine the file for information without assuming it contains the truth, or that its contents are a faithful reflection of the past.[41] Using the second of Weld's 'archival logics' also means not taking the Security Branch at face value. It means peering beyond the facade of bureaucratic efficiency and panopticon-like omnipotence suggested by Sedibe's file.

Take, for example, the constant misspelling of Julius Nyerere's surname as Ngere and Nigere in the file, or the entry on Barry Gilder. The Security Branch always confused Gilder, a tall white South African of Jewish descent, with Aboobaker Ismail, a tall Indian South African of Muslim background who headed MK's Special Operations section and went by the *nom de guerre* Rashid. One can see the Security Branch's confusion of Gilder with Rashid in the photographs submitted as exhibits in the treason trial against Dladla, Ebrahim and Maseko. Scribbled alongside Gilder's mug shot is the name Rashid. So much for the bureaucratic efficiency of the Security Branch.

According to Ray Lalla, 'It wasn't as if we were top-class operatives and the Boers [ANC-speak for apartheid police] had to mount sophisticated operations to penetrate us. We were *dronkies* [drunks], we were chaotic, we went to parties ... We were a comedy of errors; they [the Security Branch] were a comedy of errors. But they had a vicious streak. We were idealists. We believed that, as revolutionaries, it was do or die. But, when faced with the choice, we did not want to die. They [the Security Branch] had the laws, they had the audacity, they had the brutality. But they never had intelligence.'[42]

What the Security Branch did have were salacious details about people's lives. Looking at Sedibe's file, we might be tempted to think of it as filled with nothing but 'harmless prattle',[43] or deduce that the Security Branch were interested in nothing more than the obvious and the banal. However, to do so would be to miss the menace hidden in Sedibe's file. The file did more than titillate the voyeuristic tendencies of the police. It also provided them with information that they could and did use to deadly effect. Take, for example, the entry on Job Tabane (MK name Cassius Make). Sedibe describes Tabane's military history and positions in the ANC and MK. He says that Tabane and his wife – whose name he gives – live in Lusaka with their two children and that Tabane drives a beige Peugeot 504.

A South African death squad assassinated Tabane, Sello Motau (MK name Paul Dikeledi) and Elisa Tsineni Augusto on 9 July 1987 in Swaziland. Tabane and Motau had flown into Matsapha Airport aboard a Lesotho Airways flight from Maputo and were in a taxi with Augusto, Motau's girlfriend, when men travelling in a white BMW with South African number plates ambushed them under a bridge.[44] This was the same BMW that Warrant Officer Lappies Labuschagne and Colonel Johan Botha had stolen from Sheila Nyanda after abducting her in May 1987.

Tabane, who had made ANC history in 1985 by becoming the youngest member of the organisation's national executive committee, was head of MK's ordnance department, and Motau was a senior MK commander for the Transvaal. According to Kevin O'Brien, the assassinations followed information provided by Sedibe and other South African agents within the ANC and MK.[45] Archie Whitehead insisted that Sedibe 'had a hand' in the deaths of Tabane and Motau.[46] Their deaths were among 11 assassinations of ANC members in Swaziland carried out by South African agents in the year after Sedibe's defection.[47]

What does Sedibe's file tell us about how the South African policy-making and political machinery operated? Scholars such as Kevin O'Brien and institutions such as the TRC have shown that under apartheid political assassinations were a tool of state policy. O'Brien writes, 'While South Africa is not, by far, the only "democracy" to have used assassination as a tool of state policy, in comparison with other industrialised states, it did have the most effective and structured programme for the elimination of its opponents.'[48] To understand how political assassinations came to be a tool of state policy in South Africa, 'one must understand the nature of the national security architecture and composition which supported and implemented that use'.[49]

Starting in the 1970s, there developed a 'mechanised and systematised process, whereby problems were reported, targets were selected and operations implemented to remove those targets ... [seen] as a threat to the state'.[50] This process was driven by a 'national security state' and maintained by a 'security architecture run by the State Security Council'.[51] The council, established in 1972, was responsible for the National Security Management System (NSMS). This system drew in turn on the strategic and tactical work of the various police and intelligence organs of the state, from the National Intelligence Service to the foot soldiers who carried out assassinations. O'Brien remarks that, by one count, 'more than 50 opponents of apartheid' were assassinated between 1977 and 1989.[52]

Askaris such as Sedibe operated within the NSMS. Sedibe served variously as bounty hunter, intelligence analyst and, quite possibly, assassin. He participated in the interrogation of Ebrahim Ebrahim and Sheila Nyanda, even if his participation in each case was limited to his confirmation of their identities. How far-fetched is it to believe that he may also have taken part in the killing of former comrades?[53] Ebrahim commented, 'What I know is that after his abduction, they raided Swaziland and he was seen in the car with the SAP.'[54] Given the timing of his own defection, Sedibe was probably one of the key sources of the information used to set up the assassination of Tabane and Motau. We know, in other words, that the blandness of Sedibe's police file masks deeper truths about askaris.

Hearsay evidence that Sedibe was involved in the killing of ANC members comes from one of his fellow collaborators.[55] Judas Mpho Tladi, who testified as Mr X2 in the treason trial against Dladla,

Ebrahim and Maseko in May 1988, had joined the ANC in 1980 and was captured by South African agents in January 1988. When Tladi appeared as Mr X2 in the Ebrahim trial, his defection was so recent that the judge would not allow anyone in court, including the witness himself, to mention any of the personal names he had used in the ANC. Tladi told the court that he was on his way to visit his family in South Africa when he was arrested by the police in Piet Retief. He was in the boot of a car driven by a Swazi car smuggler when the police stopped the vehicle. Tladi said an ANC colleague named Joseph Dlamini had arranged with the smuggler to take him into South Africa.[56] However, when I spoke to Tladi at his home in January 2014, he told me that the askaris Sipho Ngema and Chris Makgopa, a veteran collaborator captured in Botswana in 1984,[57] had 'helped' him return to South Africa and that he, Tladi, had in fact handed himself over to the police as part of an ANC ploy to flush out apartheid spies in the ANC in Swaziland.[58] Ngema was shot dead on 6 January 1988 as he sat in a Mozambican restaurant in Manzini, Swaziland. Ngema's killer, the MK operative Kevin Mabalengwe Mandlankomo, part of a four-man unit sent to Swaziland to assassinate askaris, received amnesty for the killing in December 2000.[59]

Tladi hated Sedibe, not least because he may have had a hand in Tladi's capture. Asked about his impressions of Sedibe, Tladi replied in a mix of English and Zulu, '*Bekuyi-nonsonso yomuntu.*' (He was a terrible person.) According to Tladi, Sedibe told him sometime in 1988 or 1989 that De Kock had instructed him to put together a three-man unit to go to Swaziland to attack ANC members. Sedibe wanted Tladi to be a part of that team and told him in Pedi, '*Re-ilobetha pipe*' (slang for 'we are going to fire our guns'; literally, 'we are going to hit the pipe'). Tladi recalled, '*Ngimubhek' ebuswen' umakasho lezinto, ngizibuz' ukuthi indoda ingakhuluma kanjani kalula so ngokubulala omunye umuntu. Kunzima ukubulala umuntu ongalwi naye.*' (I would look at the expression on his face as he said this and ask myself how a man could talk about killing another human being like that. It is hard to kill a man you are not fighting with.) Tladi said that he found excuse after excuse to get out of the mission. When Sedibe realised Tladi was stalling and not keen on the mission, he (Sedibe) wanted to kill him.[60]

Asked how much Sedibe and his colleagues were paid for killing ANC members, Tladi replied, 'R5000 – *and, bheka, yin' i-R5000!*' (and, look, what is R5000!) Tladi remarked that there was no shortage of collaborators willing to work with Sedibe on his missions of murder. But Sedibe wanted Tladi to go along on his killing missions because he was still 'fresh' and more likely to know the ANC's new hiding places.[61]

There is no way to determine whether Tladi's account is truthful. He is the only person to implicate Sedibe directly in the killing of ANC members. We should also note that, of the askaris interviewed, Tladi was the only one to express open hostility towards Sedibe. Recalling his days at Vlakplaas, Tladi said, 'Life was terrible. I only felt free the day Vlakplaas shut down.' Yet, despite these sentiments, there seemed to be a faint hint of longing for the place.[62]

* * *

Although the NSMS, which provided the 'framework within which systematised assassination was developed and implemented',[63] was total in its assumptions, it was the product of serious divisions in the police and military. These divisions arose in the face of a deepening political crisis. Johann Coetzee, police commissioner from 1978 to 1985, favoured an approach that emphasised 'soft repression'. The key elements of this approach were limited coercion and the use of espionage to manage South Africa's low-intensity conflict.[64] Others, such as Major-General Charles Lloyd of the South African Defence Force, Major-General Johan van der Merwe, then the Security Branch chief, and Major-General Bert Wandrag, head of the police's C-Section counterinsurgency wing, favoured a harder approach.[65] Incidentally, a secret CIA assessment of South Africa seemed to have missed these divisions, suggesting for example that the South African military as an institution appeared to be more in favour of reforms than did the police force.[66]

The state attempted to break growing resistance to apartheid using, among other things, the Security Branch's 'holy of holies' – 'its national network of informers within the ANC'.[67] But no amount of killing and jailing would help solve South Africa's fundamental problem. As Kevin O'Brien points out, South Africa's security forces were good at finding and using tactical intelligence (such as that provided by Sedibe), but they were hopeless at providing decision-makers with the kind of strategic, far-reaching intelligence needed to solve the country's problems.[68] In fact, says O'Brien, the Department of Military Intelligence engaged in activities that did more harm than good to apartheid South Africa's political strategy.[69]

According to O'Brien, South Africa's 'total strategy' failed because it was 'fed by an intelligence apparatus which both misconstrued the quality of the ANC's revolutionary warfare pursuits, and ultimately reacted to the resonating results of its own operations'.[70] The apartheid government believed it was on the edge of the abyss – not realising that its very actions had created the abyss.

Writing of the Stasi files, Barbara Miller says, 'Much is missing and, consequently, the information which is recorded may be in danger of being retrospectively judged more significant and representative of the individual biography than was the case.'[71] The same observation applies to Sedibe and how we read his file. We know that Sedibe's collaboration extended well beyond the contents of his file. But there is much that we still do not know. For example, how many former comrades did he help recruit to the Security Branch and Military Intelligence?

When Nelson Mandela became South Africa's first democratically elected president in April 1994, it is said that he asked Niel Barnard, the last head of the National Intelligence Service under apartheid, 'for the identities of government spies in ANC ranks'.[72] Barnard refused. In another telling of the same story, it was the ANC, and not the South African government, that refused to name the spies in its ranks. According to this second telling, when it became clear that apartheid was about to become a thing of the past, officials of the National Intelligence Service suggested to their ANC counterparts that they share the names of spies within each other's ranks. The ANC refused, seeing in this suggestion a tool that could be used to blackmail individuals.[73]

Who knows what might have come out had Barnard agreed to Mandela's request? Who knows what might have been revealed had the ANC agreed to share notes with the National Intelligence Service? The truth is that outed collaborators such as Sedibe and Behr were more the exception than the norm. There were a great many collaborators, and we know much less about them than we should.[74]

7
The village

Mr Sedibe would today have been either the Head of the army or Head of the Defence Force or the Minister of Defence. So in a sense we not only destroyed his life, we also left his family with a handful of ashes. Regarding his brothers, sisters and parents, we left him in a situation where they didn't know whether or not he was a traitor or whether he could be trusted. By interfering in his fate we destroyed a person who could today have acted for us in the same stature as some of the greater military leaders that we have known. That is the man I knew. We interfered with one of the best persons available to us in the country and this is one of the things which still affect me today.

– Eugene de Kock[1]

Glory Sedibe was tall for a black South African, standing at almost six feet.[2] He had an oval-shaped face, wore his hair in a neatly combed Afro, had a moustache he liked to keep trimmed and was, by the time he was in his thirties, what South Africans like to call hefty. Sedibe was also light-skinned, though not very.[3] He was, by most accounts, intelligent and jocular: he liked a good joke and a laugh.[4] However, if Sedibe's height put him above the average black South African male, his decision to flee South Africa in 1977 and take up arms against apartheid made him more than average for a generation of black South Africans who came of age in the 1970s.

This was a generation that, in the words of Diana Wylie, knew 'how it felt to have a lid pressing down your hopes and dreams'.[5]

Sedibe was one of thousands of young people who went into exile following the 1976 Soweto rebellion. The incarceration of his brother Kaborone on Robben Island in December of that year also had a major effect on Sedibe.[6] But a look at his social background suggests that, in addition to his anger and heartfelt grievance against the state, his personal and social circumstances contributed significantly to his decision. To say that Sedibe's resolve to leave South Africa, join a banned organisation and undergo military training in Angola, East Germany and the Soviet Union was driven in part by his background is not to say that he was a pawn pushed this way and that by the forces of history.

It is instead to understand where he came from.[7] It is also to understand why, despite its claims to be a 'people's army', MK always had limited appeal among black South Africans. This is not to ignore the value of MK as a resistance movement or to downplay the symbolic importance of its 'armed propaganda' in raising the ANC's profile and making many young South Africans believe that, as omnipotent as apartheid South Africa seemed, it could be challenged.[8]

When Sedibe joined the ANC, the organisation's military wing had not fired a single shot or carried out any military mission inside South Africa in almost 10 years.[9] Part of the explanation for the lull was that the government had effectively destroyed ANC activity within South Africa and reduced the ANC's physical presence in the country to a smattering of individuals, often well known to the Security Branch and isolated from the ANC in exile. As Thula Simpson points out, 'MK faced a taller order than any comparable liberation army fighting white minority rule in Africa in the late twentieth century'.[10]

MK was a 'blunted spear'.[11] But in 1977 that was about to change. The ANC was about to resume military activity inside South Africa. The change was due partly to apartheid South Africa's loss, starting in 1974, of the cordon sanitaire it had enjoyed on account of the white minority regimes that ruled Angola, Mozambique and Rhodesia. More importantly, the change in MK's fortunes was due largely to the influx of young South Africans like Sedibe who had streamed into exile following the apartheid government's brutal suppression of the 1976 student uprising.

It is one of the many ironies of this story that when Sedibe joined the ANC, the organisation was about to resume military operations inside South Africa with a campaign targeting collaborators. On 9 September 1977 MK insurgents in KwaMashu, Durban, assassinated Leonard Nkosi, a former member of MK who had defected to the Security Branch. In January 1978 MK members shot and wounded the former ANC cadre Steve Mtshali, who had turned state witness against ANC members in numerous cases. On 14 April 1978 ANC cadres in Soweto killed Abel Mthembu, former deputy president of the ANC in the Transvaal, who had also defected from the ANC and given evidence against ANC members in court. The political scientist Tom Lodge estimated that the ANC killed about 12 individuals viewed as collaborators between 1976 and 1983, and that defectors made up most of those assassinated.[12] Boasting about the assassinations, the ANC leader Francis Meli said, 'The ANC, like any African elephant, has demonstrated a long historical memory in such cases.'[13]

The irony is that Meli, one-time editor of the ANC journal *Sechaba*, was himself an apartheid agent. The National Intelligence Service recruited Meli through a Ghanaian agent named Kojo Boakye-Djan who was based, like Meli, in London. Taking advantage of Meli's alcoholism, Boakye-Djan, a former major in the Ghanaian army, used Meli to gain access to the deliberations of the ANC's national executive committee. Meli, whose real name was Allan Wellington Madolwana, was not the only senior apartheid agent in the ANC in London. Solly Smith (real name Samuel Khanyile), one-time ANC chief representative in London, was also an agent. Both Meli and Smith died mysteriously after their return to South Africa in the early 1990s.[14]

The ANC's killing of collaborators did not mean that the odds of military success were tipping in the organisation's favour by the time Sedibe joined. Taking up arms against apartheid might have been the most heroic thing to do in the 1970s, but statistically it was still a hopeless cause. Tom Lodge found that between January 1977, when Sedibe joined MK, and December 1982, the ANC carried out 'at least 160 instances of violent activity'.[15] But that heightened activity came at great cost. Howard Barrell calculated that 'Two or three guerrillas appear to have been captured or killed for every three attacks'.[16] And yet Sedibe and thousands like him still took up arms against apartheid. This was at a time when not only was apartheid South Africa a nuclear power and, through Armscor, in the top ten of the world's weapons producers, but when 'the external service of Radio South Africa was the third most-powerful shortwave broadcaster in the world', after the Voice of America and Radio Moscow.[17]

The decision to go to war against apartheid was taken first by the liberal African Resistance Movement in October 1961, in the hope of bringing the 'government and its supporters to their senses before it is too late'. The movement was followed on 16 December 1961 by the ANC and South African Communist Party with their declaration of war.[18] Stephen Ellis observes that the start of the armed struggle in South Africa was 'inscribed in the politics of the Cold War'.[19] But to limit our understanding of these decisions to the Cold War, or some communist plot, is both myopic and robs real-world actors of their agency. Mandela and his contemporaries (communist, liberal and nationalist) were justified by circumstances in taking up arms. While some commentators, like Scott Everett Couper, argue that the ANC's turn to arms in December 1961 and its relationship with the Soviet bloc 'postponed western governments' belated anti-apartheid stance',[20] this claim is belied by the evidence, as the following story shows.

On 13 November 1961 Lucius D. Battle, executive secretary of the US State Department, wrote to McGeorge Bundy, President

John F. Kennedy's special assistant for national security affairs, with a suggestion. Chief Albert Luthuli, the banned leader of the outlawed ANC, was to travel to Norway the following month to receive the Nobel Peace Prize. Battle suggested that Kennedy send Luthuli a message of support. 'A congratulatory message from the President will be a source of encouragement to him and all opponents of apartheid, and will be beneficial to us in the over-all African context. The Government of South Africa will, of course, be greatly displeased.' Kennedy rejected Battle's idea.[21]

Instead, it was Luthuli who wrote to Kennedy on 14 December 1961,[22] four days after giving his Nobel Prize acceptance speech in which he reminded the world that in South Africa the 'spirit of peace' was 'subject to some of the severest tensions known to man'.[23] Luthuli's letter was written shortly before his return to South Africa, which he had left on a ten-day passport (issued grudgingly by the government) to travel to Norway to receive the prize for his non-violent opposition to apartheid. Previously, he had been confined to his hometown of Groutville in Natal by a series of banning orders that went back to 1953.

Why would Kennedy not support Luthuli? This is a difficult question for those who assume that, but for the ANC's association with communists, Washington would have supported the struggle against apartheid from the very beginning. As we know from history and its own official archives, the US government was not opposed in principle to the use of violence for political ends. It all depended on who was committing the violence and whether they were friend or foe.

For example, on 18 June 1948 the US National Security Council issued a directive authorising peacetime covert operations by the CIA. The council had first issued such a directive in 1947 after President Harry Truman expressed concern over what he saw as the Soviet Union's lead in 'psychological warfare'.[24] The 1948 directive ordered the CIA to direct covert rather than merely psychological operations against hostile foreign states or groups, or in support of allies, 'but which are so planned and executed that any US Government responsibility for them is not evident to unauthorised persons and that if uncovered the US Government can plausibly disclaim any responsibility for them'.[25] The operations so authorised included 'propaganda, economic warfare, preventive direct action, including sabotage, demolition and evacuation measures, subversion against hostile states, including assistance to underground resistance movements, guerrillas and refugee liberation groups and support for anti-Communists in the free world'.[26]

Accepting that the declaration of war against apartheid South Africa by communists, liberals and nationalists was justified also means understanding that the Soviet bogey used to justify apartheid violence was a figment of apartheid South Africa's imagination. The Cold War was simply a 'convenient framework' used to validate apartheid policies.[27] Apartheid ideologues claimed that South Africa's violence was a necessary bulwark against Soviet expansionism in southern Africa. But, as Irina Filatova and Apollon Davidson point out, South Africa's version of Soviet policy was 'only loosely connected with reality'.[28]

As they show, Afrikaner nationalists were not always hostile to the Soviet Union. In 1920, for instance, D.F. Malan, who later became apartheid South Africa's first prime minister, compared the Bolsheviks with Afrikaner nationalists in positive terms: 'The Bolshevists stand for freedom, just like the NP [National Party].'[29] There were also extensive trade links between South Africa and the Soviet Union, which increased after 1956.[30] But, despite these ties and the fact that southern Africa was not key to Soviet strategic interests, the Cold War gave Afrikaner nationalists a useful excuse for their brand of authoritarianism,[31] even more so when the Soviets decided in 1961 to supply the ANC with arms.

The ways in which the ANC prosecuted its insurgency were to some extent determined by its opponents. As David Dirkse, the protagonist in Zoë Wicomb's novel *David's story*, tells the narrator: 'If things go off course, that course is also determined by the very system we attack. And it's enemy tactics ... that produce corruption ... by making us insecure about our own members so that we remain suspicious, incriminate the innocent, and do terrible things to our own people. Keeping your hands clean is a luxury that no revolution can afford; there's corruption in every institution.'[32]

The decision to go to war against apartheid was justified by circumstances, but this did not make violence any less problematic as a means of struggle. Any resort to violence is inherently dangerous because violence tends to eat up everything in its path. Ted R. Gurr observes, 'Worst of all it consumes men, its victims physically, its practitioners mentally, by habituating them to violence as the means and end of life.'[33] Gurr made his argument in a widely read book entitled *Why men rebel*. To understand rebellion in general, Gurr wrote, one needs to analyse popular discontent and its sources, people's justifications for political action, and the balance between a discontented group's capacity to act politically and the capacity of a government either to repress or channel that discontent.[34]

Gurr and his book play more than a passing role in Sedibe's story. When state prosecutors charged Sedibe's brother Kaborone and eight of his colleagues in January 1976 for organising the 'Viva Frelimo' rallies, they used Gurr's book to support their claim that the Black People's Convention and South African Students' Organisation were pursuing a revolutionary strategy to overthrow the government. Gurr tells the story: 'When the initial charges were brought, the defence team cross-examined the state prosecutor and asked, among other questions, the basis for the charges that [the two organisations] were following a revolutionary strategy. The prosecutor's academic advisor, political scientist Stoffel van der Merwe, said it was based on his four-stage model of revolutionary strategy. Asked by the defence what authority he could cite, he mentioned the work of an American political scientist who a few years earlier had published a major theoretical study, *Why Men Rebel*.'[35]

To refute Van der Merwe's claim and the state's case, the defence team asked Gurr to serve as *their* expert witness. Gurr agreed. He gave his testimony in June 1976, as the Soweto uprising was under way. Gurr and other defence witnesses, including Steve Biko and the political philosopher Rick Turner, helped the defence lawyers demolish Van der Merwe, forcing him 'to concede that revolutions were born of frustration, not conspiracy'.[36] Unable to challenge Gurr on the merits of his argument, the prosecutors Cecil Rees and Kevin Attwell tried to undermine Gurr by suggesting he was a tool of the ANC.

Using the 1976 riots as a frame, Gurr responded, 'I rhetorically asked whether what was happening in Soweto was a revolution. My answer was no, but the question itself elicited applause from the courtroom audience, many of them relatives of the defendants.'[37] When Gurr met the defendants briefly in the holding cells of the Pretoria Supreme Court, they wanted to know about the US civil rights movement.[38]

The state had missed the point of Gurr's book. He argued, 'Discontent is not a function of the discrepancy between what men want and what they have, but between what they want and what they believe they are capable of attaining ... If their means are few or threatened, they are likely to revolt.'[39] Kaborone rebelled because the government denied him the chance to express himself. Sedibe valorised the fact that his brother was the first in the family to go to university. Seeing his brother denied the chance to finish his university education, Sedibe very likely felt that his brother had been denied the opportunity to attain what he was capable of, leaving behind the asbestos-mining village in which the Sedibe boys had grown up. To understand Sedibe's sense of injustice at this, we must understand where he came from.

* * *

In 1907 a trader named Thomas Ward 'discovered' asbestos on the banks of the Olifants River, just under 400 kilometres north-east of Johannesburg.[40] Ward, whose find confirmed an earlier discovery by a man curiously named Charlie the Reefer, may have been acting on behalf of the Transvaal Geological Survey, which also recorded asbestos in the area in 1907.[41] Ward's discovery led to the founding of Penge (pronounced 'Penj', rhyming with Stonehenge), a small mining town in the Steelpoort River valley, in the mountains of Sekhukhuneland. Regarded in Europe and North America from the late 19th century onwards as a 'wonder' material because of its 'properties of heat resistance and tensile strength',[42] asbestos had been used by locals for years before its European 'discovery' in southern Africa. The various forms of asbestos include amosite, widely used in thermal insulation during the first part of the 20th century. Amosite – the form of asbestos found in Penge – also happens to be one of the more hazardous forms of the substance.

Amosite mining in Penge began in 1914.[43] The operation was small-scale, with Ward and his partners using ox wagons to transport ore to the nearest railway station in Belfast, about 320 kilometres further south. In 1925 British-owned Cape Asbestos bought out Amosa and Egnep (Penge spelt backwards), two companies founded by Ward and his partners. In 1937 a newspaper described the area as the 'most marvellous asbestos country'.[44] There were two mine shafts and mills, and these employed black male labourers, who worked fixed hours under a white supervisor. Until operations were mechanised in the 1960s, 'processes were rudimentary and the distinctive dry milling of asbestos created an enormous health risk that was little understood at the time by all involved'.[45] Alongside the two mine shafts, there was also a parallel form of asbestos mining, north-west of Penge, made up of family labour. White tributers would be granted licences to blast horizontal shafts for black contract workers. 'The ore was too heavy to bring down the mountain so it was generally easier to remove the softer and lighter asbestos from the ironstone on site. This was done by family groups, including women and children.'[46]

According to the Asbestos Relief Trust, 'Groups of women would sit hammering the asbestos out of the rock in a process known as "cobbing". The family units involved children, including babies, who accompanied their parents to the work sites, where they were exposed to the dust in some of the highest recorded approximated quantities of human exposure to the carcinogenic fibre.'[47] X-ray tests conducted in the 1940s found asbestosis in children younger than 12. By that time, about 25 per cent of the male asbestos mineworkers were under 16. Cape Asbestos tried to obtain exemptions from the Native Labour Regulations on the ground that juveniles were 'cheaper to employ and they did the work adult males would not do'.[48]

The Penge mines drew male migrant labourers from near and far.[49] They came from the surrounding villages and from places as distant as Natal, Transkei, Mozambique, Malawi and Ghana. Many married local women and were absorbed into nearby Pedi-speaking communities. Among those who came to Penge was Sedibe's father, Ephraim, sent by Lutheran missionaries to educate the children of mineworkers in 1947.[50] As the village did not offer much in the way of family housing, Ephraim lived among the migrant workers in a hostel in Penge while his wife, Lillian, stayed behind in Pilgrim's Rest, from where Ephraim hailed, to raise their children. Lillian would, like most migrants' wives, pay regular visits to Penge. By 1953, when Sedibe was born, the African workforce at Penge had grown to 5000.

Penge was a hard place to raise a family. In the 1950s an inspector of native labour described the town as 'wretched, unhygienic and conducive to the outbreak of disease'.[51] Black residents collected their drinking water from the same asbestos-contaminated streams used to wash laundry. But what mattered to the mine owners was that by the 1960s Penge was the largest asbestos mine in South Africa, accounting for 39 per cent of all asbestos produced in the country, and the only large-scale amosite mine in the world.[52]

At some point, Lillian and the children joined Ephraim in Penge and the family lived in a four-roomed house in the black section, a short walk from Penge Primary School, where Ephraim taught, and from the mine hostel where he later worked as a clerk.[53] David Mokwena, who grew up with Sedibe in Penge, met Ephraim in 1950. 'He was my teacher. He taught all the subjects from Standard One to Standard Three.'[54] Mokwena recalled that Ephraim was a good teacher. Mirriam Mashego, a relative of Sedibe's, whose son was also in exile, said Ephraim 'was very harsh. He was very strict.'[55] Ephraim might have been strict with his children because he wanted them to go further than he had. Glory Sedibe entered Penge Primary School in 1961 at the age of 8. A natural joker, he would have been under intense pressure to do well. 'He was good at relay, long jump and high jump,' said Asam Phiri, a classmate whose father had come from Malawi to work at the Penge mine.[56] But he was a mediocre soccer player.[57]

Penge might have been a small mining town in the middle of nowhere, but it was certainly an apartheid town.[58] When Sedibe was growing up in the 1950s and 1960s, Penge was so small that different (white) Christian denominations shared the only church building in the white part of town, taking turns to hold their services. But the town had two of everything when it came to black and white residents: two doors at the post office, at the butcher shop and at the bakery.[59] At Fraser's general dealership, black customers had to do their shopping through a window.[60] Cape Asbestos set up the town's infrastructure.[61] It sought to build an apartheid idyll in the bush, creating the perfect show village for a South African version of 1950s and 1960s social engineering: small and prosperous, with blacks who seemingly knew their place as labourers and servants.

White miners and their families lived in 'white square single-storey houses with gardens and street lighting. Other amenities included a recreation centre, a golf course and club house, and a mining hospital and several trading stores.'[62] The black area, in contrast, had no electricity and none of the facilities found in the white section. What soccer grounds and play areas there were the inhabitants had established themselves. They built their own churches. The company erected the houses and Penge Primary

School – both made, of course, of asbestos – but they were tiny.[63]

Despite these conditions, Sedibe had a happy childhood.[64] He and his friends would go swimming – against the warnings of his parents – in the Olifants River nearby.[65] He would visit cousins in other areas and get up to mischief with some of them. 'We did things together,' his cousin Bernard Malope said simply.[66]

Ephraim barely managed to keep his family above the poverty line. But he instilled in his children a love of learning and encouraged their ambitions to go far. Kaborone used his father's lessons to get himself into university, where he became an activist. Sedibe also wanted to go to university. Because Penge Primary School only went up to Standard Six, Sedibe moved to Leolo Secondary School in neighbouring Burgersfort in 1969. In 1972 he obtained his junior certificate. This was an achievement that placed him among a small elite of black South African students.[67] In 1971, 70 per cent of black students left school after four years or less of attendance, and less than four per cent entered secondary school.[68] In 1972 Sedibe moved to Ngwana Bohube High School in Pietersburg, where he obtained his matric in 1973.[69]

Sedibe wanted to pursue a Bachelor of Administration degree at university.[70] The degree would have suited him for work as a public servant in the Lebowa bantustan, the apartheid 'homeland' for Pedi-speakers. At a time when many people of his generation were opposed to homelands on the ground that these were tribal creations designed to deprive black South Africans of full political rights in their country, Sedibe evinced no discomfort at his possible choice of degree. In fact, there is every indication that he would have gone to university and registered for a BAdmin but for the fact that he lacked the money to do so. In 1974 he worked as a clerk at Roberto Construction in Elandsfontein, east of Johannesburg. In 1975 he taught at Mathibela Secondary School in Bosbokrand in the Eastern Transvaal. In 1976 he worked as a store clerk for Burton Construction in Kempton Park, also east of Johannesburg. Later in 1976 he moved to Barberton, on the border with Mozambique and

Swaziland, and worked at a tea plantation before transferring to the nearby Fairview gold mine to work as a general labourer there.[71]

At some point – his family is not sure of the exact date – Ephraim quit teaching and went to work at the Penge mine as an administrative clerk. The pay was better and the job came with the promise of bursaries for his children[72] In fact, it was a bursary from the mine that allowed Kaborone to attend Turfloop, where he registered for a law degree. David Mokwena said the Sedibes were not a political family, and Kaborone must have picked up politics at university.[73] Like all black universities in South Africa, Turfloop had been in ferment since the mid-1960s as a result of a worldwide rise in student activism but more specifically since the establishment, by Steve Biko and others, of the South African Students' Organisation in 1968.[74]

The year 1977 was a major turning point for the family. Ephraim lost his job at the mine and Glory went into exile.[75] According to Lillian Sedibe, Ephraim had been on leave. 'He worked in the mine's welfare office. The office said money had gone missing and accused him of stealing it. But he was on leave. They said he must pay the money back. He resigned.'[76] Having lost his job, Ephraim had to give up his company-owned house in Penge. He moved the family to a village some distance away named Matibidi and found a job working in a kitchen in the town of Steelpoort.[77] Ephraim died in 1992.

Kaborone recalled that his brother had told him that he planned to leave South Africa at the first available chance.[78] Kaborone said Sedibe had taken part in the 1976 student uprising (even though he had finished high school in 1973) and participated in the burning down of the Rabasotho Community Hall in Tembisa, east of Johannesburg.[79] He moved to Barberton to devise a plan for going into exile. 'He worked at the mine for about a month and gathered intelligence from migrant labourers about how to cross the border,' Kaborone said.[80] According to his police file, Sedibe had intended to skip the country together with two friends, George Mokone and Baska Moabi, in 1976, but had changed plans and moved to Barberton after the two friends were arrested.[81] Finally, in January 1977, Sedibe crossed into Swaziland near the Josefsdal border post.

If Kaborone's claims that his brother was an anti-apartheid activist before he left South Africa in 1977 are true, that would place Sedibe among those young South Africans who had, in the words of Colin Bundy, 'learned the practical science of making a petrol bomb; the street sociology of taunting armed soldiers; the pavement politics of pamphlet distribution and slogan painting; the geography of safe houses and escape routes; and the grammar and dialectics of undercover operations'.[82] But Sedibe's life as a political refugee in Swaziland began on a more bureaucratic note. He reported to the Mbabane police station as required by law and from there was sent to the Mawelawela refugee camp on the road between Manzini and Mankayane, the town from which he would be abducted in August 1986.[83]

Stanley Mabizela, a South African exile and MK operative who fled to Swaziland in 1965 and received military training in the Soviet Union, visited Mawelawela regularly to recruit refugees to the ANC.[84] Mabizela – whose 'day job' was that of a schoolteacher at a Catholic boys' school in Manzini – was one of the key ANC figures in Swaziland. There was fierce competition between the ANC and the PAC for recruits, and ANC and PAC representatives had to act fast to ensure that newly arrived refugees did not join their opponents. During one of his visits, Mabizela met Sedibe and recruited him to the ANC.[85]

It is unlikely that Mabizela would have had much persuading to do, given that Sedibe's brother was on Robben Island, and Sedibe came from a part of the country with a long tradition of migrant labour and ANC activism. In March 1977 Mabizela took Sedibe to his house in Manzini. From there, Sedibe moved to a house near the University of Swaziland to await instructions from the ANC about how to proceed, because he had said he wanted to undergo military training. Sedibe spent a few days here before being introduced to

Henry Chiliza, another ANC operative. Chiliza took Sedibe to the Swaziland–Mozambique border in April 1977 and helped him jump the fence into Mozambique.[86]

As we picture the 24-year-old Sedibe, paperless and stateless, jumping over the border fence to begin his military training, we might recall the man who only four years earlier was thinking of a career in a 'homeland' administration. This sort of twist was common in a society full of contradictions. If his family had had the means, Sedibe might indeed have gone to university and then got a job as a bantustan bureaucrat. But that would not necessarily mean that he had embraced apartheid. As Timothy Gibbs shows, the 'homeland' elites constituted networks that, paradoxically, 'made the boundaries between opposition and collaboration permeable'.[87] We cannot make neat distinctions between collaborators and resisters based simply on where individuals were in their working and social lives during apartheid.

What in Sedibe's social background might help explain why he chose the path of insurgency? Ironically, to answer that question, we have to go to the scene of the most public enactment of his collaboration: his testimony in 1988 in the treason trial against Dladla, Ebrahim and Maseko. The explanation for why certain men rebel was provided by Mark Orkin, a University of the Witwatersrand sociologist, who had been asked by the court to prepare expert written evidence on behalf of the accused 'in mitigation of sentence'.[88] Orkin conducted about six hours of interviews with Ebrahim, Maseko and Dumisane Nkabinde (an MK operative who had been charged separately in another political trial) before they were sentenced.[89] The state had found Ebrahim and Maseko guilty of the charge of treason and the prosecution had asked for the death penalty. Orkin's job was to argue for a lesser sentence.

Orkin reported, 'The men's families were urban, of intermediate social class, with the husband in formal employment ... The mothers all stayed at home, but still had to do informal-sector work to supplement the income. In all three cases, then, the parents were aware enough of the importance of education to encourage the youngsters to persist with it, providing a basis of literate awareness; but unable to provide the supportive milieu ... for education to provide unproblematic access to social rewards. Instead, given the overt racial discrimination legislated by apartheid, it was inevitable that all three would not only experience material hardship, but also have vivid childhood recollections of developing the fierce sense of injustice.' Orkin concluded, 'they were not too poor to have expectations; educated sufficiently to be keenly disappointed by inequality in general and discrimination in particular; and therefore deeply enough involved in political effort to be massively affronted when this last recourse was summarily closed by the state in one way or another.'[90]

Had Sedibe been among the accused – instead of being a state witness – Orkin's conclusion would have been just as applicable to him. In fact, it would have described many of the 'militant activists at the heart of anti-colonial nationalist movements'.[91] Orkin's comment that ANC insurgents tended to come from the so-called intermediate classes would have come as no surprise to the ANC president, Oliver Tambo, who led the organisation throughout its 34 years in exile. As Timothy Gibbs says, 'More than once, "Oliver Tambo expressed concern about ... the glaring absence in the ANC camps of cadres of working class and peasant origins."'[92]

Still, saying that ANC insurgents tended to be 'disaffected aspirant *petit-bourgeois*' does not, as Orkin himself pointed out, advance our understanding of who rebelled and why. 'The point was thrown at me ... by every judge or magistrate before whom I gave evidence: innumerable other black South Africans experienced what the accused had suffered, but without themselves joining the ANC or MK and training to commit sabotage or kill members of the security apparatus. Why then did the accused in particular take their commitments to these lengths?'[93]

Orkin replied that in addition to who they were and where

Glory Lefoshie Sedibe, photo from a security police file

Penge, the asbestos-mining village in Limpopo, where Glory Sedibe grew up

The Sedibe family home in Penge

Sedibe family collection

Sedibe family collection

Above: Glory Sedibe (lower left) with friends

Below: Glory (left) with a friend travelling by train

The Mankayane police station in Swaziland, on the South African border, from where Glory Sedibe was abducted by South African security police in August 1986

The entrance to Vlakplaas, the security police death squad base, from where Sedibe operated as an askari

National Archives, Pretoria

National Archives, Pretoria

Mandla Maseko, one of three MK operatives and former ANC colleagues against whom Glory Sedibe testified in a treason trial of 1988; photos taken from security police files

National Archives, Pretoria

National Archives, Pretoria

Simon Dladla, one of three MK operatives and former ANC colleagues against whom Glory Sedibe testified in a treason trial of 1988; photos taken from security police files

Photos of ANC members and MK operatives from a security police album used to identify suspects

Paul Dikeledi, MK operative killed by South African security police in 1987

Cyril Raymonds, MK operative and apartheid spy, who died in ANC detention in 1988

Francis Meli, senior ANC leader in London and apartheid spy

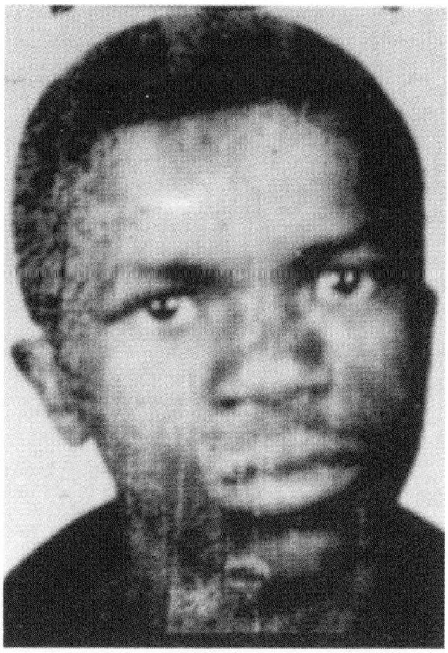

Job Tabane (MK name Cassius Make), senior MK operative who was assassinated by a South African death squad in 1987

Still from an SABC documentary of 1987 on the ANC, showing an askari wearing a balaclava said to have been Glory Sedibe (Photo courtesy of SABC)

Glory Sedibe's gravesite

they came from, those who took up arms against apartheid also 'possessed the extra ineffable quality that made them exemplary citizens. They happened to be the minority we all admire in everyday life, who play football like Maseko rather than merely spectating the game or watching it on TV; or stand for the local party branch committee, like Ebrahim or Nkabinde, rather than merely come to branch meetings or vote in elections. Sociology here reaches the limit of individual prediction.'[94]

Orkin wrote that in the context of apartheid, the men 'were also acting in a substantively moral fashion'.[95] He said that 'despite the hopeless odds and MK's relative lack of military success, the three cadres and thousands like them have provided a moving example of what Marcuse called the power of "negative thinking", a refusal to bow to the seeming unassailability of the dominant political order ... In becoming MK guerrillas they were simply acting in brave conformity to such principles [as democracy and nonracialism]. What really needs explaining is why the rest of us did less.'[96]

For our purposes, what needs explaining is why, having committed himself to an armed struggle against the South African state, taken all kinds of risks and seen his brother languish in prison for organising a public rally, Sedibe would turn against his former comrades. Here, too, the social sciences reach the limits of individual prediction.

In their attempt to undermine Orkin's conclusions, judges and magistrates would essentially ask: if apartheid was so bad for blacks, why did so few blacks take up arms against the system? Of course, this question was a cynical attempt to show that, far from acting out of legitimate grievances, ANC insurgents were dupes of Soviet communism or some other bogey bent on destroying so-called Western, Christian civilisation as 'everyone' knew it in southern Africa. But there is another dimension to the question. Throughout its 46-year history apartheid was neither ideologically coherent nor bureaucratically consistent.[97] Different apartheid ideologues believed different things at different times, and the application of rules was uneven, depending on what the government could achieve at any given time. Even Prime Minister H.F. Verwoerd, seen by many as the 'intellectual' father of apartheid, could be pragmatic. P.C. Swanepoel, a long-time intelligence officer for various apartheid spy agencies, remarked, 'Dr Verwoerd was not doctrinaire, but he suffered from a dearth of brave men around him.'[98]

Few will be convinced by Swanepoel's portrait of Verwoerd as an otherwise well-meaning visionary who suffered the misfortune of having weak advisers.[99] But Verwoerd, a sociologist, was certainly aware of social distinctions among blacks; he knew that blacks of different social backgrounds were affected differently by the apartheid system. Verwoerd saw bantustans as one avenue through which the black elite could develop along their so-called own lines. He was not alone in this type of thinking. Yet this awareness of the differential effects of apartheid on black South Africans was missing from the kinds of questions put to Orkin.

His questioners took for granted a commonality of experience among black South Africans. They assumed that, if black life under apartheid was as bad as the ANC said it was, then surely every black person would have joined the ANC and taken up arms against the regime. The fact that relatively few blacks chose this option was self-serving proof to Orkin's questioners that apartheid was not so bad. This spurious argument, as cynical as it is, lives on in democratic South Africa. Apologists such as former president F.W. de Klerk, former apartheid spy Maritz Spaarwater and ex-cop Herman Stadler claim that, for all its wrongs, apartheid as a bureaucratic system at least worked.[100] Some even go so far as to say that apartheid built bridges, houses, schools and many other amenities.[101] Besides, the argument goes, the armed struggle was an isolated project conducted by a small group of people.

Yes, relatively few blacks took up arms, but that in no way means most blacks accepted apartheid. Yes, apartheid governments built infrastructure, but that infrastructure was always skewed in favour of whites. Yes, it built schools and black education in fact boomed under apartheid.[102] But we should not forget that this was Bantu education conducted in generally inadequate facilities. Sedibe, for example, had to live away from home at least twice just so that he could finish school. There were simply not enough schools for people like him – and certainly not the kind of opportunities someone of his background might have expected.

* * *

In the view of Eugene de Kock, Sedibe never abandoned the political convictions that led him to the ANC in the first place, even as he was hunting down those who still held and acted on those convictions.[103] De Kock claimed that he understood why black South Africans took up arms against apartheid and that if he were black he probably would have done the same thing. The Nazi war criminal Adolf Eichmann made a similar claim during his trial in Jerusalem in 1961.[104] Keen to give the court the impression that he was no anti-Semite and that he in fact had nothing against Jewish people personally, Eichmann tried to argue that if he were Jewish, he too would have opposed Nazism. Eichmann's self-serving argument became the source of Hannah Arendt's controversial portrayal of him as a thoughtless bureaucrat who was only doing his job. Even though the 'job' consisted of shipping millions of people to their deaths, he was, argued Arendt, too thoughtless to put himself in the shoes of his victims.[105]

But, as David Cesarini says, Eichmann was no cog in a murderous system but a moral agent who made certain choices in the journey that was his life. What's more, he was a rabid Jew-hater. For people like Eichmann, 'their course was not fore-ordained ... they made informed choices along the way, and ... they had to accommodate to the consequences of their acts'.[106]

Sedibe was no Eichmann but he, too, was a moral agent who made informed choices along the way.[107] He decided to become an insurgent. The structure of apartheid society did not decide that for him, even though it shaped the conditions under which he took that decision. He was forced, at the risk of death, to become a counterinsurgent. But he persisted with that 'choice' and took to it with apparent relish. He helped hunt down and kill people pursuing the beliefs he claimed to believe in himself. How do we explain that?

* * *

Today, Penge is a derelict monument to the folly of apartheid. It became an all-black town following the exodus of whites and jobs after the mine closed in 1993. The town was incorporated into Lebowa in that year, but Lebowa, like all bantustans, disappeared into the proverbial dustbin of history in 1994.[108] Today, Penge, its years of prosperity long gone, gives visitors the impression of a town on the verge of extinction. With no jobs in the town itself, many of its inhabitants subsist on government welfare.[109]

Our account of Penge has an interesting twist. After being turned, askaris underwent extensive counterinsurgency training. According to the former askari Gregory Sibusiso Radebe, 'we did intense physical training at places like the Penge mine and Maleoskop [near Pretoria] and later, just before Vlakplaas was shut down, we did the normal police course at the police college in Hammanskraal with emphasis on detective work. There was not so much theory, though De Kock liked to have us watch war movies – he seemed to like the movies of the Vietnam War.'[110]

If Sedibe did participate in the training at Penge, what would have gone through his mind? What would he have thought as he saw, once again, the separate entrances to public buildings for blacks and whites? What effect, if any, would the drive down memory lane have had on Sedibe and his new commitments? Sedibe is not here to answer our questions. In his absence, we are left to wonder about the work of memory on Sedibe, the possible pricks of conscience and the role of place in identity formation. Sedibe left South Africa to fight for a different future. He returned to it as a servant of his former enemies.

8
The oaths

Ek is 'n Suid-Afrikaner in die ware sin van die woord [I am a South African in the true sense of the word].

– Mr X1[1]

Sedibe took four important oaths in his life. The first was in 1968 when, aged 15, he was confirmed in the Lutheran Church. The second was in 1979 when, aged 26, he swore loyalty to MK. The third was in 1987 when, aged 34, he pledged allegiance to the SAP, which he had joined formally in February that year at the rank of constable.[2] Each oath came with a ceremony and a set of commitments that defined him as a person. We do not have extant accounts of the ceremonies that attended the first and third oaths, but we do have a vivid description of an MK oath-taking ceremony. James Ngculu, who swore allegiance at an ANC camp in Angola in 1979, says:

> This was an oath of allegiance and loyalty to the ANC and MK. O.R. Tambo, the ANC president, and Joe Modise, the army commander, would visit the camp and people would be called according to detachments. Before this we had rehearsals: Your name would be called and you would march forward towards the President. The commander would then present you to the President (the commander-in-chief). The president would present a spear to you. You would accept the spear from the President and say the following: I, —,

> do solemnly declare that I am a soldier of the South African revolution serving in MK. I place myself in the service of the people, the movement and its allies. I promise to serve with discipline and dedication at all times, maintaining the integrity and solidarity of MK, the people's army. Should I violate any of these I accept that I should be punished by all means not excluding death. A tooth for a tooth; an eye for an eye and a life for a life. O.R. Tambo would then ask, 'Do you understand and accept this oath of MK?' The cadre would respond thus: 'With the spear of the nation, till victory or death.' Then about-turn and back to your formation.[3]

Ngculu, who may have taken his MK oath at the same ceremony as Sedibe, writes that recruits could not volunteer for the oath. They had to be nominated by a senior member of the organisation. 'Oath-taking made one proud but those who were not afforded the opportunity were deeply hurt and terribly embarrassed', because among those denied the chance to pledge their allegiance to the ANC were people of 'questionable biographies and backgrounds'.[4]

When Sedibe took the stand against his three former comrades in 1988, he swore a fourth oath, vowing to tell the court the truth. Leonard Gering and Kessie Naidu, the defence advocates whose job it was to challenge Sedibe's integrity, used this pledge to place Sedibe within a moral framework in which all oaths were sacrosanct. Wanting to shame him, they asked him about the contents of each of the major oaths he had sworn. What did it say? What did it mean? Limited by Sedibe's court-sanctioned anonymity as Mr X1, Gering and Naidu used a religious idiom that relied in part on Sedibe's past commitments as a Lutheran and a senior member of MK to remind him of the meaning of loyalty and betrayal. Sedibe most likely recognised what the lawyers were trying to do and refused to play along. He knew that, unable to damn him in the eyes of the court and the police for being a turncoat, the lawyers were trying to remind him of what he had once believed in.

Sedibe knew what the oaths meant. Recalling his church confirmation, Sedibe said this was a vow not to be 'tossed about from membership to membership' but to be a steadfast Lutheran;[5] his oath to the SAP was a pledge to 'conduct or perform my duties in the service properly' as well as a promise not to 'disclose the secrets of the SAP to enemies of the SAP'.[6] Tellingly, Sedibe could not recall the wording of his MK oath: 'No, I cannot remember the whole wording because it was a long-worded oath but what I remember is that towards the end of this oath, when we were to hold onto the Spear of the Nation together with Modise and Tambo, the words we uttered were "With the Spear of the Nation till victory or death".'[7] This was a curious memory lapse, especially considering that Sedibe could remember otherwise banal details (such as missing teeth and limps) about his former ANC comrades.[8] Sedibe had said in public that he was willing to kill or be killed for the ANC. How could he forget such a vivid promise?

If Sedibe's Security Branch file constituted one form of collaboration, his performance as a state witness marked another. The contents of Sedibe's file may have been literally beaten out of him; his performance in court was not. Initially, Sedibe may have been a reluctant collaborator. But there is a certain bravado and sarcasm to his voice (as 'heard' through the trial transcripts) that suggests that, as a state witness, he was collaborating with gusto. Years later, Ebrahim Ebrahim remembered Sedibe the witness this way: 'He was quite arrogant. He appeared to be quite confident. He was not shy about giving evidence against us.'[9]

According to Sedibe's testimony, the MK oath, complete with its ceremonial staging and use of props such as a spear, was introduced in 1979 in the midst of growing paranoia within the ANC about the presence of apartheid spies.[10] In September 1977, about 500 residents (90 per cent of the total) of Novo Catengue, an ANC camp in the south of Angola, came down with a severe case of food poisoning. James Ngculu, who was present when the incident happened, recalled comrades 'bending low and holding their stomachs, vomiting, unable to control their bowels, and complaining of pain and dehydration'.[11] No one died, but the incident, which came to be called Black September by the ANC, was blamed on apartheid spies and agents provocateurs. The episode may in fact have been a simple case of food poisoning. ANC camps in Angola, established in 1976 following the collapse of Portuguese rule in Africa, were the 'scene of numerous hardships' and food shortages were common.[12] In 1979 the South African Air Force bombed Novo Catengue, killing one MK member and a Cuban soldier, and injuring 14.[13]

The 'general atmosphere of suspicion' inside the ANC was not unfounded.[14] Starting in 1959–1960 with the reorganisation of the police Special Branch into the Security Branch and the formation in 1963 of Republican Intelligence (the initial forerunner of the National Intelligence Service), the South African government had targeted the ANC for surveillance and penetration.[15] This focus began with little sign of the menace that was to define it by the end of the 1960s. Commenting in 1969 on the change, the ANC said, 'The oafs in raincoats, riding around in their Volkswagens and who used to hang about the edges of our political meetings taking copious notes, were not going to be of much use now – everyone in the movement could smell one of them a good mile off. Apartheid had to find new methods of dealing with us – learn to attack us from within.'[16] That meant cultivating informers and planting agents within the organisation; it meant sowing seeds of doubt and mistrust. The ANC, which did not have much of a security apparatus in its first decade in exile, believed somehow that solidarity on its own was sufficient protection.

In truth, the ANC's biggest problem was not so much enemy infiltration as it was how to integrate the thousands of young members, such as Sedibe, who joined in the wake of the 1976 uprising. In 1965 the organisation's military wing had about 800 members. By 1975 the number had grown to 1000. By 1980 it had jumped to 9000, with the bulk of new members coming from the 1976 generation.[17] Ivan Pillay, already in exile when the influx took place, noted that many of the new members lacked 'life experiences' and 'useful regimes'.[18] They were young and had not had many responsibilities in life. This was the context in which Sedibe joined MK.

There is no reason to doubt that Sedibe was sincere when he took his oath of loyalty to MK, swearing to lay down his life for the revolution. He was as seized as the rest of the ANC by the fear of betrayal. Shortly before his abduction in August 1986, Sedibe had ordered Raymond Molapo, an ANC operative whose MK name was Clement, to 'eliminate traitors' – referred to in Zulu as *izimpimpi*.[19] Indeed, on the day of his arrest by the Swazi police, Sedibe and Humphrey Mkhwanazi, a fellow MK operative who was a lecturer at the University of Swaziland, were on a mission to hunt down traitors. Mkhwanazi recalled that Swaziland was teeming with apartheid agents at the time. 'It was so bad that we ended up running away from *izimpimpi* instead of them running away from us.'[20] Mkhwanazi said that he, Sedibe and another MK comrade named Vusumzi John Khumalo (MK name Bricks) had found a homestead with a secluded garage, a car not known to anyone in the ANC, a tape recorder and blank cassettes that they planned to use to take down confessions from apprehended agents. The mission was so secret that when the Swazi police arrested Mkhwanazi and Sedibe, both men immediately suspected the Swazi national from whom they had rented the garage of selling them out.[21]

Bricks narrowly missed being arrested with his two comrades because, when Mkhwanazi and Sedibe met him at the appointed hour, he insisted on finishing the two beers he had just bought. They left him alone as Sedibe had two errands to run. The first was a secret meeting with a touring group of South African students from Turfloop university; he wanted to give them ANC propaganda material to take to South Africa. The second errand was in the centre of Manzini, the commercial capital of Swaziland. Sedibe, who never slept in the same place twice for fear of South African attacks, had a mistress who worked at the Barclays Bank in Manzini.

He asked Mkhwanazi to drive him there so he could tell the woman he would be spending the night at her place. As there was no parking in front of the bank, Mkhwanazi parked outside a Spar supermarket nearby. 'We were confident because no one knew the car,' said Mkhwanazi.[22] Sedibe went inside the bank and returned shortly thereafter. He climbed inside the car. 'I found her. Everything is fine,' he told Mkhwanazi.[23]

Mkhwanazi continued: 'As I am starting the car, suddenly there are guns everywhere pointed at us. It's a special paramilitary unit. It was just a shock. In fact, it was an ambush.' 'Out! Out! Out!' the members of the paramilitary unit shouted.[24] Manzini is a small city, and Mkhwanazi and Sedibe were chained together and frog-marched to the police station nearby. Mkhwanazi believed that a South African agent named Andrew Kemp had spotted Sedibe, who was a poor driver, in the new car on the highway between Manzini and the capital, Mbabane. Kemp then informed fellow South African agents within the Swazi police force, who proceeded to mount a paramilitary operation. According to Mkhwanazi, the Swazi police who arrested Sedibe did not know who he was. All they knew was that they had nabbed a big MK fish – one of interest to the South Africans. Mkhwanazi said that the 'Swazis struggled to work out who September was. They did not know who September was at the police station.' They were only able to identify him after the South Africans gave them a copy of his identikit.[25]

By the time he appeared in court as Mr X1, Sedibe had changed from being an *impimpi* catcher to being an *impimpi* himself – not that Sedibe agreed with this characterisation. Advocate Leonard Gering, who represented Mandla Maseko and Simon Dladla, asked Sedibe during cross-examination about the orders that Sedibe had given Raymond Molapo, one of his MK subordinates, to kill *izimpimpi* inside South Africa. 'And seeing that you yourself used the word *impimpi* in your own evidence, would you regard yourself in the situation which you now find yourself, would you regard yourself as falling within the description of the word *impimpi*?' Sedibe answered, 'No, the police would not refer to me as an *impimpi*, but the ANC will.'[26]

GERING: 'I am not asking you whether the police would refer to you as an *impimpi*. My question is specifically designed as to whether you yourself having used the word *impimpi* in your own evidence, whether you yourself will now regard yourself in the situation you now find yourself as being within the description of *impimpi*?'

SEDIBE: 'With regard to?'

GERING: 'I say that would you yourself, having regard to the position in which you now find yourself as a witness testifying for the SAP against former colleagues in the ANC, would you regard yourself as falling within the description *impimpi*?'

SEDIBE: 'I regard myself as a member of the police. I do not regard myself as an *impimpi*. They may regard me as an *impimpi*, but I do not regard myself as such.'

GERING: 'Why do you say they "may" regard you as an *impimpi*? Isn't it quite clear from your evidence, beyond any shadow of doubt, that they would regard you as an *impimpi* on the evidence which you have given to this court?'

SEDIBE: 'That is so, yes.'

GERING: 'So when you said they may regard you as an *impimpi*, that is not the whole truth, is it?'

SEDIBE: 'When I say?'

GERING: 'That they may regard you as an *impimpi* that is not the whole truth?'

SEDIBE: 'Well, I said this agreeing with what you were saying, that is what they may regard me as.'

GERING: 'I do not know whether in the Zulu language there is a distinction between may regard you and would certainly regard you, and what I am saying to you is may regard is not the whole truth. On your evidence they would certainly regard you as an *impimpi*, to use your phrase.'

SEDIBE: 'Well, since they are also here we could ask them what they regard me as.'

GERING: 'I am not asking you what the three accused might or might not regard you as, what I am saying to you and I would be glad if you would listen to the question, what I am saying to you is this that on your evidence there is no shadow of a doubt that the ANC would regard you as an *impimpi*, to use your own word.'

SEDIBE: 'I understand that.'

GERING: 'And you agree with me?'

SEDIBE: 'Yes.'

It is important to bear in mind that the exchange between Sedibe and Gering was in fact a three-way conversation conducted in two languages (English for Gering and Zulu for Sedibe), mediated by a court interpreter. When Sedibe took the stand and was sworn in as Mr X1, he told the court he wanted to testify in his 'mother tongue' – Zulu.[27] Yet, Sedibe was not a native Zulu-speaker. 'He was a deep Mopedi. He spoke broken Zulu,' said Mkhwanazi, himself a native Zulu-speaker.[28] In fact, his home language was Pedi. Why did he lie to the court about his home language? Why did Sedibe elect to testify in a language of which he had a poor command? He certainly spoke better English, as even Police Commissioner Johan van der Merwe acknowledged when he later praised Sedibe's 'valuable service' to the police.[29]

Sedibe might have chosen to testify in one of his weaker languages as an act of psychological distancing. He might have decided to make Zulu his language of betrayal – except that he and the defence lawyers could not even agree on the meaning of 'betrayal' in Zulu. Here is Gering cross-examining Sedibe about what he understood by betrayal. When the cross-examination goes nowhere, because Sedibe will not agree that his actions constitute betrayal, Gering falls back on a religious idiom:

GERING: 'What I have been saying and what I am about to say is not intended in any way to reflect on the SAP but what I am going to put to you is this, you told us you took an oath as a Lutheran?'

SEDIBE: 'Yes.'

GERING: 'You must be aware of the reference in the New Testament to 30 pieces of silver?'

SEDIBE: 'I seem to remember that vividly though I cannot specifically remember to what this refer [*sic*] to, the 30 pieces of silver.'

GERING: 'It is a reference to the price paid for betrayal.'

SEDIBE: 'No, that I do not remember. What I remember is something said about Judas and Jesus.'

When Gering fails to wring a concession out of Sedibe, Gering's colleague Advocate Kessie Naidu, representing Ebrahim, has a go at Sedibe:

NAIDU: 'Now, the interpreter, when he dealt with the cross-examination by my learned friend when he used the word betrayal [he] used a word *thengisa* if I am correct about that.'

SEDIBE: 'That is so.'

NAIDU: 'What do you understand by the word *thengisa*?'

SEDIBE: 'It means *thengisa* in the manner that you would understand it.'

NAIDU: 'Please tell us, Mr X, what do you understand by that word, the equivalent of the English word betrayal.'

SEDIBE: 'According to how I understand it I would say so, yes.'

NAIDU: 'Then will you please tell us what you understand by that? What is it to betray somebody in your understanding of it?'

SEDIBE: 'It means betrayal in the manner that I have said I understood it.'

NAIDU: 'Can you please tell us again how you understand it?'

SEDIBE: 'That is *thengisa*, the word *thengisa*, that manner of *thengisa* ...'

NAIDU: 'Mr X, I do not know why you – even while my learned friend was cross-examining you and now I am cross-examining you I am asking you quite clearly [to] tell us in your own words what you understand is the concept of to betray.'

SEDIBE: 'This word was not coined by me originally. It is a word that I got to know and I understood it as meaning betrayal.'

NAIDU: 'Mr X, unfortunately I am going to persist until I am stopped by the court, but you are requested to answer the question and the question I am asking you and if you do not understand the question I will repeat it, is what do you understand by the concept to betray a person?'

SEDIBE: 'If you would perhaps help me, guide me in answering in the manner that you want.'

NAIDU: 'No, I am not going to guide you and I do not want ...'

JUDGE DANIELS: 'Well, if somebody says to you he was betrayed, what do you understand? What is he saying, what is he telling you? I know he uses the word betray, but what does that convey to you what happened to this person? What, to use the example that Mr Gering quoted, what do you understand happened between Judas and Jesus?'

SEDIBE: 'It is the example that I quoted when I made mention of Jesus Christ and Judas Iscariot. Jesus Christ said that he had been betrayed by Judas.'

JUDGE DANIELS: 'Yes. Now, what do you think he meant when he said that he was betrayed by Judas?'

SEDIBE: 'What I understand in that is that these people were together, they belonged to the same group, but that in the course of time one of them deviated from their manner of operating or behaviour. He was no longer in that group.'

NAIDU: 'And do you agree then, to complete this scenario, that person actually moves over to the opposing group, the enemy?'

SEDIBE: 'I understand.'

NAIDU: 'And do you agree also, to finalise that scenario, that the one person who moves from one group to the enemy group betrays his colleagues when he tells to the enemy group what happens that lets down his first group, his own group. He lets them down, he sells them out as it were.'

SEDIBE: 'No, I do not know if you expect me to say yes to this suggestion because you see when I decided to change or to deviate the decision was taken by me for my own self. I wanted to start a new life.'

NAIDU: 'Mr X, I want to suggest that you are anticipating a question that I may ask you five or six questions later, but the question presently is not about your decision, it is not about your role, it is not even about the ANC and I am only going to ask you this the last time and if you prefer to answer it the way you want to do it. My question to you is that do you agree that it is betrayal for a person from one group to say to the members of the enemy group things that let down the first group to which he belongs?'

SEDIBE: 'Yes, that is so.'

NAIDU: 'You see there are people belonging to the group that he has left [who] will say about this person who has left them, "he has betrayed us" but the people in the group to which he has gone will not say "he has betrayed those". At least, I am pleased to say that you appreciate the concept of betray. Did you do English in matric?'

SEDIBE: 'Yes, even in JC [Junior Certificate] I did.'

NAIDU: 'Did you pass English in matric?'

SEDIBE: 'I passed my matric.'

NAIDU: 'Would it be correct to say, Mr X, that when the questions are put to you in English you have a good understanding of them?'

SEDIBE: 'No. You see, it depends on the level of the English used. If it is the English of the level of your education then I would not understand it.'

NAIDU: 'Are you suggesting in any way, and I would like you to think carefully about this, are you having any difficulty understanding or were you having any difficulty understanding the questions as they were put to you by Mr Gering in English?'

SEDIBE: 'There were points where I could not understand him.'

JUDGE DANIELS: 'Just as a matter of interest, when one gives evidence through an interpreter and in particular now you standing there, do you actually find yourself listening attentively to the question which is put to you or do you wait for the question to be translated?'

SEDIBE: 'I mainly wait for the interpretation.'

The court record gives us Sedibe in his own voice, despite the mediation of the interpreter. The transcripts show sides of Sedibe that many of those who knew the man remembered about him. There is the bombastic fellow, on the one hand, and the Jim-comes-to-Jo'burg country bumpkin, on the other. Although a smart man, Sedibe would often pretend to be less intelligent than he was – as can be seen in his exchange with Naidu and Daniels. Ray Lalla remarked, 'I found him very rural in outlook. He came out as a person who, although he sounded educated and bright – what struck me was his ability to sound naïve and innocent.'[30] Delilah Rekisa, among the first women to be turned into askaris and one of Sedibe's closest friends after he turned, also commented on Sedibe's seeming naivety. Rekisa said, '*Glory un' atletsi buPedi.*' (Glory was too Pedi.) This was a crude way of saying that Sedibe was raw and unsophisticated.[31]

The transcripts also show that while Sedibe refused until the end to accept the label *impimpi* or to admit to betrayal, he was compelled by the nature of the drama in which he was a leading actor to justify himself. He was forced to explain how he came to be where he was: a former senior member of the ANC now working for the police against the ANC.

Political trials in apartheid South Africa were traumatic events in which the accused and the state witnesses were compelled to face each other as what we might call intimate strangers across a courtroom. Judas Mpho Tladi, who testified as Mr X2 against Dladla, Ebrahim and Maseko, called his turn on the witness stand one of the most difficult moments in his transformation from resister to collaborator.[32] Recalling his cross-examination by Kessie Naidu, Tladi, shaking his head, said, '*Ngimubheke, ngith' ukub' uyaz' ukuthi ngifike kanjani la.*' (I would look at him [Naidu] and say to myself, "If only you knew how I got here.")[33]

Tladi felt that the hardest part of his cross-examination was when Naidu asked him to say how he knew that one of Ebrahim's *noms de guerre* was Mzwandile. Tladi, who had only been captured two months before the police ordered him to give evidence in this trial, commented that what made this part particularly difficult was that the police had asked him similar questions during interrogation and he had resisted – until his interrogators produced minutes from a secret ANC meeting in Swaziland at which both he and 'Mzwandile' had been present, confirming that he knew that Mzwandile was Ebrahim. Tladi did not say this, but that moment – when he was confronted with secret ANC minutes that could only have come to the police through betrayal – was perhaps when he started to turn. It was probably the moment when he felt the eight years he had dedicated to the ANC begin to disappear. Naidu's questions reminded Tladi of what he might have considered his moment of weakness.[34]

Oscar Linda Moni, who testified as Mr X4 against Dladla, Ebrahim and Maseko, also found his 'performance' as a state witness traumatic. Moni, captured in South Africa in January 1986 and turned through torture, said that he held out for 16 months after his capture, giving his interrogators some information but withholding what he considered to be more important material. However, the last of his defences crumbled the first time he had to appear in court to testify against former ANC comrades in the terrorism trial *State* vs *Buthelezi and others*. His exchange with Naidu bears quoting at length. At the centre of the exchange are Naidu's questions about how Moni knew Ebrahim and where they had met.

NAIDU: 'When was the first time that you discussed or mentioned accused no. 3 [Ebrahim] to any policeman after your arrest?'[35]

MONI: 'If I am not mistaken I would say it was during my interrogation after my arrest.'

NAIDU: 'Can you say whether it was in the same month of your arrest, the same year of your arrest? Can you give us some idea when was the first time you mentioned accused no. 3 to any policeman?'

MONI: 'I cannot be certain because you see my interrogation

lasted for about a year and six months. This is the time that I was in detention. The police would now and then come to me to take me for interrogations and I am in no position to say when or at which period of time I spoke of any particular person.'

NAIDU: 'And had you already mentioned accused no. 3 to some policeman before you spoke to Mr Deetlefs [the same senior policeman who took part in Sedibe's abduction and tortured Ebrahim] or was mention of him first made when you spoke to Mr Deetlefs?'

MONI: 'I mentioned all the people I knew with reference to an album that had been used or that was being used during my interrogation.'

NAIDU: 'Were you shown this album at the early stages of your interrogation or at the late stage of your interrogation?'

MONI: 'Well, I would say I saw this album throughout the period of my interrogation.'

NAIDU: 'The first time – just try and apply your mind to the question I am asking you, the first time that you were shown this album, would you say that was the early stages of your interrogation or the late stage of your interrogation because according to you you were interrogated for about 18 months from January 1986.'

MONI: 'I would say it was about immediately after my arrest, but it is a distortion of what I had said to say that my interrogation lasted for 18 months. I said about 16 months.'

NAIDU: 'Please forgive me, it is probably what I misheard, but I got the impression you said 18 months.'

NAIDU: 'You said you saw this album in the early stages of your interrogation, so do you recall that a photograph depicting accused no. 3 was shown to you or you saw it at the early stages of your interrogation shortly after your arrest?'

MONI: 'Yes.'

NAIDU: 'And on that occasion when you first saw him, did you mention to the policeman or policemen interrogating you that you had seen this person previously and in what circumstances and when you saw him?'

MONI: 'Well, I may perhaps not have said some of the things that I knew of, you see, because I was at that stage still resisting.'

JUDGE DANIELS: 'When you were shown this album, were you told who the people were or rather were you told – were the people depicted in this album, were they actually identified to you by the investigating officer? Did he say to you this is Mr A, do you know him, or how did you go about identifying these people?'

MONI: 'What was happening is that the investigating officer would be seated on a table on the other side, this is now on my opposite side, he would then be having this album before him, take a photograph and show it to me in his hand, the photograph in his hand and show it to me, then I would say I know that person, then he would put it on one side, take another photo and similarly show it to me as well and I would respond.'

NAIDU: 'Did you at that stage when you first saw his photograph mention at least the times when you saw this person Achmed [one of Ebrahim's *noms de guerre*] that you know him as?'

MONI: 'Well, I would not be able to say specifically what I said about every person because at the time I was still tense and especially because of the knowledge I had of accused no. 3. I did not have so much knowledge of him, but what I said was I had seen him, I knew him.'

NAIDU: 'And you said in an earlier reply that you did not tell him everything, some of the things you did not tell him because you were still resisting. What do you mean by that?'

MONI: 'What I mean is that I was still withholding the facts or what I knew.'

NAIDU: 'And how long did you continue to withhold these facts before you actually stopped resisting as it were?'

MONI: 'Well, I would say until I became tamed.'

NAIDU: 'Yes, it seems so, but tell us when you became tamed? When approximately? You were arrested in January and some 16 months later you were released from your detention.'

Moni: 'I got tamed when I entered a witness stand and I was being told that I was to give evidence for the state.'

Naidu: 'Do you mean the first time that you had entered the witness box and told that you were going to be giving evidence for the state, that is when you got tamed?'

Moni: 'Well, you see I had also then properly thought about my conditions, conditions of life on earth, conditions at home.'

Naidu: 'Now, but I would like you to please answer my question. You say that you stopped resisting, in other words you stopped withholding information and facts, when you got into a witness box and told you were being [*sic*] giving evidence, now I want to know from you by that do you mean that you stopped resisting, you stopped withholding facts on the day you got into this witness box when you first gave evidence for the state?'

Moni: 'Well, what I am trying to say is that day was the first day that I put the lives of my comrades at, what I would say, at stake or shall I say that was the first time that I did what is said to be betrayal. That was the first time that I did what is said to be a traitor.'

This exchange underscores the role of language in the business of collaboration. We speak often of people 'breaking' under torture. We speak also of 'breaking' animals as a way of domesticating them. It takes Moni's talk of being 'tamed' to show us the ease with which talk of 'breaking' and 'taming' animals shifts to talk of 'breaking' and 'taming' insurgents. De Kock described Sedibe shortly after his abduction as 'wild'. In other words, he had yet to be brought under control; he had yet to be 'tamed'. It is significant that, for Moni, the moment of his 'taming' did not come during his long interrogation, during his multiple identifications of his comrades pictured in the Security Branch photo album. It came the first time he had to face his former comrades from the witness stand. As he said in court, giving evidence for the state was the first time that he 'did what is said to be betrayal. That was the first time that I did what is said to be a traitor.'

We could focus here on Moni's faltering grammar, his apparent discomfort at this moment in his testimony. But that would not take us far. As the writer and artist Allan Sekula puts it, the police identikit does not capture the subversive himself, merely his likeness.[36] Moni knew that by betraying the photograph, he was not betraying his comrades themselves. His betrayal only became real once he betrayed them in person. The political trials might have been shows, but they were real, and the betrayal built into them was also real. That is how Moni was 'tamed'.

9

The show trial

The show trial is both an exemplum – with the presentation and severe punishment of sinners and the demonstration of the strength and determination of the state – and at the same time one of the most important forums where the legitimacy of the state is asserted by pointing to the threat coming from the ever-present danger of subversive activities.

– Istvan Rev[1]

As Mr X1, Sedibe was the star attraction in a show trial. In the Soviet Union show trials were elaborately staged dramas in which the accused were assigned lines and parts. In South Africa it was the state witnesses who were assigned parts by the prosecutors, and were constantly reminded by them of the threat of prosecution under which they played their roles. State witnesses were fed lines by prosecutors and were directed by police investigators, who sat behind the prosecutors – all the better to ensure that they did not stray from the script, and maybe to remind them of the torture that had brought many of them there in the first place.

To call political trials in South Africa show trials is not to say they were all form and no content. Each trial had unique material and psychological substance that extended beyond its scripted nature. Lives were at stake. If these trials derived their form from the rituals that governed them, their content came from the physical and psychological price that both the accused and state witnesses paid to attend the performances.

In the Dladla, Ebrahim and Maseko trial, the four askaris who served as state witnesses, with Sedibe playing the lead, were each summoned from a chorus (of collaborators) through dialogue with the prosecutors, placed on stage (the witness stand), and called on to sing the virtues of the apartheid state. Each witness had to say who he was, explain his association with the ANC, and tell how he came to see the light, how he came to be a state witness against an organisation he had vowed to defend and die for. It is through this scripted dialogue with the prosecutor that we get Sedibe's version of how he changed from an insurgent to a counterinsurgent. The police and judicial system marked Sedibe's version as official, thereby making it the standard version heard each time Sedibe – who became, among other things, a 'professional witness' for the Security Branch – took the stand against former comrades.

Sedibe's version went as follows: he and Mkhwanazi were driving around Manzini on 13 August 1986 when the Swazi police arrested them. The Swazis tortured him, leaving him with a scar down one side of his nose. Sedibe had R8000 in a red wallet for an MK mission. The Swazi police confiscated the money and transferred him to the Mankayane police station. One night, a team of MK operatives sprang him from prison. As he could not stay in Swaziland or go to Mozambique, where his wife and daughter lived, he decided to hide out in South Africa while considering his options. He crossed illegally into South Africa and, while walking alone in the bushes near the border, resolved to hand himself over to the police.

He walked to the Piet Retief offices of the Security Branch and there presented himself to Warrant Officer Freek Pienaar. Sedibe said that he told a stunned Pienaar he was a senior member of MK but was tired of life as an insurgent and wanted to turn himself in. 'He told me he did not believe what I was telling him. He knew about me, he had heard of me and he wanted something concrete by which he will believe me and then I told him that Bernard and

Tolman [*sic*] were to come to a certain spot where I were [*sic*] to go and meet them.'[2]

In Sedibe's version, Pienaar decided to check out Sedibe's story about Bernard (real name Mbongeni Kone) and Tallman (real name Assen Jeremiah Thimula), two MK operatives on a mission to infiltrate South Africa from Swaziland. Sedibe's tip-off proved true and the two men were killed in a Security Branch ambush. This, according to Sedibe, was the turning point. Pienaar now believed he could trust Sedibe. Pienaar told Sedibe to go 'home' and think about his future. Sedibe had two options: to go back to school or look for a job. Sedibe said he decided after a few days at 'home' to join the police. He went back to Pienaar to communicate his decision. Pienaar welcomed him to the fold and by February 1987 Sedibe was a member of the SAP.[3]

Nowhere in this version is there a word about abduction and torture by the South Africans. In fact, Sedibe publicly denied being tortured by the Security Branch. He said the only people who tortured and scarred him were the Swazi police who arrested him. To hear Sedibe tell it, he became a counterinsurgent because he was tired of being an insurgent.[4]

When Gering suggested during his cross-examination that the deaths of Kone and Thimula were due to his betrayal of them and that their killing must have been 'pursuant to the information' he gave the police, Sedibe denied betraying his two comrades.[5]

GERING: 'Now, I put it to you that when I said to you you betrayed your two former comrades when you informed the security police that they were going to be coming into South Africa, surely you must agree with that?'

SEDIBE: 'Well, I do not know that. You would know how I betrayed them in doing this.'

GERING: 'To give information to the security police as to the approximate time and the approximate place of crossing into South Africa of two members of Mkonto [MK] who had served with you in Mkonto in Swaziland, I put it to you that on any ordinary meaning of language that must amount to a betrayal by you because you did this knowingly.'

SEDIBE: 'No. I do not know that. What I know of is that I went to the police and I told them the truth.'

GERING: 'Yes, as a matter of fact by telling them the truth on this I say you knowingly betrayed them because you knowingly knew, you deliberately knew that if the police acted on your information they would fall into a trap.'

SEDIBE: 'I am listening to what you are saying if you are simply telling me that.'

GERING: 'Let me put the facts to you very simply. You knew that Bernard and Tolman [*sic*] were going to be coming into South Africa within a day of your leaving them?'

SEDIBE: 'Yes.'

GERING: 'You knew they were going to be bringing arms and ammunition into South Africa?'

SEDIBE: 'That is so.'

GERING: 'You knew they were planning to cross in the vicinity of Nerston?'

SEDIBE: 'Yes.'

GERING: 'You knew that in a military operation by the ANC it is crucial not to disclose to the enemy of the ANC the proposed infiltration into South Africa by members of Mkonto?'

SEDIBE: 'That is so.'

GERING: 'You say that you had training in military intelligence?'

SEDIBE: 'That is so.'

GERING: 'Surely it must follow that when you give such information knowingly to the security police, you are in effect betraying your colleagues because they will fall into a trap once the security police know the approximate time and place of their proposed infiltration?'

SEDIBE: 'Yes, I knew that if the police accepted what I told them then they would go to see these people.'

GERING: 'I am glad you finally come round to that because

that in effect means that you realise ... I put it to you that your conceding that ... your conceding that amounts to an admission that you knowingly betrayed your former colleagues by giving this information to the security police.'

SEDIBE: 'I did not intend to betray them. I was simply telling the police the truth. I mentioned this to prove to them that I had told them the truth after having surrendered myself.'

Sedibe was lying. He had nothing to do with the betrayal and killing of Kone and Thimula. The same death squad that had abducted Sedibe a day earlier killed the two men on 14 August 1986 on the border between South Africa and Swaziland. Eugene de Kock, who led the death squad, later admitted, 'There was no way MK September could have known of the operation [against Kone and Thimula].'[6] The operation had been planned before Sedibe's abduction. Why, then, did Sedibe confess to something he had not done? Sedibe's brother Kaborone believed the police lied to Sedibe, telling him that the intelligence for the operation came from him. 'De Kock compromised him. They killed some of the guys he was to meet to make it look as if my brother had sold them out. He could not go back to the ANC after that. They were going to kill him,' said Kaborone.[7] Sedibe, who knew about Kone and Thimula's mission, might have mentioned it during his interrogation shortly after his abduction. But, unknown to him, he confirmed what the police already knew about the two operatives.

There is another reason why the Security Branch might have lied to Sedibe about his connection to the killing of Kone and Thimula: to protect their agents in the ANC. Having removed Sedibe from the ANC picture, as it were, they could use him to take responsibility for the actions of their agents still in the ANC, thereby protecting them. When Kone and Thimula were killed, they were travelling in an ANC van with Vusi Sindane, a fellow MK member, and Shadrack Sithole, a Swazi national who served as a courier and driver for the ANC. But Sithole had sold the men out to De Kock's death squad, having been arrested a week earlier and 'turned'.[8] He had been promised R10,000 in cash (and full-time employment as a South African agent) to deliver the three men. Sithole stopped at a prearranged spot on the South African side, where De Kock and his men cut the three men down. Kone and Thimula died immediately. Sindane, injured, fled to a peasant homestead in the border area. Unfortunately for him, the homestead belonged to a police informer, who promptly called the police. They arrested Sindane. Meanwhile, as Sithole was driving back to Swaziland, De Kock asked the Piet Retief Security Branch commander if Sithole could be trusted. The commander said no and added that it was '100 per cent that he will betray us sooner than later, but betray us he will'. De Kock remarked, 'I made a decision then that I in later years had to explain to the TRC in detail. We shot him as well.'[9]

Mandla Maseko was the first person to raise the red flag about Sithole. Already in detention in the Piet Retief police station when Kone and Thimula were killed, Maseko had spotted the ANC van in the parking lot of the police station a day before the two men's killing. Thinking Sithole, who he knew worked for the ANC, had been arrested, Maseko asked prisoners working in the grounds who it was that had driven the van to the police station. 'A policeman,' they answered. Maseko suspected then that the ANC had been penetrated, but his suspicions were not confirmed until the following day, 15 August 1986, when the police took him to the government mortuary and ordered him to identify Kone and Thimula. Maseko said in a note, dated 5 March 1990, prepared for his lawyers and the ANC, 'It is clear that they [the police] wanted to eliminate Sithole because they did not want witnesses, even though he was their own informer.'[10] Regarding Sedibe's claim to have been the one to tell the cops about Kone and Thimula, Maseko commented, 'This was clearly an attempt to hide the fact that they had got their information from Sithole.'[11]

In De Kock's view, 'There has always been some universal emotion of disgust and loathing reserved for traitors, no matter whose traitors they are. One fact has always been a constant through the millenniums, and that is that a traitor can never be trusted.'[12] Although De Kock would not say this, Sithole was expendable because the Security Branch had no shortage of agents in the ANC. The police had agents in all sectors of South African and Swazi society, including the criminal networks on which the ANC relied for everything from money and infiltration to vehicles. According to Humphrey Mkhwanazi, police penetration of the ANC was so extensive that the 'Boers would get some of these smugglers to sell us cars. The cars were bugged.'[13]

Police Commissioner Johan van der Merwe and Eugene de Kock claimed that Sedibe himself was betrayed long before he betrayed the ANC.[14] The police had penetrated his network. According to De Kock, when Sedibe was abducted in 1986, he had recently returned to Swaziland from Mozambique. He had fled Swaziland a few months earlier following the assassination by an apartheid death squad of a group of ANC operatives under his command. Said De Kock, 'The source was an ANC member working for the Soweto [police] intelligence service and was the one who pointed out the house for us that night, and also knocked on the door for the people inside to open the door.'[15] De Kock mentioned that Sedibe was betrayed even before he left Maputo for his fateful return to Swaziland. 'A fellow ANC operative informed on Sedibe to the Middelburg Security Branch, who in turn informed the Swazi police, who then arrested MK September on his first day in Swaziland.'[16] The ANC agent in Mozambique who betrayed Sedibe did so, according to De Kock, for 'sordid monetary gain'.[17] Apparently, Sedibe was 'on the road from Namahashe, Mozambique, to Manzini, Swaziland' when the Swazi police arrested him.[18] But according to Humphrey Mkhwanazi, who was with Sedibe when the Swazis arrested them, the arrest took place outside the Spar supermarket and near the police station in the centre of Manzini.

But De Kock is not the only unreliable narrator in this account with little narrative clarity. Asked by the defence lawyer Leonard Gering during his state witness testimony in the 1988 treason trial if he still believed in 'everything that the ANC stood for', Sedibe deflected the question by stating, 'I am now a policeman.'[19] Asked why he had surrendered, Sedibe replied, 'I was just tired of being with the ANC in Swaziland and having to be hiding myself.'[20] Nowhere did he acknowledge the threat of imprisonment that a return home entailed. Nowhere did he say that he stood a greater chance of going to jail for longer than the five years his brother had spent on Robben Island. Sedibe did not mention any of this because his decision to become a collaborator removed the threat of jail. He owed the police his freedom – and life. Gering tried to press Sedibe on this, saying, 'You have a great indebtedness to the South African Police.' Sedibe responded, 'What indebtedness now? To whom?'[21]

Sedibe's story of disillusionment, defection and conversion would very likely have been the only version in the official archive but for Almond Nofomela. A member of the squad that abducted Sedibe, Nofomela had been on death row for two years for the murder in 1987 of a farmer (a crime unconnected to his police job) when he told the world about police death squads. Nofomela and an accomplice had killed the farmer during a robbery. Expecting his police bosses to get him out of jail, Nofomela was disappointed when, on the eve of his execution, Eugene de Kock sent word that the police were not going to free him. He was told to 'take the pain'. Nofomela did not want to take the pain.[22] So, on 19 October 1989, he wrote an affidavit asking for a stay of execution. He had information about police death squads that would be of interest to the state, he announced. The government granted the stay. Nofomela talked: he detailed political murders as well as abductions committed by the police. Among the abductions he mentioned was Sedibe's.[23]

Nofomela would not have known this at the time, but his revelations confirmed some of the stories that Dirk Coetzee, Nofomela's first death-squad commander, had been trying to tell members of the parliamentary opposition and the anti-apartheid media in South Africa. Coetzee, a star student at the police college, had been demoted from his job as commander of Vlakplaas after falling foul of his bosses' puritanical ways. Coetzee, a man with a healthy regard for his own talents, was embittered by his demotion and sought revenge. But no one would believe his stories about death squads – until Nofomela talked.

Nofomela's affidavit described Sedibe's abduction from Swaziland in 1986. He said De Kock had ordered him and a few other members of Vlakplaas to go to Swaziland to kidnap a 'certain member of the ANC by the name of September'.[24] Nofomela recalled that before they kidnapped Sedibe, De Kock warned that 'there should not be a shooting because it has been arranged with the commissioner of police in Swaziland that there will be no policeman [*sic*] who are going to be armed at that stage'.[25] The men kidnapped Sedibe and took him to a farm in Piet Retief. 'Then from there September was interrogated most especially about the whereabouts of his comrades ... From there he was being assaulted all the time.' De Kock and Paul van Dyk led the assault. It was not long before Sedibe was 'telling them stories'.[26] Sedibe was then taken to the Piet Retief police station. Nofomela said that he did not see Sedibe again until 1988, when 'I met him in Krugersdorp. He was in the company of other askaris, then he told me that he is working with them.'[27]

Nofomela's revelations forced President F.W. de Klerk to appoint a commission of inquiry 'into certain murders'. Chaired by Louis Harms, a judge of the Pretoria Supreme Court, the commission could have investigated the death squad allegations in detail. From the beginning, however, Harms seemed more interested in discrediting Coetzee and Nofomela than in testing their claims. Sedibe would most likely not have participated in the commission's proceedings but for the fact that Nofomela had named him in his affidavit – and had offered an account of Sedibe's defection at variance with what Sedibe had told the court in his testimony against Dladla, Ebrahim and Maseko. Sedibe's police and military bosses were openly contemptuous of the Harms Commission, despite the judge's sympathy towards them. They gave evidence in disguises so ridiculous that they must have intended them as a joke. Still, they ordered Sedibe to appear before the commission to counter Nofomela's story.

Sedibe's appearance began with a ruling that his identity must be protected, which meant that journalists covering the proceedings could not identify him. In giving his testimony, Sedibe stuck to his story: he had defected to the police because he was disillusioned with the ANC.[28] Harms duly issued a report that exonerated the police and branded Coetzee a liar. But the death squads had been revealed. Vlakplaas had been exposed or, in the words of a secret Security Branch report, 'contaminated'.[29] The Security Branch tried to spin the story. They claimed that, far from being a death squad camp, Vlakplaas was in fact a centre for 'rehabilitated terrorists'. These were described as people who had seen the errors of their ways. The Harms Commission might have been a whitewash, but it did provide information that would come in handy six years later when the TRC began its work.

* * *

Deborah Posel writes that the TRC was intended to serve as a 'nation-building exercise to create a "shared" national history' and that, as such, it did not 'require a comprehensive, detailed narration of individual and community histories. The goal was rather to produce enough truth to demonstrate and exemplify the inequities of the past. A sample of the truth rather than the whole would suffice to establish the desired consensus.'[30] Sedibe became a part of that sample – one illustration among many of the 'inequities of the past'. By treating Sedibe's case this way, the TRC added yet another version to the 'strange saga of Mr X1'.

The TRC's version was partly the result of Eugene de Kock's application for amnesty for his role in Sedibe's abduction. Having been arrested in May 1994, a month after the formal end of apartheid, for crimes committed while he was head of Vlakplaas,

De Kock turned to the TRC for a chance at freedom. Having been sentenced already to more than 200 years in prison, De Kock had little to lose. He declared before the TRC that his crimes had been politically motivated. He also accepted full responsibility for the actions of the men who served under him and only implicated people of his rank or those above him.

De Kock's amnesty application led to a flood of applications by other cops. Fearful of being the one left without a chair when the music stopped, each of these men tried to implicate others, or feigned amnesia as the result of post-traumatic stress disorder. Men who had spent years making it their business to know everything there was to know about their enemies suddenly could not remember the most spectacular details of their operations. The journalist De Wet Potgieter called this an 'amnesia of epidemic and ... terminal proportions'.[31] Having lost their cause and *esprit de corps*, they did not know what their colleagues would say. It was every man for himself. So, in cases where a lot of information was already in the public domain, they gave frank confessions. As a result, De Kock's amnesty application for Sedibe's abduction from Swaziland was joined by those of seven of his colleagues during a hearing in February 2000.

Christo Deetlefs told the committee that he had been in Swaziland on a routine visit to see his Swazi counterparts and meet with his agents when the Swazi police informed him that they had arrested Sedibe and were about to deport him to Zambia, where the ANC had its headquarters. The Swazis told him where Sedibe was detained. Deetlefs knew from his agents in the ANC that Sedibe was an alcoholic. 'He used to consume large volumes of liquor and this created the impression that if I could get in touch with him, I might be able to convince him to cooperate with us.'[32] To shield his Swazi counterparts from blame, Deetlefs denied that they had colluded in Sedibe's abduction. Deetlefs said he had summoned De Kock and a few of his men to Swaziland for the operation.

The other applicants corroborated Deetlefs's story. While they all agreed that Sedibe was assaulted when he was abducted, they denied that he was tortured once on South African soil. Except for Nofomela, who said Sedibe was assaulted in Piet Retief, the other applicants claimed that once in South Africa, Sedibe defected voluntarily. Freek Pienaar, the officer credited with 'breaking' and 'turning' Sedibe, began his testimony by telling the committee that, in addition to seeking amnesty for Sedibe's abduction, assault and the 'illegal transgression' of the Swaziland border, he was also seeking amnesty for perjury. 'How do we get to perjury?' asked Judge Sisi Khampepe of the TRC Amnesty Committee. Harry Prinsloo, the lead prosecutor in the trial against Dladla, Ebrahim and Maseko but now a private lawyer representing Pienaar, answered, 'He gave evidence during the trial of Mr Ebrahim [and] Maseko and he gave false evidence with regard to how September came from Swaziland to South Africa. The evidence was not disclosed that he was abducted, instead it was presented that he had independently moved from Swaziland to South Africa.'[33]

Khampepe refused to accept Pienaar's application for amnesty for perjury. She ruled that the count of perjury was separate from the charges of abduction, assault and the violation of Swaziland's sovereignty. 'Do we have jurisdiction to hear it?' Khampepe asked Prinsloo. When Prinsloo answered yes, Khampepe asked, 'What is the connection between this incident [Sedibe's abduction] and perjury?'[34] The exchange offers a stark illustration of the limitations the Amnesty Committee imposed on itself. As Madeleine Fullard and Nicky Rousseau have shown, members of the committee, lawyers mostly, adopted a strict, legalistic approach to their work. They interpreted their briefs so narrowly that they allowed amnesty applicants, especially former members of the army and police, to give only as much information as they thought the committee needed – or information that was already in the public domain. Members of the committee failed to pursue lines of questioning or follow clues that might have yielded more truth than the applicants intended.[35] Although the applicants' testimony invited obvious questions about askaris, these questions were not asked. Pursuing the charge of perjury, for example, might have opened up lines of inquiry leading to Sedibe's life as a collaborator.

It is a curious feature of the Amnesty Committee's hearing into Sedibe's abduction that he was presented only in one guise – that of a victim. The committee froze Sedibe in time. It said nothing of the eight years he had spent as a collaborator. There was even a lawyer, Percy M. Leopeng, paid for by the state, appearing 'on behalf of the victims, the brother of the deceased and the wife of the deceased'.[36] Sedibe was indeed a victim. But he was also a prominent askari. Presented with a rare chance to question the men responsible for turning anti-apartheid combatants into collaborators, and delving into how such collaborators worked, the committee passed on that opportunity.

Instead, it spent the better part of the three-day hearing trying to establish whether Sedibe had been tortured in South Africa, and what scars, if any, could be seen on his body. To be sure, mention was made a few times of his life as an askari. But that did not interest the committee. They did not ask what it meant to be an askari. They did not ask how askaris operated or about the grey zones askaris inhabited. They did not ask how the police decided whom to 'turn', whom to imprison and whom to kill. Deetlefs said he knew Sedibe was an alcoholic and that he might be turned. But as De Kock told the committee, 'With regard to his drinking habits, everybody drank, the ANC drank, the SAP drank, this had absolutely nothing to do with his thoughts of defecting.'[37]

Deetlefs described Sedibe as an askari. 'He provided us invaluable information which was of great assistance to the Security Branch at that stage. And indeed he gradually did become a member of the Security Branch.'[38] Asked what made him so confident that Sedibe could be turned into an askari, Deetlefs answered, 'It was just a feeling that I had because I knew that he was uncomfortable in Swaziland and that is why I made the assumption. It is a chance one takes. One can never be certain.'[39]

He insisted that Sedibe was not tortured in South Africa. This was because 'everything was aimed at getting so far as to the point that he would assist us. We wanted him to assist us on a voluntary level. We did give him a drink. He was quite a heavy drinker and it wasn't very long thereafter that his tongue loosened and we were all getting along quite well with each other.'[40] But Sedibe's widow, Ção, told a different story. She said that after Sedibe was subdued and tied up, he was force-fed whiskey.[41]

Among those applying for amnesty, De Kock alone denied that Sedibe was an askari. Asked to define an askari, De Kock replied, 'As I understand it, it was here a person who decided or a person from one of the liberation movements who decided to go over to the police. In other words, one could call him a traitor.'[42] He said that Sedibe never changed his pro-ANC political views even after he started working for the police, but was a 'hostage of circumstances and he did not have a choice'.[43] De Kock added, 'I did not send him out with the askaris, he was not treated as an askari because he was not an askari as far as I was concerned. He did not ever supply any information that led to the apprehension of any MK members or of any attacks to the neighbouring states. He did testify in a case and that was unfortunate.'[44] But the Amnesty Committee failed to ask De Kock to elaborate on how exactly he used Sedibe, if not as an askari. As a result, they missed the opportunity to hear from De Kock's perspective what exactly Sedibe did for the Security Branch and the DCC.

According to De Kock, 'Mr Sedibe was not the sort of person who could be classified under the normal term of askari, he wasn't like those persons who had been made an offer instead of having to serve out a prison sentence and so forth.'[45] De Kock claimed that when he asked Sedibe how much ANC information he had given to the police, Sedibe replied it was about 10 per cent. 'When I asked him why so little, he said that was enough for them to keep him alive. He also mentioned that the Security Branch already had much of the information, he only had to confirm it. And in my mind he never turned out to be an *impimpi*. He was an intelligent man, he gave them just enough to satisfy them and to keep them happy, but it was about his survival.'[46] Yet the committee did not pick up on the discrepancies between De Kock's testimony and that of his former colleagues, who all insisted that Sedibe was an askari.

Louisa van der Walt, a prosecutor in the trial against Dladla, Ebrahim and Maseko but now a private lawyer for ex-cops Schalk Visser and Paul van Dyk, challenged De Kock's image of Sedibe as a special type of collaborator. A devoted state prosecutor under apartheid, Van der Walt had well-pronounced rightist views. When Dladla, Ebrahim and Maseko were found guilty and sentenced to lengthy prison terms on 16 January 1989, the three men gave the clenched-fist salute while their supporters in the public gallery sang anti-apartheid songs. Van der Walt, still in her prosecutor's robes, responded by shouting, 'Long live the AWB!', in reference to the neo-Nazi Afrikaner Weerstandsbeweging. When Van der Walt's colleagues, including Harry Prinsloo, told her to restrain herself, she shot back: 'Why do you have to shut me up when others are allowed to sing?'[47] When apartheid ended, Van der Walt quit her job as a state prosecutor and began to represent Afrikaner right-wingers in various cases, including the Boeremag trial, the first treason case in post-apartheid South Africa.[48]

Van der Walt had led Sedibe's evidence in the trial against Dladla, Ebrahim and Maseko. She had kept him on the witness stand for six days of the six weeks he spent testifying and being cross-examined as Mr X1. In short, she knew her security police and their collaborators well. So when De Kock claimed during his amnesty application that Sedibe was not an askari, Van der Walt asked, 'Do you remember Miriam Williams?'

DE KOCK: 'Miriam who?'

VAN DER WALT: 'Miriam Williams.'

DE KOCK: 'No, Chairperson, I do not have a recollection of this person. If you could perhaps link the person to something, I might be able to refresh my memory.'

VAN DER WALT: 'Miriam Phumla Williams. She was identified by Mr Sedibe at the Baragwanath Hospital where the nurses' buses stopped and she was also charged later.'

DE KOCK: 'I don't have any knowledge of this.'

VAN DER WALT: 'Sedibe did not testify in that matter, but you know that he testified in the Ebrahim matter.'

DE KOCK: 'Yes, I am aware of it. The reason why I say that I am not aware of the person that he identified is that I would have been the one to fill out the claim and to instate the claim and there was no claim for that identification.'[49]

This exchange created an opening that, if taken, might have enriched our understanding of how askaris operated. De Kock suggested, for example, that bureaucratic processes, separate from the payment of regular salaries to askaris, governed payments of bounties for the identification of members of the ANC. What were the sums? How were they calculated? How did the bounty payments compare with regular askari salaries? These are all questions the Amnesty Committee failed to raise.

In 2013 I asked Miriam Phumla Williams to give me an account of her capture in 1988. She recalled that she was getting out of a minibus taxi outside Baragwanath Hospital in Soweto on 29 June 1988 when Sedibe, accompanied by other askaris and police officers, arrested her.[50] 'When the taxi arrived and I was about to alight from the taxi, I immediately recognised September as I had been with him in Swaziland and at some point in Mozambique. As I was staring he immediately alerted other plainclothes members of his team who I did not recognise. At that point I started screaming as he dragged me out of the taxi. I screamed to alert the people around there as I had realised I was being arrested.

'I was taken to Protea Police Station and was handed over to a policeman called Mr Terblanche. I can't remember the names of the others. The interrogation started there with the focus being to establish who I was going to meet. I just had a brainwave of directing them to my family's house as a way of alerting them I was already in the country. I knew such arrests very often resulted in people never being found,' she said. Williams told her abductors she had been on her way to meet her mother. 'That really helped as they all went home and arrested my pensioned mother, and my sisters, aunts, for questioning. They were kept for about two to three days and released thereafter as they [the police] realised they knew nothing,' she said. Williams's 'brainwave' probably saved her life, as it helped publicise news of her arrest.

Three days after kidnapping Williams, the police transferred her to Piet Retief for interrogation. 'Amongst the people who were used to persuade me to work for the askaris were September and his Mozambican wife whom I also knew from Swaziland. I was subjected to an intense interrogation with endless hours of questioning with no breaks. They would take me every morning and bring me back in the evening for sleeping. This happened for roughly three months before they took me to court and formally charged me.'

Williams said of Sedibe: 'I had no doubt I was sold out by him. He was the one who recognised me at the Bara taxi rank. What became more shocking to me was the discovery during interrogation that he had been working with them even in Swaziland. The reason I know that was that during one of the interrogation sessions, I was confronted with a letter which my boyfriend then (Vuso Shabalala, who later was to be my husband) wrote and gave to him from Swaziland to bring over to me in Mozambique. That letter never reached me and we had just assumed it got lost in the message services we were using at that time. The wife of September was brought to my cell one day to supposedly visit me and to bring me some food. She was the one who was brought to tell me "the Boers are not as bad as we have been made to believe in the ANC". Those were her words in heavily accented English, as she was Portuguese. Unfortunately, she got a rude awakening, discovering that I was not as easy as she was made to believe. I told her to leave my cell with her food and go back to Mozambique where she belongs. That was the last time she was sent.' Sedibe did not participate in Williams's interrogation. 'Not directly. He was brought to my cell alone to supposedly chat with me. Unfortunately, his involvement did not work at all because he came once or twice. And I simply did not talk at all. Not even respond to his greeting gestures. In fact, his wife was brought after they failed to use him to talk me out of supporting the ANC and turn and be one of the askaris.'[51]

On 16 March 2001 the TRC's Amnesty Committee granted amnesty to Eugene de Kock, Izak Bosch, Freek Pienaar, Eugene Fourie, Johannes Koole, Schalk Visser, Paul van Dyk and Christo Deetlefs for their role in the abduction of Sedibe. Judges Sisi Khampepe and Ronnie Pillay said the committee was 'satisfied that all the Applicants have complied with the formal requirements, that they acted with a political objective as required by the Act and that all Applicants have made a full disclosure of all relevant facts. Accordingly, apart from the Applicant Nofomela whose application will be dealt with by another Panel, amnesty is GRANTED [their emphasis] to all the other Applicants listed above for any offence or delict flowing from or directly associated with the abduction of Glory Sedibe and the consequent unlawful detention.' Nofomela received his amnesty separately later.

As his brief exchange with Van der Walt showed, the work of De Kock and his men included many 'dark areas'. But even these areas were governed by bureaucratic procedures.[52] That the committee failed to pursue the clues dropped by De Kock and others is reflected in the final report of the TRC, which even gets the date of Sedibe's death wrong. The report states that Sedibe died in 1992.[53] Sedibe in fact died at his house in Verwoerdburg, Pretoria, on 20 March 1994. The report, as Posel says, 'reads less as history, more as a moral narrative about the fact of wrongdoing across the political spectrum'.[54] The reason for this stems in part from the commission's inability to deal with what Posel calls the 'problem of agency'.[55] The commission failed to deal with the fact that Sedibe was more than a victim; he was also an askari who sold out his former comrades.

10
The location

Memory can be an unreliable mirror. It shifts and shifts, now and then emphasising the dramatic, now and then leaving out detail, now and then flushing out detail at surprising moments.

– Mongane Wally Serote[1]

In 1979 the South African government announced plans to move the residents of Oukasie, a township near the agricultural town of Brits, about 90 kilometres north-west of Johannesburg, to a new location called Letlhabile, about 25 kilometres further north, on the 'border' of the Bophuthatswana bantustan. The move was intended to make way for the expansion of Elandsrand, a white suburb of Brits. Oukasie and Brits were right next to each other, as is often the case in small-town South Africa. The local town council had lured whites to Elandsrand with the promise that Oukasie would be moved.[2]

In 1985, when Letlhabile was ready for occupation, a third of the estimated 12,000 residents of Oukasie made the move. Most agreed to the transfer because of the opportunity it gave to improve their quality of life. Letlhabile had 'water-borne sewerage, taps to each plot, proper drainage, graded roads, electricity and large plots'. In contrast, Oukasie relied on a bucket system for sewage disposal and 50 outside taps for the whole township; it had no electricity, and suffered from abysmal roads and drainage. Oukasie was one of the oldest and smallest townships in South Africa, but the government had subjected it to 'deliberate neglect' since its founding in the 1930s.

No new houses had been built since its establishment and there was a freeze on its extension, making it one of the most congested residential areas in the country.[3] Many Oukasie residents, however, fought against the move. They used legal and popular means – such as the courts and street protests – to challenge the removal, and Oukasie became a cause célèbre among community struggles against apartheid in the 1970s and 1980s. The government replied with vigilante violence, arrests and assassinations, but these measures failed to compel people to leave.

People did not want to move for various reasons, but a 'common theme is their view of Oukasie as an organic community which they identify with and know intimately'.[4] In other words, a sense of community and bonds of solidarity compensated for Oukasie's material inadequacies.

Being a new township, Letlhabile did not yet have the social networks that defined Oukasie. But there was a group of people for whom Letlhabile's lack of history made the township particularly attractive: askaris. Here, these men and women, who carried multiple identity documents and passports and used false names as a matter of course, could live in relative anonymity. Knowing that many of the new township's residents came from different parts of Oukasie and elsewhere, askaris could fashion new identities for themselves. They could become 'public servants' in a township popular with civil servants in Bophuthatswana. Goodman Twala, an askari captured in December 1985, who moved to Letlhabile in 1986, said there was no discussion allowed of the matter. Askaris were simply told by their bosses at Vlakplaas that they would be moving to Letlhabile and that the SAP would help them get bank loans to pay for the houses.[5]

There was already a small community of askaris in Letlhabile when Sedibe, his wife, Ção, and their daughter moved into a modest house in January 1987. The house was 'small', not much bigger than the four-roomed asbestos house in which Sedibe grew up in Penge.[6] But it was theirs, a good start for a family aspiring to join the black middle class.[7] Sedibe and his wife immersed themselves in the social life of the township. In fact, such was Ção's integration into the life of the area that soon she acquired fluency in Pedi and Tswana.[8] Brits and the surrounding agricultural towns were considered right-wing bastions of Afrikanerdom. But, speaking to Nadja Manghezi, Ção recalled 'with a smile that she was the first Black to go to the White hospital in Brits because her child was ill'.[9] The Sedibes had their second child, another girl, in Letlhabile in 1987. Beyond the veneer of normality, however, life was not as it seemed.

Ção 'was not allowed to contact her family or anybody else in Maputo'. She also noticed that Sedibe would not visit his parents in the Eastern Transvaal. 'He said they could risk to get their house burnt down if he visited,' Ção told Manghezi.[10] Ção's account contradicts those given by Sedibe's fellow askari Gregory Sibusiso Radebe and Sedibe's cousin and childhood friend, Bernard Malope, who each told me that Sedibe travelled freely and visited his parents often.

The Sedibes seem to have lived as full a life as possible in Letlhabile itself. Glory, keen on soccer but not good at playing the game himself, was a founder-member of Morning Star, one of the top football clubs in the township. It was through the club that he met Stephen Phiri (not his real name), a veteran of the South African Defence Force and Military Intelligence, who was to become one of Sedibe's close friends and colleagues.

A few policemen and askaris lived in Soshanguve and Atteridgeville. Nofomela mentioned that, for years, De Kock asked him to move to Letlhabile, but his friends and social life were in Soshanguve, where he had grown up. 'He wanted us all in Letlhabile because he could control us there.'[11] De Kock did not like old townships like Soshanguve because they were not, claimed Nofomela, as well ordered as Letlhabile. De Kock treated his black and white subordinates the way his strict father raised him.[12] He saw himself as a father figure who did not believe in sparing the rod. However, there was a more compelling reason why De Kock wanted members of his squad to live in Letlhabile: it was close to Vlakplaas, being only about 60 kilometres from the farm, or half an hour's drive.

Sedibe, who was by all accounts devoted to his two daughters, used Letlhabile to attain a semblance of the 'normal' life he had claimed he wanted.[13] This might be surprising coming from a member of a police death squad. But studies abound of killers and torturers, from Nazi Germany to Latin American dictatorships, who led otherwise normal lives, returning home to their wives and children after long days at the 'office'.[14] For Sedibe, normality also extended to his promise – first made when he fled South Africa in 1977 and repeated in 1987 after his defection – to return to school. He signed up with the University of South Africa (Unisa) in the late 1980s for an undergraduate BJuris degree, popular among those interested in law as a career.[15] Unisa is a correspondence university and Sedibe used Letlhabile as his address to receive study material. This was perhaps a place from which he could envision a different future.

Letlhabile was not Sedibe's only address. He had a mailbox registered in his name in a Piet Retief township called New Location. Piet Retief was a logical base for Sedibe the askari. After all, it was where he was first detained after his defection. During his detention, Sedibe, Ção and their daughter would be together at the Security Branch offices (but not in the interrogation room) during the day and part ways in the evening, with Ção and the daughter going back to the Moolman Hotel and Sedibe to the 'hostel' he claimed to be staying at. 'Until she said that she couldn't go on living like that. He had said he had a house for them, but it wasn't true.'[16] Ção and the daughter moved in with the family of a black policeman in New Location while Sedibe remained in his 'hostel'. The Sedibes finally moved to Letlhabile in January 1987.

Recalling their life in Letlhabile, Ção said 'it seemed to her that they were doing well'.[17] They did even better when Sedibe joined

Military Intelligence in 1990. His educational background and his employment by the apartheid government made him one of the first black beneficiaries of the collapse of petty apartheid. Because Sedibe's transfer to Military Intelligence coincided with the demise of racial segregation, Sedibe and his family could buy property in the formerly whites-only suburbs. They chose a neighbourhood called The Reeds in Verwoerdburg, near Pretoria. This was where Sedibe died on 20 March 1994, depressed but in middle-class comfort, as the system he had served was collapsing all around him.[18]

Named after the founding father of apartheid and popular with public servants – especially those in the police, military and intelligence services – Verwoerdburg has since been renamed Centurion. It remains popular with public servants, most of whom are now black. Stephen Phiri, the veteran Military Intelligence member with whom Sedibe became fast friends, grew so close to Sedibe that the families would exchange weekend visits. Phiri and Sedibe were colleagues at a secret Military Intelligence base outside Pretoria called Fontana. When Sedibe moved his family to Verwoerdburg, Lieutenant-Colonel Anton Jan Nieuwoudt, Phiri's commander, ordered Phiri to buy Sedibe's Letlhabile house for R40,000. He refused. Phiri, who still lives in Letlhabile, remarked, 'I had paid R30,000 for my house and did not want to get into new debt.'[19]

Like any township, Letlhabile was stratified socially, as were the askaris themselves, though their stratification was along lines of income and rank at Vlakplaas. Gregory Sibusiso Radebe lived in a working-class section called Zone 10 Mapantsuleni. 'Among us, the best-paid lived in [a section called] Bester,' he said. According to Radebe, the better-paid askaris included Sedibe, Michael Matikinca and Chris Mosiane. Radebe, who claimed he joined the ANC at the age of 15, before he had finished high school, said that askari salaries were based on one's level of education. When he joined Vlakplaas, his starting salary was R600 a month. 'There were payslips, bank deposits. You could live [on the R600].' However, askaris made the bulk of their money through incentives. 'I think it was R8000 to point someone out. There were different amounts of money for finding an AK-47 rifle, a grenade and a pistol. For a man it was about R8000, for a rifle about R7000.'[20]

Askaris knew one another. They lived in the same neighbourhoods, their children went to the same schools and their families worshipped at the same churches. One askari, Tlhomedi Ephraim Mfalapitsa, served as pastor of a born-again congregation called the New Life in Christ Church. Individual askaris might not have known how others came to be askaris but they knew what it meant to be one – that one could not be trusted. In fact, some of them became askaris after they were kidnapped by comrades-turned-askaris. Judas Mpho Tladi, for example, would not talk about this, but he was most likely kidnapped from Swaziland in January 1988 by Sedibe and Chris Makgopa.[21]

Peter Harris writes, 'The askaris, like most traitors, are not trusted by their police colleagues. They are all highly trained and experienced in combat and may, in the view of their commanders, defect back to the ANC. In order to prevent this, some of the established askaris are paid to inform on the new askaris ... In addition, their movements are strictly monitored.'[22] In fact, askaris could and did move around when they were not 'at work'. Sedibe, for example, would go on long drives and visit relatives in places such as Alexandra township in Johannesburg.[23] Gregory Sibusiso Radebe would go on long trips by himself to visit friends and girlfriends when he was not 'on duty'. Asked if he had considered defecting back to the ANC, Radebe commented, 'There is a possibility to escape. The question is, if you escape – *uyaphi*? Where do you go?'[24] Asked what kept askaris in place, Nofomela replied, 'Fear. They were afraid of the South African police force, afraid of jail, afraid of death.'[25]

Ray Lalla observed that 'fear broke many people. When I look at the askaris, the common thread in their stories is fear.'[26] Two askaris confirmed the role of fear in their conversion from insurgents to counterinsurgents. Mfalapitsa described his association with Vlakplaas as a 'relationship in which I was formed by fear of these people'.[27] Oscar Linda Moni remarked that he was 'extremely scared' of Eugene de Kock. 'I had the fear of God that was instilled in me,' Moni told a TRC Amnesty Committee hearing in October 1999.[28] According to Moni, life as an askari and at Vlakplaas was governed by violence. There was 'extreme military discipline at Vlakplaas, which was accompanied by occasional beatings, almost on a weekly basis, on the various members who happened to indulge in unauthorised use of alcohol or who happened to ill-treat their wives.' The beatings, dispensed by De Kock, cut across racial lines: 'anybody was a candidate if they should transgress the disciplinary lines that were set'.[29]

Not surprisingly, the lives of askaris were marked by a lack of mutual trust. Yet the absence of trust did not prevent them from socialising with one another. Askaris were notorious for their constant and copious consumption of alcohol and marijuana, and for casual sex.[30] Goodman Twala reported that he lived on alcohol and dagga. 'Life was bad. We lived like we did not care. A man would be alive today, disappeared tomorrow. I did not care about life. I could die any minute. I had no plans for the future.'[31] Speaking of life among askaris, he noted, 'There was no trust. We talked about everything – women, soccer – except politics.'[32]

Radebe observed that askaris lived and operated in cliques, even if they were neighbours. 'It depended on how you understood each other when you communicated. There were groups. People related to each other as groups. You checked all the time what you said. We avoided talking politics. We only talked social issues.'[33] Judas Mpho Tladi recalled, 'We drank all the time. We were always drunk. Life was terrible.'[34] Even though askaris were given 'proper' police training and absorbed into the police force before the formal end of apartheid in 1994, they were not treated like regular police officers. Radebe said, 'They called you a policeman but you never became a real policeman. You just remained their hostage.'[35] The experience of askaris was highly racialised. As Tladi stated, 'We lived in fear. A white man [at Vlakplaas] would look at you and you would start wondering if you were next.'[36]

Askaris' lives were profoundly violent. Stories abound of Eugene de Kock subjecting both askaris and white members of his death squad to merciless beatings.[37] Radebe told of how once, during an exercise at a shooting range, De Kock sjambokked him because he did not like the way Radebe was handling his firearm. 'The man could be human; at the same time he could kill you at the snap of a finger.'[38] Askaris were notorious, too, for domestic abuse and for failing to support their families. De Kock would intervene often in the private lives of his askaris. According to Radebe, 'The wives would come to De Kock to complain about their husbands.'[39] De Kock would drive to Letlhabile and beat up husbands in front of their wives and children.

Nofomela claimed he argued with De Kock about this. 'I told him he was not a social worker.'[40] But De Kock was not the only source of violence. Askaris were often brutal towards each other. Twala alleged that De Kock would use askaris to eliminate other askaris. Speaking of his former colleague Radebe, Twala said, 'That man was evil. He killed someone once and claimed it was an accident.' De Kock had apparently ordered Radebe to kill the man, as he could no longer be trusted.[41]

Delilah Rekisa said she was once at a party in Soshanguve, with her then husband, Chris Makgopa. When Rekisa, who usually 'worked' from home because she did not want to work in the same place as her husband, was introduced to a new askari, the man made the mistake of pointing to a woman he had met earlier with Makgopa, saying that he thought *she* was Makgopa's wife. Makgopa beat up the new man so badly that he ended up in an intensive-care unit with broken ribs. Rekisa recalled, 'Chris has never beaten up a person like that before!'[42] The woman who the new askari thought was Makgopa's wife was in fact a police officer who had been having an affair with Makgopa. Immediately after the incident she was granted a transfer to Durban, as Rekisa had told the mistress that she was going to kill her.[43]

Nofomela, a teetotaller, mentioned that when he and his colleagues went to a shebeen to socialise, he would order the askaris to deposit their firearms in a hessian sack which he kept in the boot of his car. 'These people were anarchists,' said Nofomela, 'they were wild.'[44] Although he never touched alcohol, Nofomela said he had a weakness for women. In fact, every Nofomela war story revolved around women. 'God has created a beautiful thing – a woman,' he would repeat over and over again.[45] He was not unique in that regard. Askaris were constantly chasing booze, dagga, women – and, of course, insurgents. Tladi related the account of a colleague named Jimmy Mbane, a former ANC mechanic who became an askari sometime in the 1980s. Mbane, whom Joe Mamasela described as a mentally unstable serial killer and child rapist,[46] was driving around Letlhabile with Tladi one day when they came across a woman hitchhiking. Mbane, who was driving, had an Uzi semi-automatic pistol on the floor next to the front passenger seat. He stopped to give the woman a ride and ordered Tladi to move to the back seat. As soon as the woman sat down, Mbane placed the Uzi on her lap and told her not to touch it. Tladi, seeing where this was going, asked to be dropped off at home. 'The woman had her hands up,' Tladi said.

When he went to Mbane's house later that afternoon, he found Mbane walking around the house with a towel around his waist and the woman in the shower. He and Mbane never talked about the episode. That was simply a way of life for askaris.[47] Mbane, we may recall, was one of the askaris involved in the operation against the Gugulethu Seven. According to Mamasela, he also ran taxis between Soweto and Pietersburg and contracted himself out as a paid assassin.[48]

Violence among askaris extended to the family. Brian Ngqulunga, an askari killed by the police in July 1990 after he talked to the ANC about rejoining the organisation, shot his wife, Catherine, in the stomach while she was pregnant with their child. She survived, but the baby died.[49] Joe Mamasela said that this shooting took place after the 'whole exposure' in the media of police death squads. 'He couldn't take it. He was on the verge of a complete breakdown and as a result he shot his wife three times, his pregnant wife.'[50] Catherine, a packer at a supermarket in Pretoria, had trouble keeping her job afterwards as a result of her injuries. Delilah Rekisa, who accompanied Catherine Ngqulunga to the TRC's amnesty hearings into Brian Ngqulunga's death in Pretoria in September 1999, declared that it was after sitting through those hearings that she decided to have nothing to do with the TRC. 'It was full of only lies,' she told me.[51] She did not say where the 'lies' came from.

Rekisa, who was married to the long-time askari Chris Makgopa, told me that she knew she had to get a divorce after she woke up one night to find a drunk Makgopa standing astride her on their marital bed, pointing his gun at her, and threatening to kill her and their two sons. 'It was either me or him. He was either going to kill me first or I was going to kill him first.'[52] She mentioned that once, while Makgopa was away, she opened the family safe, took all his firearms, loaded them into a bag and took them to the Sunnyside police station in Pretoria. 'I called and told him what I had done.' Makgopa rushed to the station and, when he got there, opened a case of attempted murder against her. 'I was sitting in the charge office and the senior police came in to arrest me. I said, "How can you arrest me when you can see I am just sitting here?"' Rekisa, who used her severance pay from Vlakplaas to start a business selling handbags, believes that Makgopa was responsible for a robbery and attempted car hijacking in Pretoria during which she lost all her money – about R40,000 – which she planned to use to buy more stock.[53]

According to Rekisa, the stress of being an askari was made worse by Makgopa's womanising. She had become an askari because of him; she had abandoned the PAC for the Security Branch because of her love for him – so when he left her for other women, it made her 'sacrifices' appear worthless. She took it out on their sons. Her eldest son came home drunk one night soon after he started a new job in Pretoria. The boy had never touched alcohol before and his new colleagues had, as part of some initiation prank, spiked his drink. 'He was misbehaving. I beat him black and blue. I hit him like I was hitting a man my size.' Rekisa reported that the boy's colleagues refused to believe him when he told them the following day that his mother had beaten him up so badly. 'That is what I did to my own child.' Rekisa said that her sons sometimes joked about that beating, reminding each other not to get on her wrong side. Asked how her sons coped with what must have been a stressful household, Rekisa replied, 'The kids learned to accept it.' We must wonder what this means. Rekisa's eldest son lost his job in Cape Town in 2013 after he assaulted a colleague at work. In February or March 2014 the same son suffered a heart attack. He was 29.[54]

The Vlakplaas unit apparently included five female askaris, including two who were named Susan and Thandi.[55] Save for Xolelwa Virginia Shosha, whose name cropped up in a few cases examined by the TRC in the late 1990s, the story of female askaris has yet to be told.[56] According to Jacques Pauw, Shosha went into exile in 1980, joined the ANC and received military training in Angola, East Germany and Libya. She was captured in 1984 and became an askari that same year.[57] That is all we know about her. Because so little is known about female askaris, those interested in the stories they have to tell do not know where to begin. This is a pity because, as Jacklyn Cock said in her study of *Women and war in South Africa*, the twilight war in South Africa was very much a gendered conflict. As Cock wrote, 'People go to war as "nationalists" and "patriots". But they do so in their gender identities as "men" and "women".'[58]

Rekisa was 22 and pregnant with their first child in 1984 when her husband, Makgopa, was arrested in Botswana. She had been working as a courier for the PAC, operating between Botswana and South Africa. Makgopa was handed over to the South African security police and held at a game lodge in Zeerust. The South Africans sent word to her that she could see her husband. 'I had to meet these fearsome Boers on my own. My father insisted that my brother go with me. Obviously, he was not in the interview.' Rekisa recalled that the police knew a lot about the couple and the work they had been doing for the PAC. 'They knew things about me. They had pictures of me in a remote village where Chris and I thought we were hiding.'

It would appear that by the time Rekisa met the police at the lodge, Makgopa had already turned but wanted his wife and unborn child to come with him to South Africa. Rekisa said it took time to turn her. 'It was gradual. There were debriefings and it was during those debriefings when you would realise there was no turning back.' The debriefings included the ubiquitous police album and its mug shots.[59]

'They [the police] wanted me to work at Vlakplaas. I refused to work in that place. I refused to work in the same place as my husband. Me and Chris – never!' Rekisa said. 'We were promised houses. We got those houses. But we had to pay for them. We were put on the police payroll. That meant we qualified for a bond.' The couple bought a house in Soshanguve. Because she refused to work alongside her husband, she was allowed to operate from home. This meant that she was given 'special tasks' and would travel to Vlakplaas when needed. 'Eugene [de Kock] would call me, give me a job to do, and then I would report to him afterwards.' Speaking of her life after turning, Rekisa said, 'We had comfortable lives. Not rich but comfortable. We were OK.' She and her husband earned about R650 a month each, but this was supplemented by allowances for subsistence and travel.[60]

According to Rekisa, her tasks included running apartheid agents in Botswana and collecting intelligence.[61] Notably, Rekisa, the only woman among the five askaris I spoke to for this book, was the first and only person to talk unprompted about the violence she committed in the course of her work, as well as the violence that marked her domestic life. Nofomela and the other askaris talked mostly about women only in relation to sex. The two exceptions concerned his descriptions of two female askaris, Xolelwa Virginia Shosha and a woman known only as Susan. Speaking about Shosha, Nofomela said, 'That woman was so ugly we called her Mashamplan.' He did not remember much about her life and work as an askari – only that she was ugly. He was full of compliments for 'Susan' – 'That woman could handle an AK. She would hit targets running. And, eish, she was beautiful!'[62] Nofomela disclosed that Susan was an MK operative and that he helped persuade her to turn after apartheid agents captured her in Swaziland in the late 1980s. But Nofomela never talked about the violence he perpetrated as a policeman during my conversations with him. He had spent 22 years in prison for murder and had confessed to the TRC to various murders, but he did not raise the subject with me.

Rekisa, in contrast, talked openly about violence. The first 'work-related' story she told me as we sat down for a three-hour conversation at a restaurant in a Pretoria shopping mall was about killing one of her agents in Botswana. 'I had to eliminate him. He became greedy, too greedy. I had to eliminate obstacles.'[63] According to her, the agent was a young man who ran a small business in Botswana. He was connected to the PAC, and, when South African agents found out that his business was struggling, they recruited him. They offered to prop up his business in return for information, with Rekisa as his handler. The arrangement worked well. 'But then he got greedy.' Rekisa said the young man was approached by another South African intelligence agency (she would not say if it was the National Intelligence Service or Military Intelligence) and asked to spy on the PAC. Instead of turning the request down, the man saw the chance to double his income. 'He lied about how much we were paying him so these other guys would pay him more,' Rekisa said. He boasted about this to Rekisa. 'I know you won't kill me,' he reportedly told her during one of their meetings.

'That boy did not know who he was dealing with. I was worried he was going to expose me. I had to eliminate him.' Rekisa would not mention how she eliminated the man, save to say, 'He drove a motorbike. I had to use that motorbike.' Rekisa also spoke openly about her use of firearms. 'I don't pull out my gun unless I am going to use it,' she said at one point. This was after she told me how she had threatened to kill one of her husband's mistresses. 'I was going to kill her,' she said. Rekisa also told me that when *Mmegi*, a newspaper in Botswana, wrote a story about how she had helped Eugene de Kock 'disappear' anti-apartheid activists in Botswana, she called the journalist who had written the story and threatened to 'disappear' him. She told the man that his family would never know what happened to him. 'I believe he resigned and left the newspaper the following day.' If these were boasts, they were not delivered in a boastful manner. Rekisa was soft-spoken and matter-of-fact in her delivery.[64]

Thrown by her seeming celebration of violence, I found Rekisa to be the most difficult interviewee of the askaris to whom I spoke. This is not because I had been seduced by 'myths of female innocence'.[65] I had simply not expected to meet a person who appeared to celebrate and even miss her life as an askari. Asked about her time at Vlakplaas, Rekisa said, 'There were good things and bad things at Vlakplaas.' When I asked her to elaborate on the 'good things', she said, 'The good things were the parties we had.' What about the 'bad things'? She answered that life at Vlakplaas was like 'walking on eggshells. A lot of people disappeared from that place.'[66]

What did it mean to be a woman askari at Vlakplaas? 'Being a woman didn't make a difference,' she said. 'Remember, I was the only girl in a family of boys, so I have always been more comfortable among men than among women. Women gossip and I don't like to gossip.'[67]

There was, it seems, a status dimension in the way the 'women of Vlakplaas' related to one another. Rekisa claimed that when she started working with Vlakplaas in 1984, she was the only trained insurgent among the women. 'They [other women] would gossip about my meetings with Eugene [de Kock] but what did they know?' Most of the women attached to Vlakplaas were wives and girlfriends whom the male askaris 'found' after they had been turned – and most had minimal schooling. Rekisa, the daughter of middle-class parents who left South Africa for Botswana in order to avoid apartheid, had little in common with these women.[68]

Some commentators have presented Glory Sedibe's defection as a function of his 'weakness' for liquor and the easy life; others have suggested that he became an askari because he could not take pain, presumably the way a 'real man' would.[69] In these accounts, Sedibe's collaboration becomes a personal failing that forecloses the possibility of raising questions about the predominantly masculinist narratives of the struggle against apartheid.[70] Curiously, the language of masculinist failing is what Rekisa used to talk about Sedibe's demise – though in her mouth the language was gendered in such a fashion that his demise came about because of his failings as a man and a father, not because of the crimes he committed as an askari. Speaking of Sedibe's death in March 1994, Rekisa said, 'He would have killed himself if they had not killed him first. The closure of Vlakplaas and DCC hit him hard. He had a wife and two daughters – how was he going to provide for them? He was seriously depressed. He was going down. He would not eat, he would not sleep, he would not get out of bed or wash himself.'[71]

Rekisa said that Sedibe lost his job in Military Intelligence after F.W. de Klerk shut down the DCC in 1993. Sedibe could have minimised his losses by moving out of Verwoerdburg and back to Letlhabile, to a house he and his family could afford. Rekisa commented, 'Ção put pressure indirectly on her husband. I would say he was weak. She would say, "I will never go back to the township. What would people say!"'[72] So Sedibe opted to stay in a house he could no longer afford.

'Come the new government, September lost his job,' wrote Nadia Manghezi. 'He got some money as one pay-off, but it was not enough. Now was the time that he really went for the drinking. He refused to do anything. Stayed at home drinking heavily. By that time Conceição had tied [*sic*] some of her old contacts with family and friends.'[73]

On 17 June 1994 the *Government Gazette* issued a 'Notice to creditors in deceased estates' in connection with 3 Yeland Street, The Reeds, Verwoerdburg. It announced that Sedibe had died and that creditors had 30 days to lodge claims against the estate.[74] We do not know how long it took to wind up the estate. But Ção never moved back to Letlhabile. She took her two daughters and returned to Mozambique. Rekisa, who has visited Sedibe's widow in Maputo, said that she encouraged the widow to go back to school. In Rekisa's telling, Ção did so and now has a degree and a good job at a university in Maputo. The widow and her daughters, one of whom was married in 2013, visit Sedibe's family once a year. But when Manghezi interviewed Ção in Maputo, she had 'problems making ends meet and finding money for the school fees. Should she go to the ANC and get the same support as other freedom fighters' widows and children?'[75] asked Manghezi. Sedibe's old friend Humphrey Mkhwanazi has also visited Ção in Mozambique. 'She is so anti-ANC,' he recalled. 'She says they sold them out.'[76]

11
The archive

If it is true, then, that people do not collaborate by chance, but under the influence of certain social and psychological laws, it seems appropriate that we should define what is known as a collaborator.

– Jean-Paul Sartre[1]

Gregory Sibusiso Radebe remarked to me, 'Sometimes it is easy to say "This guy was an askari". But have you ever asked yourself: What makes an askari?'[2]

To answer this question, I suggest we examine the explanations given by askaris themselves for why they switched sides. These are not straightforward or innocent explanations. Many askaris were tortured and turned, though some may have defected without such compulsion. No two askaris were the same. Yet the testimonies they gave in court as Mr X or Ms Y followed a similar script in which South Africa was represented as a normal society and apartheid itself a legitimate order.[3] This meant that any challenge to the status quo was abnormal. Askaris who testified for the state against former comrades had to renounce their former political allegiances while endorsing the existing order.

To write this book, I needed to talk to as many askaris as I could. For obvious reasons, most refused my requests. A typical example occurred in May 2013, when I had a brief telephone conversation with Steven Mbanda, who was one of the longest-serving askaris and who is named in various TRC reports as such. When I called him to request an interview about Sedibe, he fobbed me off. 'To be honest, I never worked with that guy. He was one of the trusted.' Speaking of his own role at Vlakplaas, Mbanda said, 'They never trusted me. I was a guard there. I was not inside.'[4] I asked Mbanda if we could meet and talk in person. He refused. He had nothing to add.[5] Mbanda's story did not tally with what others said. Joe Pillay, a South African refugee abducted from Swaziland by the Security Branch in February 1981, testified to the TRC in a written statement that Mbanda had assaulted him severely while he was detained at Vlakplaas.[6] Nofomela and Rekisa told me that Mbanda was one of the most trusted askaris, used to spy on his colleagues.[7] But because Mbanda would not talk to me, I could not put any of this to him.

So I turned to the archives, not in the hope of finding *the* truth, but to pick up the scraps that contained within them something of the past. These scraps might be of suspect provenance, they might dissemble, they might even be fake. But they were of the past. As Achille Mbembe says, the archive is like a cemetery 'in the sense that fragments of lives and pieces of time are interred there, their shadows and their footprints inscribed on paper and preserved like so many relics'.[8]

It was in the archives that I dug up fragments of Mbanda's life. He evidently came from the Camperdown district in Natal. He joined the ANC in 1977 after fleeing South Africa while training to be a teacher. He received military training in Angola, and was arrested on 27 December 1979 in the Durban area while on a mission to recruit for MK and smuggle weapons into South Africa. The police first used him as a state witness in April 1980 in the Soekmekaar and Silverton Trial, in which nine MK insurgents were charged with high treason, murder, attempted murder and robbery. Three of the nine accused were found guilty and sentenced to death. Mbanda, who appeared on the witness stand under the name Joseph Zakile Zulu, told the court that he had defected to the Security Branch on 27 December 1979. 'I was against violence, and the killing of people, citizens of the land ... innocent people.'[9]

Asked in Afrikaans by Advocate C. Rudolph Jansen, the prosecutor, to say what were the aims of the ANC, Mbanda, speaking through a Zulu interpreter, responded, '*Kan ek dit liewers in Engels stel? Ek vind dit 'n bietjie moeilik in my taal.*' (May I explain that in English rather? I find it a bit hard to explain it in my language.) Mbanda then said in English, 'The main aim of the ANC is to overthrow the South African Government and to establish a democratic type of Government.' (Perhaps he had yet to be 'tamed' at this stage.) Mbanda tried to move between Zulu and English during his cross-examination by the defence lawyer Jules Browde, but Browde would not let him. 'I think you better just stick to your language, otherwise there is going to be confusion. You speak in your language and I will speak in my language and I think we will be able to get on better that way.'

Browde, as a defence attorney, was perhaps trying to unsettle Mbanda with his aggressive and patronising tone. He may also have been frustrated with the way his cross-examination was going. Mbanda claimed that his defection was a voluntary act that had nothing to do with any inducements from the police. Browde challenged this. He questioned Mbanda, who was training to be a teacher when he went into exile, about his reaction to the June 1976 student uprisings.

BROWDE: 'Up to that time, up to the end of 1976 when you passed your first year at the [teacher] training college, were you happy in South Africa?

MBANDA: 'By happy in South Africa, do you mean that I had enough money and enough clothing, or what do you mean by that?'

BROWDE: 'I mean, were you content with your life here?'

MBANDA: 'You see, I am not quite clear with your question. You said something about happiness. Will you just, please, elaborate on that for me to understand what you mean, because you may mean that I had enough money or clothing or whatever the case may be. Will you just put the question clear to me?'

BROWDE: 'Were you content to go on living in South Africa in 1976?'

MBANDA: 'Yes, I was. In fact, I intended staying in South Africa.'

BROWDE: 'Do you remember the unrests that started in June of 1976?'

MBANDA: 'Yes, I do.'

BROWDE: 'Did that have an effect on you?'

MBANDA: 'No.'

BROWDE: 'Did you feel nothing about that?'

MBANDA: 'I was hurt by the children, because the children decided not to go to school. I was not happy about the children not going to school.'

BROWDE: 'Did you know why the children weren't going to school?'

MBANDA: 'No, I only heard of this.'

BROWDE: 'What did you hear?'

MBANDA: 'That they want Bantu education abolished.'

Try as Browde might to show that Mbanda's decision to abandon his studies as a teacher, go into exile and join the ANC was in part a reaction to the June 1976 student rebellion, Mbanda would not budge. Asked if he, a matriculant in 1975, had any opinion about Bantu education, Mbanda said no. 'I never gave it a thought because I was at school. I was attending school. I had learned a lot of things.' Mbanda tried to paint a picture of normality in which happiness was tied to material well-being as opposed to one's political position in a country. But Mbanda's testimony does not read only one way towards the direction of collaboration. Notice his answer to Jansen's question about the political aims of the ANC.

When I met Goodman Twala on 23 January 2014, I was in the company of Almond Nofomela. I suspect Nofomela's presence was the only reason Twala had agreed to talk to me. The two men might both have been down and out, chasing small-scale government contracts – Nofomela for a job erecting flagpoles for the hoisting of the South African flag in schoolyards, Twala for a project building fences around schools – but they had not completely abandoned the roles they had assumed at Vlakplaas. Nofomela was still the dominant figure and Twala the dominated. The residue of this old relationship between the two men tainted my interaction with Twala. But having Nofomela there was the only way to get Twala and (later that same day) Judas Mpho Tladi to talk to me. When Nofomela and I met Twala in Brits, he did not know that I knew he had testified against two MK insurgents named Mthetheleli Mncube and Mzondeleli Nondula in 1987. Mncube and Nondula were convicted of murder and sentenced to death, but their sentences were later commuted. To test Twala's reliability, I asked what trials he had been used in as a state witness. 'There was one case in the Free State somewhere,' he said.[10]

Twala was being less than candid. We know from the archival record that he was a key witness in camera against Mncube and Nondula.[11] Before Twala was sworn in, Advocate R.S. Black, representing the two accused, had objected to the use of secret witnesses. 'It is an undesirable practice that justice is not seen to be done and people are not prepared to give their evidence in open court.' Mr Justice P.O. de Villiers, the presiding judge, sympathised, though only to a point. 'I will agree with you. It is an undesirable practice, a court is held with open doors.' But De Villiers still allowed Twala to testify in secret.

Twala had left school after Standard Eight in 1977 and found a job as a fork-lift driver. He went into exile early in 1982 to join the ANC, travelling through Mozambique. The Mozambican government detained him for seven months and he was able to join the ANC only in August 1982 after the ANC secured his release from a local jail.

Asked during cross-examination in the Mncube and Nondula trial if he had joined the ANC because he was concerned about 'black living and political conditions', Twala said, '*Ja, maar alles was nog nie vir my duidelik nie.*' (Yes, but not everything was clear to me yet.) Arrested on 9 December 1985 – two days after returning to South Africa on a mission to recruit and train people for combat – Twala told the court that he had defected to the Security Branch because he wanted revenge against the ANC, which he held responsible for the death of a friend in a Mozambican jail. The friend had left South Africa with Twala in 1982 and was arrested along with Twala by the Mozambican police that year. Twala stated in court that he had lost his faith in the ANC when his friend died. He said that when he was arrested in South Africa, the police offered to take him to a 'rehabilitation centre'. Asked why the police would choose to send him to this centre instead of charging him, Twala answered, '*Omdat hulle besef het dat ek berou gehad het, ek was jammer oor wat ek gedoen het.*' (Because they were aware that I had remorse, I was sorry for what I had done.)

BLACK: 'What was the purpose of you going to a so-called rehabilitation centre?'

TWALA: '*Daar is niks spesifiek wat ek daarso gedoen het nie, behalwe dat dit is werk.*' (There was nothing particular that I did there, except that it was work.)

BLACK: 'But you are spending your time now working for the security police in order to get, either by way of testifying or by other methods, to get back at the ANC, is that correct?'

TWALA: '*Ja.*'

BLACK: 'I can understand you, because you are almost in a position of an informer, not so?'

TWALA: '*Ja.*'

BLACK: 'But why did you decide to join the security police?'

TWALA: '*Omdat ek my rug teen die ANC wil draai.*' (So I can turn my back on the ANC.)

BLACK: 'Had you shown in the past any interest in joining the police before you went up to Mozambique and Angola?'

TWALA: '*Nee.*'

BLACK: 'So your sole reason for being, joining the security police, is to get your revenge on the ANC?'

TWALA: '*Ja.*'

When Twala and I spoke on 23 January 2014, he did not know that I had read the transcript of his testimony. Asked if the

Security Branch tortured him after his capture, Twala said that nothing physical was done to him. 'I would say it was psychological torture.'[12] T.F. Makuleni, another askari who testified in camera against Mncube and Nondula, used a line that – while less personal than Twala's search for revenge – was common among askari testimonies.[13] Simply put, the stock response was that people became askaris after growing 'tired' of the ANC and of life in exile. Makuleni was arrested in February 1987 but told the court that he had defected to the police voluntarily. Why? '*Nee, ek was nou moeg van hierdie ANC.*' (No, I was now tired of this ANC.) Asked during cross-examination why he joined the ANC in January 1984, he said it was to fight.

BLACK: 'For what, what do you want to fight for?'

MAKULENI: '*Hierdie vryheid waarvan hulle gepraat het.*' (This freedom that they talked about.)

BLACK: 'What did you think about your – the community and the people that you – fellow friends and black people, were living under at the time? Were they free, were they oppressed, was there a need for this?'

MAKULENI: '*Ek gee nie om van ander mense nie, ek kyk maar net na myself. As die ander persoon voel hy is onderdruk ensovoorts, dan is dit sy besigheid, nie myne nie.*' (I don't care about other people. I am only looking after myself. If another person feels he is oppressed and so forth, then that is his business, not mine.)

In Makuleni's evidence we see the 'exaggerated individualism and sense of aloneness' that Jacklyn Cock has argued are the outcome of torture.[14] According to Cock, torture was not only a means of obtaining information, it was also intended to destroy an individual and that individual's sense of solidarity. 'Guilt and isolation dislocate the individual from any sense of identification with the group.'[15] Solitary confinement, used extensively by the police under apartheid, disoriented victims and left them thinking, as the narrator in Achmat Dangor's novel *Bitter fruit* puts it, that they were 'among friends, that the questions being put to you, casually, in well-practised, jocular township voices, were part of some innocent banter among buddies'.[16]

Judas Mpho Tladi, Mr X2 in the treason trial against Dladla, Ebrahim and Maseko, also sounded the fatigue theme in his testimony as a way of justifying his turning against the ANC after he was arrested in January 1988.[17] 'Well, let me just clearly say this, that when I got arrested I immediately told the police, "People, I have already grown tired of the ANC". I was handcuffed and even when they were handcuffing me I said to them but there is no need for this. I have told you that I am already tired of the ANC.'

ADVOCATE KESSIE NAIDU: 'Were you in fact honest when you told the police that you had grown tired of the ANC?'

TLADI: 'I was.'

NAIDU: 'When did you in fact grow tired, when did you begin to despair of the ANC?'

TLADI: 'Well, I had had numerous times of feeling tired of the ANC and this was because of my experiences.'

Oscar Linda Moni, Mr X4, said something similar when asked about his turning.[18] When Naidu questioned him about his 'change of heart', Moni replied, 'It is because I had grown disillusioned with the ANC. I had lost interest.' Sedibe himself, as Mr X1, told the court, 'I was just tired of being with the ANC in Swaziland and having to be hiding myself.'[19]

We cannot entirely discount the idea of fatigue simply because it repeats itself so often in askari testimonies. Insurgents were caught, to use the words of the novelist Alan Furst, in a 'prison of borders, passports, false names, and de facto non-existence'. They were 'citizens of nowhere'.[20] This precarious existence was preyed upon by both the police and the state prosecutors. The police would capture an insurgent, 'break' him through torture, and then offer him a chance of leading a 'normal life'. As Sedibe said in his testimony against Dladla, Ebrahim and Maseko, 'I just thought to myself that I would be leading a better life if I was back home.'[21]

On the face of it, Sedibe was a successful man with the means to buy property in a formerly whites-only suburb, and to entertain his friends and colleagues with little care for how much that entertainment cost.[22] But inside he was a mess. Delilah Rekisa recalled that Sedibe, in emotional turmoil about the things he had done as an askari, would check himself into a Pretoria hotel and drink himself into a stupor. He would not eat. At home, first in Letlhabile and then in Verwoerdburg, he would lock himself in the main bedroom and drink himself sick.[23]

Ção, Sedibe's widow, reported that Sedibe resumed contact with his family after he lost his job in Military Intelligence around 1993. 'But very few people realised how serious his situation was. He was very good at hiding it.'[24] Sedibe was chronically depressed. Goodman Twala also talked about the contradiction between what askaris said about life as collaborators and the real emotional, physical and psychic content of their lives. When I interviewed him in Letlhabile in January 2014, he told me, 'People pretended everything was normal above the surface, but below the surface things were bad.'[25] Speaking in May 1999 during his amnesty application, Mfalapitsa said, 'A concept such as askari, former terrorist, you know, all those concepts they bring a multiple [*sic*] of danger and feeling of helplessness and alienation to those who were so named.'[26]

Mfalapitsa's tense exchange with Advocate Leah Gcabashe, a member of the TRC Amnesty Committee, provides some insight into the post-traumatic stress disorder that seems to have been a hallmark of the askari experience. To gain amnesty, Mfalapitsa had to tell the truth, prove that there was a political motive behind his actions and show that the actions were proportionate to the threat perceived. In this exchange, Mfalapitsa cast himself as a helpless and alienated victim of circumstances. Gcabashe refused to let him get away with this. The exchange opens a window into the tortured and tormented world of askaris. It gives us some insight into how collaborators 'lived' with themselves. It also helps us understand what a cataclysmic episode the TRC's advent was for many askaris.

As Mfalapitsa told the Amnesty Committee, 'the announcement of the TRC itself was almost like an apocalyptic event'.[27] Mfalapitsa admitted that he had even contemplated suicide to avoid having to account to the commission for his crimes. Speaking of fellow askaris, Oscar Linda Moni said that 'most of us and in particular myself, had serious misgivings about the TRC. I heard that there were going to be prosecutions, etc., etc., and I never had applied or seen anything like the TRC before and I knew where I was standing with regards to the criminal Courts.'[28]

These misgivings might explain why, according to the TRC, only 35 of 47 white officers at Vlakplaas and only seven black askaris applied for amnesty.[29] Not knowing how their stories would be received, and undoubtedly hoping that the secrets of the past would stay buried, the majority of askaris kept well away from the TRC. Those who did come forward, like Mfalapitsa and Moni, did not do so out of a sense of altruism. They testified because the families of their victims demanded an account of what had happened, insisting that the askaris say what had befallen their loved ones. Mfalapitsa, pleading for understanding, stated during his TRC appearance, 'it is no mean act to stand here facing this nation to admit to acts like this one, without putting extraneous circumstances of the history of this country'.[30]

Asked by Gcabashe why he had betrayed Zandisile Musi and Musi's three friends – 'Was it fear? So was it just self-preservation or were you doing this because you believed that you were actually promoting the interests ... of your employer and therefore of the State of that particular political leaning?' – Mfalapitsa replied: 'I think fear in this position [is] a part of human nature ... Every human being wants to preserve themselves in the circumstances and people in normal circumstances will express their ethical viewpoint in order to also acquire higher values. But with me, illiterate as I was, the three [*sic*] was not an education to arm me with an intellectual power to confront ethical issues and so on. I was ignorant of such issues. I was coming from a fear background.'

Mfalapitsa declared that while he worked for the Security Branch at Vlakplaas, he did not once share the police's beliefs and principles. He said the 'forces that motivated them are forces that did not motivate me'.

MFALAPITSA: 'Actually, here I'm setting straight a history which was my part, which began as political and which [went] terribly wrong. And it's not my own problem alone. There are many people in South Africa who have this historical problem with their past, some being leaders in this country. Even though perhaps they might be exonerated in terms of their status. But in a sense we all grapple with this history and this history we didn't invent it, invent it somewhere in the ghettos or in the backyard of my mother. It was invented in the arena of politics in South Africa.'

GCABASHE: 'Mr Mfalapitsa, it's not that broad history, you know, that I'm looking at. I am really trying to understand, you know. My understanding of your evidence was had you not reported on Mr Musi's approach to you, you thought you might be putting yourself in danger.'

MFALAPITSA: 'That's correct.'

GCABASHE: 'Yes. Now that to me spells self-preservation ... The fact that you didn't really believe in their [the Security Branch's] cause, your cause was not the same ... That again spells to me self-preservation, no alternative in the sense that you had nowhere else to go essentially. But it doesn't say to me that you were doing this because you were committed to a particular political cause, to promote a particular interest, to ensuring, you know, that the internal security of the State should not be breached by these four youths who you knew were just youths who had no military training. I don't know if you understand my dilemma?'

MFALAPITSA: 'I think that your problem is that you are, you are dissecting, you are, you are, you are mutilating my history.'

GCABASHE: 'It's my job to do that.'

Finally, Advocate Chris de Jager, Gcabashe's colleague on the TRC's Amnesty Committee, interrupts: 'The problem is far more serious. The problem is that if it's not dissected, like my colleague is doing, you have no chance of getting amnesty.'

Mfalapitsa then interrupts: 'Sir, sir.'

De Jager: 'So listen to what she is asking you, because it's our duty to help you people ...'

Mfalapitsa: 'Yes, yes.'

De Jager: 'And listen to her questions and don't interrupt her because she is asking you cardinal questions that could affect your amnesty, that it may be because of your answers that you wouldn't get amnesty or you can get amnesty.'

Mfalapitsa: 'That I understand quite well, and I don't say she must not interrogate me, as it is her right. But I have a problem when she want [*sic*] to run away with one part of my integrity, sir, and make it my motive. Once she want [*sic*] to say I was, you know, inspired by my self-preservation. I don't think that is right. I was inspired by all forces taken together. I was one person. I was one person who had fear.'

In 2001 the Amnesty Committee denied Mfalapitsa amnesty for the killing of Eustice Bimbo Madikela, Ntshingo Mataboge and Fanyana Nhlapo, as well as for the grievous bodily harm inflicted on Zandisile Musi. The committee also refused to give amnesty to Jan Carel Coetzee, Willem Schoon, Abraham Grobbelaar and Chris Rorich – all Mfalapitsa's seniors at Vlakplaas and in the Security Branch. The committee stated that the applicants had failed to prove that the killing of the three youths and the harm done to Musi had a political motive. The committee also found the applicants' actions disproportionate to the threat allegedly posed by the four youths.

* * *

The court and TRC testimonies examined here are part of what we might call 'literatures of betrayal'. They are important sources for anyone trying to understand the phenomenon of collaboration.

Although they cannot be considered innocent, they are a significant depository of voices from the 'wrong' side of history, demonstrating that the men and women who first fought against apartheid – and then fought on its behalf – were all too human. Many were initially people of principle, who believed in the justness of their cause. But among them were people who could be bought, sold and turned. They were not unique. Every political conflict has its share of treachery.

As recounted in earlier chapters, among the first ANC insurgents to turn counterinsurgent was Bruno Mtolo, the state's star witness in the 1963–1964 Rivonia Trial against Nelson Mandela and other leaders of MK. Mtolo was a founding member of MK and among its first saboteurs when MK launched its operations in December 1961. A convicted criminal turned activist, Mtolo had been sentenced to four years in prison in 1950 for stealing from a railway truck. In jail he met an ANC activist who introduced him to the organisation and its literature. An ambitious man who had taught himself English while working with the Royal Air Force at a British military base in Durban during the Second World War, Mtolo joined the ANC in 1957. In 1960 he was recruited to the South African Communist Party. The party had been underground for almost ten years after opting to disband and relaunch in secret, rather than be banned, following the passage of the Suppression of Communism Act in 1950. The ANC, together with the PAC, was outlawed in 1960.

Mtolo was arrested on 3 August 1963 after a police crackdown on MK and then tortured. The police took advantage of his drinking, financial and marital problems to turn him against the ANC. By his own count, Mtolo served as a state witness in ten political trials, including one involving Ebrahim Ebrahim, the man who was to be betrayed again in 1988 by Sedibe. Mtolo's testimony helped condemn many of his former comrades to long terms on Robben Island. Natoo Babenia, an MK operative who spent 16 years on Robben Island for sabotage, later wrote that Mtolo's testimony in court was 'all tangled lies'.[31] Looking back at his life as an activist and MK operative, Babenia said, 'Sadly, my feelings for this pivotal point in my life have often been ones of betrayal and shame.'[32] This was because of his betrayal by Mtolo. Ronnie Kasrils, who worked with Mtolo in the MK underground before the latter's arrest, described Mtolo as a weak and ill-disciplined alcoholic.[33] After his turning, the ANC condemned Mtolo to death, declaring that his treachery would not go unpunished.[34]

In 1966 Mtolo published a memoir titled *Umkhonto we Sizwe: The road to the left*. The book sought to explain why he had switched sides. Mtolo said he had lost faith and no longer had hope that the ANC would triumph. He did not want to die for a lost cause. Mtolo claimed that his disillusionment with the ANC began before his arrest. He recalled visiting the Soweto home of Walter Sisulu, one of the leaders of the ANC. 'His house looked like one of the showrooms in West Street, Durban.'[35]

Although Sisulu, an estate agent, and his wife, Albertina, a midwife, were middle class, it is doubtful that their house was the epitome of luxury. Mtolo's was a standard conversion tale according to which a believer starts losing faith after exposure to the hypocrisy of the leadership. Mtolo claimed to have become an anti-communist and had no regret about his betrayal.[36] 'I had no guilty conscience and I was not scared of anybody who might say I was a traitor.'[37] Mtolo expected his former comrades to go after him. 'It may be that someday the communists will act against me.'[38] ANC assassins killed him sometime in the 1970s.

Another collaborator who wrote about his experience was Daluxolo Luthuli. His book, co-written with another ex-MK operative called Thula Bopela, is titled *Umkhonto we Sizwe: Fighting for a divided people*. Luthuli went into exile in 1963 to join MK at the age of 15. He was sent to the Odessa Military Academy in the Ukraine for training. Because of his age, Luthuli could not join his fellow recruits when they went to the bars of Odessa after hours, so he spent his time on the shooting range. He soon became 'one of the best shots' in the ANC.[39] He returned to Africa and was arrested following the failure of the Wankie and Sipolilo campaigns. When Luthuli escaped into Botswana, he was betrayed to the Rhodesian and South African police by Leonard Mandla Nkosi, a fellow MK member on the mission. ANC assassins killed Nkosi, who had become a security policeman, on 10 September 1978. Luthuli was transferred to South Africa and sentenced to ten years on Robben Island. After leaving the island in 1980, he joined Inkatha, the Zulu nationalist movement founded by Mangosuthu Buthelezi.

When Buthelezi decided in the mid-1980s, together with the apartheid government, to develop Inkatha as a paramilitary force, Luthuli was named commander and political commissar of a 200-strong unit of killers known as the Caprivi trainees. South African Military Intelligence and Special Forces trained the men in offensive and defensive techniques. They were then divided and deployed around different parts of what is now KwaZulu-Natal, forming death squads and serving as bodyguards for the leadership of Inkatha. With Luthuli at the helm, they targeted opponents of Inkatha for assassination. Luthuli's book suggests that he turned against the ANC because he had been betrayed and, he felt, because the ANC was targeting Zulus.

He rejoined the ANC in the early 1990s after realising, he said, that the South African security forces were using him to fan so-called black-on-black violence.[40] Of his betrayal of the ANC and his campaign of murder and mayhem against the ANC, Luthuli wrote, 'I accept that I have betrayed the ANC, but that's history.'[41] Luthuli went on to serve as a senior officer in the South African National Defence Force after 1994.

Some traitors draw the ire of their former comrades more than others. Gerard Ludi is one such case. Ludi, who may have started out as an anti-apartheid activist, was one of the state's star witnesses against Bram Fischer, a senior member of the South African Communist Party and one of Mandela's advocates in the Rivonia Trial. In his book *Operation Q-018*, Ludi claimed to have always been a government agent whose mission was to infiltrate the Communist Party and the white left. Ludi recalled a conversation with his police recruiter, Att Spengler, who told him, 'The people we are asking you to mix with are immoral, peculiar, and some of them, I am convinced, are stark raving mad.'[42] In Ludi's words, 'a driving curiosity was one of the main reasons I had consented to being recruited as a Secret Agent. Remember, in those days James Bond was still an unknown and becoming a Secret Agent did not have any romantic appeal whatsoever.'[43] Ludi's book tried to paint a complex picture of his motives, suggesting both innocence and an aversion to communism as reasons for his betrayal of his comrades. 'So my motives were somewhat more complicated than just the thrill and danger of a secret agent's life.'[44]

Despite such loquacious descriptions of his motivations, Ludi's publication, described by the ANC as a 'nasty, boasting little book, full of crude Special Branch propaganda',[45] fails to mention the reason why he turned against his comrades. Ludi had in fact been arrested under South Africa's Immorality Act for a liaison with a woman classified Indian under apartheid, and faced at least five months in prison for sex across the colour line.[46] Given a choice between that and turning against his comrades, he chose betrayal. Ludi's betrayal did not end with Bram Fischer. He became a member of the apartheid secret services and left only in the 1990s, after suffering an attack of conscience. Ludi gave his reasons for quitting the security forces in a 2011 book titled *The communistisation of the ANC*. 'Some violent and ruthless criminal-based [police] special units were being created to wreak havoc among the countries [*sic*] enemies. I wanted no part of this.'[47] Like many ex-apartheid agents, Ludi has reinvented himself as a businessman and consultant specialising in risk analysis for corporations wishing to invest in Africa.

Luthuli's and Ludi's books are just two examples of what the ANC called 'political pornography'.[48] They illustrate in different ways the many guises in which collaborators appear. No two collaborators are alike. Take the case of Mwezi Twala and his book *Mbokodo! Inside MK*.[49] A senior member of MK trained in the Soviet Union after leaving South Africa in 1975, Twala defected after falling out with the ANC over issues of discipline. In the early 1990s Twala became the face of an organisation called the Returned Exiles' Coordinating Committee, a South African Military Intelligence front intended to embarrass the ANC by talking about the brutality of life in ANC camps in exile.[50] But his association with Military Intelligence had the effect of blunting the import of his message about ANC torture. To be fair to the ANC, the organisation did respond to stories of torture in its camps, appointing three commissions over a ten-year period to look into the subject, though minimal action was taken against perpetrators.

The testimonies examined in this chapter try in their different ways to deal with what Mfalapitsa called the 'broader context' of the political conflict in South Africa. They force us to come to terms with the idea of complexity. However, as we see from Mfalapitsa's testimony and his exchange with Gcabashe, complexity can only take one so far. It was well and fine for Mfalapitsa to say that the 'broader context' was complex and messy, but complexity is no argument by itself. Saying that things under apartheid were messy is not saying much. What needs explaining is why individuals acted in the way that they did. Each of the collaborators examined in this chapter tried to put his choices down to circumstance. That is not enough. Human beings never stop being moral agents.

12
The infamy

When one accommodates oneself to power, the act of betrayal becomes complete. The discourse produced from this operation can provide a sense of redemption.
– Patricia Espinosa Hernández[1]

In 1992 Sedibe drove more than 400 kilometres to Louis Trichardt, an agricultural town near the border with Zimbabwe, to visit Philipos Mamabolo Nwedamutswu. A member of the ANC in exile, Nwedamutswu had returned to South Africa after the unbanning of the organisation in February 1990. While Nwedamutswu and Sedibe had been friends in exile, Sedibe's visit to Nwedamutswu's home in the bantustan of Venda was both unsolicited and unwelcome. Nwedamutswu was still bitter over Sedibe's betrayal and the havoc wreaked on the ANC. As there was no one at home when Sedibe arrived, he scribbled a note for his former friend. It said 'Dois M' the name of Mozambique's best-selling beer and Sedibe's favourite, which was also Sedibe's nickname from exile. Eventually, the two men agreed to meet at a restaurant in the centre of Louis Trichardt.

Despite the ANC's unbanning and the opening up of political space, returned exiles such as Nwedamutswu were being harassed by the military and police, their proxies in the bantustans and by state-sponsored vigilante groups. Nwedamutswu did not trust Sedibe – who had become, after all, a police constable and a leading askari – so he took a few comrades along to the meeting.[2] It is not clear what Sedibe hoped to gain by seeing Nwedamutswu. Perhaps he was reaching out to old comrades. But Nwedamutswu knew what he wanted from the meeting: to ask Sedibe why he had utterly betrayed the ANC. Sedibe had met some of his erstwhile comrades, including Humphrey Mkhwanazi, since the organisation's unbanning and he must have come to expect the question.[3] When it came, he responded: 'I wanted to save my life because these people were going to kill me.'[4]

But that wasn't all. Sedibe directed responsibility for his acts of collaboration at the ANC, telling Nwedamutswu: 'I had expected that, as a golden rule, all the plans that I was involved in would be stopped or changed significantly. But this was not done. They continued regardless of my circumstances.'[5] Sedibe was reminding his former comrade of the golden rule that governed MK activity: captured insurgents always talked, especially when tortured. Some might hold out longer than the 48 hours they were supposed to give each other. But they always talked. Those who were free had to change every plan known to the captured combatant. In Sedibe's case, the ANC and MK did not do so. This might have been a matter of incompetence or the fact that, as Barry Gilder and Elias Masilela argue, Sedibe knew so much that no change of plan would have made a difference.[6] Nwedamutswu was clearly not impressed by this explanation. As he told Elias Masilela, Sedibe 'did not show remorse. He was plainly arrogant.'[7] Some of Masilela's informants were more blunt in their reaction, saying, 'In MK there are no cowards but sell-outs and traitors.'[8]

There is indeed something troubling about Sedibe's explanation. It only takes us into the torture chamber. It takes us as far as his all-too-human decision to give his abductors information in order to live. But it does not explain how his decision to talk under duress turned into collaboration as a career choice. This is not to suggest that Sedibe should have chosen death or that he was, as Nwedamutswu said after meeting Sedibe, an arrogant coward. Neither is it to insist that Sedibe should have accepted what Achille

Mbembe calls the 'otherworldliness of freedom', meaning the authority given in narratives of the anti-apartheid struggle to death as a fundamental guarantee of one's commitment to that struggle.[9]

We find this authority of death in the PAC president Robert Sobukwe's 'National Heroes' Day' address on 2 August 1959, in which he praised the 'heroes of Afrika's past' who 'nourished the tree of African freedom and independence with their blood'. We find it in the statement that Nelson Mandela read out from the dock on 20 April 1964 during the Rivonia Trial. Mandela declared, 'I have cherished the ideal of a democratic and free society in which all persons live together in harmony and with equal opportunities. It is an ideal which I hope to live for and to achieve. But if needs be, it is an ideal for which I am prepared to die.' We find it in the last words the ANC insurgent Solomon Mahlangu reputedly said on 6 April 1979 shortly before the South African government executed him, 'My blood will nourish the tree that will bear the fruits of freedom.'[10] We find it especially in the MK oath of loyalty that Sedibe took in 1979, vowing that he would fight against apartheid 'till victory or death'.[11] When faced with the real choice between life and death, Sedibe chose life. This is what made Sedibe a coward in the eyes of his former comrades. He would have remained a hero if he had chosen death.[12]

Death is valorised often in descriptions of South Africa's freedom struggle. Consider the story of Phila Portia Ndwandwe, an MK insurgent who – when given the choice to collaborate and live, or refuse and die – 'chose' death. Security Branch police abducted Ndwandwe, who had joined the ANC in 1985 while a student at the University of Durban-Westville, from Swaziland in October 1988. They took her to a farm near Pietermaritzburg for interrogation. They stripped her naked and kept her in a concrete room. When she refused to 'turn' in return for her life, the police blindfolded her, threw her into a shallow grave and shot her in the head. Ndwandwe had a two-month-old son named Thabani at the time. When the TRC dug up her remains on 12 March 1997, following disclosure by her killers, her skeleton was lying on its back in a foetal position. In 2001, five Security Branch policemen received amnesty for her murder.[13] The South African government posthumously awarded Ndwandwe a silver medal for bravery and valour in April 2010.

Ndwandwe's story has been celebrated and told by commentators ranging from journalist David Beresford to artist Judith Mason.[14] In 1995 Mason produced a triptych titled 'The man who sang and the woman who kept silent'. As Mason explains on her website, the triptych was inspired by two stories from hearings of the TRC that she listened to on the radio. 'They told of the execution of two liberation movement cadres by the security police. One was Harold Sefolo, who ... asked permission to sing *Nkosi Sikelel' iAfrika* before he was shot; the other Phila Ndwandwe, who was tortured and kept naked for ten days and then assassinated in a kneeling position ... Before Ndwandwe was killed, she fashioned a pair of panties for herself out of a scrap of blue plastic.'[15] The South African Broadcasting Corporation had reported that, while in detention, Ndwandwe improvised underwear for herself by using discarded plastic bags.[16]

For a part of her triptych, Mason made a blue dress using plastic bags. She inscribed the following text on the dress: 'Sister, a plastic bag may not be the whole armour of God, but you were wrestling with flesh and blood, and against powers, against the rulers of darkness, against spiritual wickedness in sordid places. Your weapons were your silence and a piece of rubbish. Finding that bag and wearing it until you were disinterred is such a frugal, commonsensical, house-wifey thing to do, an ordinary act ... At some level you shamed your captors, and they did not compound their abuse by stripping you a second time. Yet they killed you. We only know your story because a sniggering man remembered how brave you were. Memorials to your courage are everywhere; they blow about in the streets and drift on the tide and cling to the thorn-bushes. This dress is made from some of them. *Hamba Kahle* [Farewell]. *Umkhonto* [Spear].'

Albie Sachs, at the time a Constitutional Court judge, who was acquiring artwork for the new court, saw an early version of Mason's piece. He asked her to 'soften' the work. She reworked the piece and thus was born the triptych.[17] Sachs so loved the piece that he not only purchased it for the court but also used an image of the centrepiece from the triptych on the cover of his book *The strange alchemy of life and law*. Sachs writes of Ndwandwe's bravery in the preface to this work, recounting elements of the same story.[18]

Mason and Sachs were simply working with the information they had at the time. But it appears that the widely circulated story of Ndwandwe's final days is not entirely true. Ndwandwe did not die in silence. Hendrik Botha, one of her killers, told the TRC that when Ndwandwe was interrogated she gave the police new information about MK operations and confirmed details already known to the police. But when he asked her to become an informer, 'None of the signs he was looking for [in Ndwandwe] was forthcoming, not in her body language, nor in her communication. She did not raise the issue of her safety. She did not ask who else would know of it or how communication would work.'[19]

The following day, Ndwandwe continued to cooperate with her abductors but gave no signs that she would accept Botha's offer. 'It became clear that she would not be turned, certainly not without some delay, which would render it impossible to replace her in Swaziland without her finding it impossible to explain her absence and whereabouts over a long period of time.'[20] The police had no intention of charging Ndwandwe. They could not afford to release her because that would have exposed the two informers who had led her to their trap and whom they refused to name in the hearing. So they killed her.

We could say that, by refusing to become an informer, Ndwandwe chose death. We could say that, in contrast to Sedibe, she took the honourable option. But that would be a dubious assertion. While the proposition is driven by the noble sentiment that freedom is worth dying for, it minimises the culpability of her killers. To say

Ndwandwe chose death is to suggest that her killers gave her what she wanted. It is to reduce her to a means for the ends of freedom. It throws the uniqueness of her life and her brave moral stance into the river Martyr, forever flowing with the blood of revolutionaries. More than that, it risks absolving her killers of their responsibility for her death.

In fairness to Ndwandwe, she did make the honourable choice. She responded to her torture the best way she could, telling her captors some of what they needed to know. But she would not, and did not, take that final step and become a traitor. She collaborated but refused to become a collaborator. Therein lies the difference between her and Sedibe.

* * *

Many people throughout history have faced the 'choice' between death and collaboration. To date, this has been little discussed in South Africa – perhaps because so many of the country's secrets lie buried in a shallow post-apartheid grave. But these are questions that continue to confront five former political prisoners who survived Argentina's dirty war between 1975 and 1983 by collaborating with the military junta. Munu Actis, Cristina Aldini, Liliana Gardella, Miriam Lewin and Elisa Tokar were left-wing activists taken by the military. As they say in *That inferno*, the book recounting their experience: 'We are not sorry to be alive.'[21] The book expresses the women's 'frustration at having been taken alive and our frustration at the cyanide pill as a symbol of liberation and sacrifice for others'.[22] As insurgents fighting against the military dictatorship, they carried cyanide pills to swallow in case of capture. However, things did not turn out as planned. As revolutionaries, they were expected to choose death over capture. But for different reasons, they did not. Miriam Lewin, for instance, found her cyanide pill defective when she tried to take it.[23]

That inferno is dedicated to the children of the thousands of political activists and ordinary citizens 'disappeared' by the military junta during its seven years in power. 'We want them to understand the human dimension of this story and to use that understanding to reject a Manichean view of good and evil, because it is impossible to live up to the demands of absolute heroism. The truth is that, aside from brief episodes of heroism and saintliness, real history was made by human beings with all their inconsistencies.'[24]

The five were held in a torture camp at the Naval School of Mechanics in Buenos Aires. They were, as Elisa Tokar says, 'defenceless, primitive beings at the mercy of lunatics'.[25] Very likely they would have been killed, like thousands of their comrades, but for the junta's decision to use their talents. The junta employed the five, all educated, to translate documents and newspaper reports into Spanish and other languages; to help prepare intelligence briefs for the military; to forge documents for use by members of the junta's death squads; and, bizarrely, for company. The women tell how they would be tortured during the day and then 'invited' out to dinner by the same torturers at night. One torturer even complained to the women that he had better and more fulfilling relationships with them than he did with his wife.[26]

Collaboration was no guarantee of survival, however. Some people who collaborated were still killed.[27] The women said that part of the problem with the Naval School of Mechanics was that, as Liliana Gardella put it, it 'had no bars to separate the victims from the victimisers. As a result, it was even harder there than in a prison for captives to maintain their integrity.'[28] Even though they were not chained and could move around parts of the facility, the inmates never stopped fearing that they too might be disappeared. Liliana Gardella remarked, 'the pressure is always there, because you carry the terror inside you. As long as you're a captive, or you're dependent on them, they don't have to be physically present for you to feel the pressure.'[29] For Munu Actis, being an inmate brought her close to death. 'I felt death. You never completely return from that point.'[30] But the junta did more than use the women's brainpower and expose them to death. In the words of Liliana Gardella: 'What they did was to mine our ideals, force us to adapt to their behaviours in order to survive.'[31] The junta sought to change revolutionaries who had wanted to change the world, into cynics who could not trust anyone.

The women accepted that they collaborated with the junta for their own survival. They did not agree, however, on how to treat those who collaborated beyond the dictates of survival. Miriam Lewin argued that while it was understandable for a captive to break under torture and to divulge information, it was not acceptable for the same person to be socialising with his or her captors six months later, drinking *mate* tea.[32] Liliana Gardella challenged Lewin on this point, saying that it placed her on a slippery slope to moral judgement. 'I don't make that distinction, because otherwise you never come to the end of dividing out the good and the bad.'[33]

Indeed, part of the difficulty with the phenomenon of collaboration is that it covers a gamut of activities. If, for example, Ndwandwe had lived, would she still be considered a hero even if the information she gave under torture led – as it reportedly did – to the capture and killing of some of her comrades? If Sedibe had lived, would we be more understanding of the choices he made?

Miguel Krassnoff Martchenko, an officer in Chile's National Intelligence Directorate (DINA),[34] Augusto Pinochet's secret service, once asked Luz Arce, socialist-turned-DINA collaborator: 'Tell me, and what does a traitor feel?' Arce answered: 'Lieutenant, all I can tell you is that, in this war of yours, I am on the losing side. From a loser to a winner, you only gave me two options: To live or die. I chose to live. How do I feel? That is my problem, Sir.'[35] Arce was a Socialist Party activist and a member of President Salvador Allende's security detail. She went into hiding when Pinochet deposed Allende in a military coup on 11 September 1973. She was captured by the DINA in March 1974, having been lured into a trap by a fellow socialist who, unbeknown to her, had already fallen to the DINA. Arce decided to collaborate when the DINA 'broke' her brother, a fellow socialist, through torture and threatened her son. The DINA later killed the brother. Arce was tortured and raped.[36]

Asked by Michael J. Lazzara about how she started collaborating with the DINA, Arce said, 'Strangely, when I was a prisoner, I *always, always, always* maintained a certain degree of lucidity. There were many times when I was literally unconscious, either because I had been beaten, or because of hunger, or whatever. Consequently, I have forgotten entire days, weeks. I remember that when I'd open my eyes and see that I hadn't died, I would think that I had two options: to live or die. So I decided that I would act as if I were going to live. That was permanent. I kept listening. I kept trying to find things out, to gather information. I never dreamed I would testify later. Never! But I needed that information to survive. I want to say that I lied to DINA about many things. In other words, my collaboration was never 100 percent. In fact, if someone were to take the time to examine who I turned in – unfortunately four people died, but it was because there was no logic in the detention centres – they'd see that I didn't even turn in a single party nucleus leader. What I'm saying is that I tried to find the least painful way to collaborate.'[37]

Arce was recruited formally to the DINA on 7 May 1975, almost 14 months after she had been detained, tortured, raped and shot in the foot. According to Lazzara, her collaboration was 'complex and multifaceted'.[38] She gave up names of comrades (four of whom were subsequently disappeared); she took part in the DINA's entrapment of leftist activists; she used her knowledge of the inner workings of the revolutionary left to draw up organisational diagrams for the DINA; she gave Pinochet's military officers classes on Marxism; she participated in espionage operations in Uruguay on behalf of the DINA; and she had sexual relations with a number of Pinochet's military officers. She also served in an administrative capacity for the Metropolitan Intelligence Brigade in Chile's capital of Santiago, and as an intelligence analyst for the DINA.

Together with Marcia Alejandra Merino Vega (nicknamed La

Flaca) and Maria Alicia Uribe Gómez (also known as Carola) – fellow leftists who had also been tortured and turned – Arce was given an apartment in Santiago and paid a salary for her collaboration. She spent six years working for Pinochet's secret service and military government as a collaborator. She tried three times to resign during that time. But it was only on 16 March 1980 that the secret service accepted her resignation. She disappeared from public life 'so that she could confront her shame and trauma privately'.[39] She moved to Europe and only returned to Chile in 1990 to take part voluntarily in Chile's National Truth and Reconciliation Commission, also known as the Rettig Commission.

Not surprisingly, despite her participation in the commission, Arce remains a controversial figure in Chile. In the words of the Chilean academic Patricia Espinosa Hernández, Arce is a 'definitive part of our national history of infamy'.[40] In fact, while it is acknowledged that 'collaboration was the norm rather than an exception' among political prisoners in Chile,[41] and that many people, including those who were later disappeared, collaborated in some way, Arce has come to stand for the phenomenon of collaboration; she is the collaborator par excellence. The Chilean journalist Gloria Elgueta Pinto says that even though Pinochet's junta depended on a degree of 'social collaboration' for its conditions of possibility, it is the 'figure of the traitor or collaborator who, when considered individually, is often saddled, in the eyes of society, with all responsibility for what happened. In short, the figure of the individual collaborator ends up serving as a sacrificial lamb for individual or collective responsibility.'[42]

As Arce herself told Lazzara, 'The scope of collaboration [in Chile] still doesn't get discussed – although it's mentioned much more often today than in the nineties, for example. In the 1980s and 1990s, it was just Marcia, Carola and me. Period! No one else collaborated. Do you see? In this country, no one else collaborated! We were the only ones.'[43] What makes Arce such a controversial figure in Chile, however, is the depth of her treachery, the content of her justification and the terms of her defence.

In many ways Arce's case parallels that of Sedibe.[44] But unlike Sedibe, Arce refused to say she had no choice. She said, 'In all honesty, I'm not going to utter the sentence "I had no choice".' According to Arce, she collaborated because she was 'terrified'.[45] She was convinced that her captors were going to kill her. 'Fleeing wasn't a solution. I had no resources to hide from DINA. I had to create a situation in which they'd *let* me live.'[46] But Arce's critics are not persuaded by her explanation. This is because Arce's rationale does not, for instance, account for what Lazzara calls the 'bureaucratisation' of her collaboration, her 'becoming a functionary of DINA and accepting a salary'.[47] Diamela Eltit, a Chilean novelist, sees Arce's collaboration as a compensatory act designed to accommodate herself to power and, more importantly, to rebuild her shattered ego after it was 'broken' during torture.[48]

What would Glory Sedibe have done if he had lived? How might he have explained his collaboration to people other than his former comrades? Like Arce, like Mfalapitsa, or like his Vlakplaas and Military Intelligence colleague Chris Mosiane? Asked on 16 October 2000 by the TRC Amnesty Committee if he had anything to say to the Mxenge family, whose house he had petrol-bombed, Mosiane declared: 'To the families of Mr Mxenge, I ask for forgiveness from the depth of my heart because I know and understand well that they suffered for a long time because they were freedom fighters. I was used in an inhuman way to oppress freedom fighters like members of the Mxenge family. With those words, you would recall that these terrible acts which I took part in were not directed particularly to the Mxenge family only, but they were directed to each and every person who took part in the struggle, therefore in this way I say I did not affect the Mxenge family only, but I was put in that position because I struggled, then I was fighting against myself, that is why I understand the pain they suffered, they endured, through the acts of the previous Government ... The people I ask forgiveness from have an opportunity and an ability not to forgive me. I would not complain, because I understand the situation they were in during these incidents. I would end by saying I suffered a lot. This would be a mark in my life, I would not forget this. Even if they may forgive me, I will not forget this.'[49]

Could Mosiane honestly 'understand' the pain suffered by the Mxenges? This, after all, was a family that lost Griffiths Mxenge to askari savagery and Victoria Mxenge, Griffiths's widow, to askari violence. Mosiane said he 'suffered a lot', but could his suffering ever give him insight into how the Mxenges suffered? Mosiane was indeed the victim of a police abduction. He probably was tortured and forced to become an askari. But his experience of apartheid violence does not mean that he can possibly know what the Mxenges went through. Mosiane agreed to become an askari. He agreed to kill and destroy for apartheid. We cannot downplay Mosiane's experience of torture – or that of Sedibe. But, at the same time, we cannot limit our attempt to understand why some became askaris to the torture chamber. Men like Sedibe and Mosiane may have lived in the deepest chambers of hell, but they never ceased being moral agents, and it is as moral agents that we must think of them.

13
The psychology

> *My legs were killing me. My head was thumping. I knew I was going to break. It was the very worst moment of my life. I knew we would all eventually do what Adrian was doing. We all* did *the same eventually. But why was he setting me up like this, apparently manipulating the way the stories were to be squeezed out of me? He wasn't just giving our names; now he was playing* their *game for them, writing* their *script.*
>
> – Hugh Lewin[1]

In his essay on French collaborators under Nazi occupation, Jean-Paul Sartre speaks in definite terms about the 'psychology of the collaborator'. He says: 'It is not enough just to have determined the social space of collaboration: there is a psychology of the collaborator from which we can draw some precious lessons.' Sartre remarks that while it would be convenient to blame self-interest and ambition for collaboration, this would only serve to make it easy to classify and condemn collaborators. It would not necessarily be the truth. According to Sartre, some French collaborated because they could, not because they stood to gain anything from the Nazis; others because they were seduced by the chance to wield power, even if this meant subordination to German diktats. 'If we want to understand the attitude of the collaborators we must, then, examine them dispassionately and describe them objectively on the basis of their words and deeds.'[2] These observations are useful for understanding how collaboration is rationalised.

As Sartre said, 'The collaborator suffers from that intellectual illness that may be called historicism.' In Nazi-occupied France, collaborators justified their collaboration on the grounds that the 'historical event' happened and there was no point in challenging it. All one had to do was to be 'realistic' and accept and accommodate oneself to the situation as it was. Speaking of historicist scholars, Sartre said they had a 'tendency to ratify events simply because they have occurred. They are here confusing the need, insofar as they are scholars, to submit to the facts, with a certain inclination, insofar as they are moral agents, to approve those facts morally. The collaborators took over this philosophy of history. For them, the dominion of the facts went together with a vague belief in progress, but a decapitated progress.'[3]

In a passage that would apply equally to askaris, Sartre wrote that collaborators 'abandon themselves passively to the various emerging currents and float towards an unknown destination; they experience the delights of not thinking, of not looking ahead and of accepting the obscure transformations that necessarily turn us into new and unpredictable human beings'.[4]

According to Nofomela, Sedibe would often say: 'I can't change what happened.'[5] As we know from numerous sources, Sedibe claimed that he collaborated in order to live. He was trying to sound 'realistic'. But, to draw on Sartre again, 'Realism here conceals the fear of performing the customary work of the human being ... and [reveals] a mystical appetite for mystery, a docile attitude towards a future one has stopped trying to shape.' Sartre said the French collaborator had a 'docile attitude to facts', which meant that, instead of 'judging facts in the light of what is right, he bases what is right upon what *is*. His implicit metaphysics identifies *is* with *ought*.'[6]

We cannot accept Sedibe's claim that he had no choice. To hear Barry Gilder, Miriam Phumla Williams, Judas Mpho Tladi and Sam Mtileni tell it, Sedibe took to his role as a collaborator with some relish.[7] He seemed to enjoy travelling to Swaziland to hunt down former comrades. He seemed to delight in earning bonuses from his actions as a collaborator. He enjoyed the trappings that came with his income as a salaried employee of apartheid's bureaucracy. Where, in Sedibe's story, is the line between his 'realism' in the torture chamber and his 'enthusiasm' for collaboration outside that chamber?

As far as we know, Sedibe himself never psychologised his decision to collaborate. When he was reunited briefly with his family shortly after deciding to turn in late 1986, he told them it was all about survival. Sedibe's mother, Lillian, who had not seen her son since he went into exile in 1977, recalled that when he visited their home late in 1986, he did so under police escort. 'We were just happy to see him. We did not talk about his life.'[8] She said her son seemed happy. Starting in 1976 with the sentencing of Kaborone to five years on Robben Island, the Security Branch had subjected the family to years of harassment, which intensified when Sedibe went into exile. Lillian Sedibe said, 'They would come in at 11 pm, at 2 am. They would raid us, walk on our laundry, throw things out of wardrobes [and say], "*Jy bly soos 'n vark.*"' (You live like a pig.) She noted that the police used neighbours to keep the family under surveillance. 'The neighbours were the spies.'[9] However, none of that mattered when Sedibe returned home and told his mother he was now working for the police.

Asked what Sedibe said to her by way of explanation, Lillian Sedibe replied, 'He said "if they catch you, you do what they want." He was one of theirs [by then]. He worked for them.'[10] Lillian and Ephraim had been so afraid of the Security Branch that when Sedibe fled into exile they would not even utter his name inside their house. 'It was like [Sedibe and Kaborone] were dead.'[11] It was a month before they fetched Sedibe's belongings from a room he had been renting in Bushbuckridge. Yet, when Sedibe arrived home with his former hunters, the family were just relieved he was alive. Although the family were staunchly ANC, they did not, according to Lillian Sedibe and other members of the family, stop to ponder the ethical and political implications of his conversion. More than that, Sedibe's transformation did not alter their own commitment to the ANC and to the struggle against apartheid.

Miriam Mashego, an aunt of Sedibe's who also had a son with the ANC in exile, stated that when Sedibe rejoined the family after he switched sides, he told them he had had no choice but to work for the police. 'He was used by the Boers and when they were done with him, they poisoned him.'[12] The family appear to have accepted without question Sedibe's version of his turning. Kaborone and Ção were the only family members to attend the TRC's three-day amnesty hearing in February 2000 into Sedibe's abduction. There seemed to be convergence between the family's acceptance of Sedibe's explanation for why he turned and the TRC's treatment of him as only a victim.

Do collaborators assume the value system of the 'other side'?[13] Did Sedibe come to believe in apartheid? What were his aspirations, and did he believe that these could be realised through his services to the police and the military? When Sedibe died in 1994, a white Security Branch policeman who had worked with him told *Beeld* newspaper about an episode on a farm in the Northern Transvaal sometime in the late 1980s when Sedibe and four other askaris, three men and one woman, sang ANC songs for their white commanders' amusement.[14] The unnamed cop (most likely De Kock) told *Beeld* that even though Sedibe worked for the police against the ANC, he remained a communist. Sedibe and the policeman would spend hours debating the finer points of communism, the officer recalled. Sedibe told his brother in November 1986 that although he had joined the police, he still supported the ANC.[15]

In Chile, Luz Arce told Lazzara that while she collaborated with Pinochet's secret police, she did not abandon her political beliefs. 'I still believe in certain things, and some of them stem from those utopian, Marxist dreams – those crazy dreams, lived irrationally, with youthful energy.'[16] Gregory Sibusiso Radebe, who used his payout from Vlakplaas to start one of the biggest pyramid schemes in post-apartheid South Africa, cast himself as an economic freedom fighter. He claimed that even as an askari, he always believed in the struggle against apartheid. But none of these claims can be taken at face value.

Jean Amery, whose reflections on torture are a useful counterpoint to Hannah Arendt's claims about the 'banality of evil', offers sharp insights into what we might call the psychology of collaboration secured through torture. A victim of Gestapo torture and survivor of three concentration camps, he committed suicide in 1978. In his book *At the mind's limits,* Amery wrote, 'Whoever has succumbed to torture can no longer feel at home in the world. The shame of destruction cannot be erased. Trust in the world, which already collapsed in part at the first blow, but in the end, under torture, fully, will not be regained.'[17] What takes over the psychic space left by one's destroyed trust in the world?

'Torture has an indelible character,' he said. 'Whoever was tortured stays tortured.'[18] If this is indeed so, can one succumb to torture, turn into a collaborator and still hold onto the beliefs for which one was tortured in the first place? This is what Arce wants us to believe. It is also De Kock's argument – his insistence that Sedibe collaborated to survive but never gave up his political beliefs.[19] This claim is not very convincing.

Sedibe, like Arce, might have been seduced by his proximity to power. It is possible that, given the licence to kill by a state whose agents had brought him close to his own death, Sedibe acquired a sense of self that compensated for the shame of his collaboration. According to Barry Gilder, Sedibe was 'particularly active in pursuing us ... he was particularly vicious in torturing some of our comrades'.[20] Did Sedibe take to his new occupation with such dedication to rebuild a shattered ego, to rediscover a sense of self-worth, to find the means to go on living in the absence of any trust in the world? Sedibe might have tried to reconstruct himself by doing to former comrades what his torturers had done to him.

The psychologist Stanley Milgram's experiment on 'Obedience to Authority' provides one lens through which to examine collaboration. Milgram, according to Thomas Blass, found that the 'ability of a legitimate authority to define reality for the person who adopts his or her authority' is central to getting people to carry out orders they might otherwise find problematic.[21] Another factor that allowed a 'legitimate authority to evoke destructive obedience' was a shift in a person's experiential state, what Milgram called an agentic shift. 'The most far-reaching consequence of the agentic shift is that a man feels responsible *to* the authority directing him but feels no responsibility *for* the content of the actions that the authority prescribes.'[22] It is possible that a similar shift allowed Sedibe to respond positively *to* the authority of the Security Branch without feeling responsible *for* the contents of the actions they prescribed. Could this prepositional play between *to* and *for* explain why Sedibe could still tell his family and his captors (if they are to be believed) that he was a committed revolutionary even as he was hunting down former comrades? These are important questions to ask, but, as the following story shows, psychology has its limits when it comes to helping us understand the phenomenon of collaboration.

* * *

Early in 1964, four people volunteered for a pilot study into the effects of solitary confinement on individuals organised by the Psychology Department of the University of Cape Town. The study was led by Kurt Danziger, a social psychologist who would go on to achieve international acclaim.[23] The volunteers were locked in a small windowless room for three days with only the facilities that might be expected in a prison cell, including a naked light bulb that was always shining. They were not allowed to smoke. But there was an emergency button they could press if they felt too stressed to continue with the experiment and wanted to get out.

Danziger, known for his opposition to apartheid, had been asked to conduct the experiment by lawyers defending accused persons in a string of political trials taking place in South Africa in that period. Witnesses who had been detained and held in solitary confinement for long stretches of time had been implicating many people in the planning and execution of subversive activities. The lawyers wanted Danziger to serve as an expert witness on the possible effects of solitary confinement on the reliability of testimony. Danziger was familiar with the relevant scientific literature, but the lawyers felt it would help if he could also call on personal experience for his expert testimony. He agreed.

Recalling the experiment almost 50 years later, Danziger said, 'As you can imagine, there were significant logistical issues involved. Personnel had to be available around the clock, and so on. I certainly would not have received a research grant from any government-sponsored body for such a project at that time. So we managed as best we could with the limited resources available. In the end, I don't think we ever got beyond four subjects.'[24] The volunteers were graduate students or junior faculty members. One of them was Adrian Leftwich, a junior lecturer at the university. Leftwich was also a leader of the anti-apartheid National Union of South African Students and a leading member of the National Committee of Liberation, a group founded in 1960 by young liberals angered by the apartheid government's turn towards violence and torture as state policy, especially after the Sharpeville massacre on 21 March 1960. Members of the committee, renamed the African Resistance Movement in 1964, were the first anti-apartheid activists to turn to violence. They blew up infrastructure such as electric pylons, bridges, as well as railway carriages and lines. Leftwich and his comrades hoped that their campaign of sabotage would bring the government to its senses and lead to the abandonment of apartheid.

Danziger recalled: 'Given the police-state atmosphere of the time, some of the subjects undoubtedly volunteered to participate in this experiment in order to test their own ability to cope with such conditions of confinement. In view of the very real possibility of his arrest, it is safe to assume that this was also Leftwich's motive. Therefore, it came as rather a surprise to me when he activated the emergency button after just a few hours and declared that he could not continue with the experiment if he were not to be allowed to smoke. He was the only subject not to complete the experiment, although all the others did find the experience extremely unpleasant.'[25] Because the experiment never went beyond its pilot status (and presumably because of its small sample size), it was never published.

In fact, it is likely that the study would have been forgotten but for what happened to Leftwich shortly thereafter. In July 1964, during a raid on Leftwich's flat in Cape Town, the police stumbled upon African Resistance Movement documents detailing the making of explosives and other subversive matters. As Hugh Lewin, Leftwich's best friend at the time and a fellow insurgent, wrote in *Bandiet: Seven years in a South African prison*, the first book to detail his betrayal by Leftwich: 'He [Leftwich] had, it seemed – in contravention of his own rules – become archivist.'[26] The police used Leftwich's archive to destroy the African Resistance Movement, sending its members to jail or exile. They also roughed up Leftwich, who decided to collaborate. He testified in court against his former comrades, including Eddie Daniels, a fellow member of the group's executive who subsequently spent 15 years on Robben Island. Leftwich's testimony also helped send John Harris to the gallows in 1965. Harris, a schoolteacher and member of the Liberal Party, had planted a bomb that killed a 77-year-old woman in the whites-only section of Johannesburg's Park Station. Even the judge who presided over the trial of Daniels and others was disgusted by Leftwich's treachery, commenting, 'To refer to him as a rat is hard on rats.'[27] A weeping Leftwich said from the stand: 'I certainly hope that there will be a time when ... these people who I am giving evidence against can forgive me.'[28]

While his former comrades served their sentences, Leftwich left for England, where he resumed his academic career, completing a PhD in politics at the University of York and then joining the university's faculty. He wrote on politics, economics, democracy and development. Shunned by anti-apartheid activists, he kept away from South Africa. It was not until the late 1990s that he began to re-establish contact with the country. This followed attempts by Stephanie Kemp, whom Leftwich had recruited to the African Resistance Movement and then testified against, to reconnect and reconcile with him. Kemp was the first white female political prisoner to be subjected to physical torture in a South African prison. Leftwich followed up his reconnection with South Africa with an essay in *Granta* in 2002 titled 'I gave the names'. The essay, an apologia for what he had done, had taken him 15 years to write.

Leftwich's essay began: 'In July 1964, when I was 24, my life in South Africa came to a sudden end. The events which brought this about were of my own making. No one else was to blame. In the gulf that opened up between my reach and my limits, between my knowledge and my self-ignorance, between my fantasies and my capacities, I crashed.' Leftwich said his crash happened in public, in full view of everyone who knew him. 'For reasons which I still do not fully understand, I tried to do things which were far beyond me, and I failed. I tried to help change the world around me but in the process I destroyed my own, I betrayed my friends and colleagues and I damaged the cause which I believed in and had worked for.'[29]

Leftwich went on to write, 'I am ashamed to write about the events that followed my arrest. Whenever I think about them, there is a side of me that simply wants to die, and always will. But the bare bones can be stated quite plainly. The suddenness, speed and near-comprehensiveness of the disintegration of my will and ability to resist interrogation in solitary confinement took me totally by surprise. It took others by surprise, too. I just caved in.'[30] Leftwich spent five months in solitary confinement, 'but I was undone in the first two months, perhaps even the first two minutes of detention. Any remaining ability to resist the urge to do anything to get out of there – to crawl, to beg, to trade – dissolved that night. Whatever remaining determination I had to stand by my colleagues, whatever commitment I had to doing the right thing – and whatever fear I had of what people would say or think of me if I did not – simply evaporated.'[31] He 'gave the names' and, as he put it in the essay, 'spilled the beans'.[32] Leftwich wrote, 'Afterwards I realised that I had learned something else that night. I learned that at the root of every fear I had ever had, and every fear I would ever have, was the impossible thought, the horror, of my own extinction.'[33]

As Leftwich saw it, the choice was simple: betray and live, or refuse and be annihilated. Yet he made no mention of his participation in the Danziger experiment. Surely, what he had learned about himself in that experiment must have stood somewhere in that gulf between his 'knowledge and self-ignorance'? It must have alerted him to the gulf between his fantasies and capacities long before the police tortured him and turned him against his comrades. Perhaps the Danziger experiment was not memorable to Leftwich; maybe he simply forgot about it. However, knowing about his experience of the experiment reduces the potency of his essay. The essay has been celebrated for its honesty. Yet, once one knows about the experiment, it becomes hard to accept Leftwich's claims about his 'self-ignorance'; it becomes difficult to accept that his collapse was as much of a surprise as his essay says it was.

Despite its gaps, Leftwich's essay is an important self-reflection about the phenomenon of collaboration. But even Leftwich cannot explain why people collaborate. As he said, 'I doubt I will ever really understand the inner history of my actions. We are all capable of self-deceit, especially when seeking to tell the truth,' and 'the simplest and most obvious explanation would be to say that I was yellow: straightforward cowardice explains a lot. But why?'[34] Leftwich accepted responsibility for his actions. But even he could not answer his own question: why do collaborators collaborate?

It is not often that there develops, after the fact, a public conversation between betrayer and betrayed about the betrayal that binds them together. The damage is often too permanent, the gulf too deep, to allow that conversation to take place. Yet Leftwich's *Granta* essay led to one such conversation between him and Lewin. Their conversation took two forms: one literary and public, the other verbal and private. By publishing his apologia, Leftwich started a process of reconciliation that his former comrades could choose to join. Lewin decided, after meeting Leftwich in private and repairing a friendship that had been dead for 40 years, to take part in the public conversation inspired by Leftwich's essay. The result was Lewin's memoir, *Stones against the mirror: Friendship in the time of the South African struggle*. Recalling his response to Leftwich's essay and the acclaim that greeted it, Lewin said, 'Readers spoke about his honesty and the power of his prose. I wasn't sure how I would take it. I expected it would make me angry and that I would then brush the anger aside and feign my usual indifference. But that's not what happened. "I gave the names" affected me deeply. It was as if I'd been waiting for it for years: this explanation, which didn't duck any responsibility.'[35]

So began a reconciliation. The repaired friendship endured until May 2013, when Leftwich died of lung cancer. He was 73. Recalling his incarceration and his feelings towards Leftwich after the betrayal, Lewin said that his experience of prison made him feel 'morally unassailable, unlike those friends and comrades (black and white) who betrayed us. The ones who turned state witness. The ones who stayed outside while we circled the exercise yard. I used to believe that they had put themselves inside a different kind of jail: a jail that had no keys. We served our sentences and were released, I used to say. They bought their freedom with pieces of silver and they would live with that knowledge for the rest of their lives. It feels less simple, now.'[36] By the time Lewin wrote *Stones against the mirror* in 2011, he was more understanding and, therefore, willing to forgive Leftwich for betraying him and destroying their friendship. As he said, 'It could have happened to any of us. Perhaps it would have happened to me if they'd decided differently who it was they wanted as witnesses. I like to think not, but can I be sure?'[37]

Lewin chose to forgive Leftwich in part because he decided that he could no longer be the 'guardian of my friend's guilt'. He also did not want to continue living with bitterness over his betrayal. Having served as a commissioner on the TRC, Lewin set about a personal process of reconciliation.[38] Lewin's reconciliation was not welcomed by all who knew Leftwich in the 1960s. One former activist who was detained by the Security Branch refused to forgive Leftwich, for reasons similar to those given by people who refuse to forgive Sedibe.[39] The former activist said that it was one thing to talk under torture, which is what people like Leftwich and Sedibe did, but quite another to go beyond what even the police asked of them. Leftwich gave the police details they did not need and had not asked for; Sedibe not only gave up his comrades, but participated actively in hunting them down and interrogating them.

14

The past, the present, the future

We have entered freedom with the luggage of unsettled accounts about our history.

– Adam Michnik[1]

It is winter 1981 or 1982 (or is it 1983?). My mother and I are on a bus somewhere atop the mountains of Transkei, apartheid's first bantustan. The bus is stationary, its windows steamed up by the breathing of the people packed inside. There is fog outside, but I can make out the outlines of torches pointed at the bus. I can also hear dogs barking. We are at a police roadblock. Presently, a man boards the bus. He is wearing a thick, long overcoat. His face is behind a balaclava. He is carrying a torch in one hand. Behind him are two uniformed police officers armed with rifles. The policemen's faces are not covered. The man walks down the aisle, shining his torch into the faces of passengers on each seat as he does so.

He moves slowly. Once or twice, the man asks a passenger to show his *dompas* and travel papers. He studies these with care before passing them on to the police behind him. They, too, study the documents carefully before returning them to the passenger. The man in the balaclava and his escorts take their time. When they get to the back, they turn around. The man in the balaclava goes through his routine again, flashing his torch into the faces of passengers, seat by seat. When he and his escorts reach the bus entrance, the two policemen exchange words with the driver before getting off. The man in the balaclava does not say a word. He disappears into the fog. The bus drives off.

I would have been nine or ten when my mother and I took that bus trip. For reasons I cannot explain, the image of the man in the balaclava has been seared into my memory for 30 years.

How many South Africans had similar experiences? Vusi Pikoli, a former ANC insurgent, describes a bus trip he took sometime in 1986: 'On a bus to King William's Town, we were stopped once again and a black guy climbed on. He looked at everybody, trying to see if he could identify any ANC guerrillas. He must have been an askari but he did not notice us.'[2] Was the man in the balaclava also an askari? Why was he in a balaclava? Was it to mask the shame of collaboration? As Bernard Williams defines it, shame means 'being seen, inappropriately, by the wrong people, in the wrong condition'.[3] Was the mask worn to cloak his collaboration in anonymity? Sure, it was cold and, yes, it was winter. It is possible that the balaclava might have been just that – a balaclava.

Thinking of the event – which could not have lasted more than 20 minutes – I am struck by the ordinariness of it all: the cold, the fog, the torch and the man in the balaclava. Nothing out of place here. Yet everything out of place. That, ultimately, is the story of collaboration. I remember, too, the silence inside the bus. I remember the passengers, my mother included, staring into the man's torch as its beam of light moved from face to face, his own face hidden behind his woollen mask. What was he looking for?

What were we doing on that bus? We were, I recall, pilgrims seized by what a German theologian named Hans-Jürgen Becken called the 'Cancele craze'.[4] It began in 1980 when thousands of people from across southern Africa began flocking to Cancele, a village near Mount Frere in the Transkei, to see a faith healer named Nomapuleti Florah Ludlolo. As the *Natal Witness* said in a report dated 2 July 1981, 'Stories abound concerning the doings of this faith healer, known as *Msamariya* (Samaritan) to her followers. Her fame has grown mainly by word-of-mouth reports of numerous miracles and healings through the use of water "blessed" by her.'[5]

While I have vivid memories of the man in the balaclava, I remember little of the pilgrimage itself. In truth, for years the story of the Samaritan of Cancele did not mean much to me. Too young to understand the significance of that pilgrimage, I always thought about the man in the balaclava whenever that trip came to mind. Later, while studying archival material on Msamariya, I was surprised to learn that there was another Jacob Dlamini in the Cancele story. Msamariya, a member of the Anglican Church, had 'started her healing ministry on the strength of visions: *uThixo* (God) [had] healed her serious disease and then commissioned her to heal other people by water and prayer.' The Anglican Church became interested; it wanted to make sure that she 'exercised her ministry in the framework' of Anglicanism.[6] So it sent Jacob Dlamini,[7] the Suffragan Bishop of St John's diocese in the Transkei (and no relation of the author of the present work), to investigate. Dlamini 'discovered a lack of evangelistic emphasis on conversion to Christ' in Msamariya's sermons. 'When the bishop suggested to her that she should heal in the name of Jesus, she did not agree to deviate from her practice, explaining that she had to obey strictly the details of the commission given to her by her visions. Consequently, the Anglican Church warned their members not to go to Cancele.'[8] By 1985 Msamariya's popularity had waned and the pilgrimage stopped. People had found other prophets and prophetesses to chase.

In the months before his death, Sedibe too was looking for a new religious home. He had long since abandoned the Lutheran Church of his youth. According to his brother Kaborone, 'A week before he died, his wife called and said he was drinking too much. I drove to his house and took away all his liquor.'[9] Shadrack Chiloane, one of his fellow askaris, took him to the the Zion Christian Church [ZCC]. Kaborone said that Sedibe told him: '"I want to join the church; I want to stop drinking." People could see that something was wrong with him.'[10] But Sedibe died before he could join the church.

* * *

What about the askaris still alive, who may number in the hundreds? Did they, like the man in the balaclava, disappear into the fog of history? Who were they and what are they doing now? What secrets do they hold and what hold do they have over those with whom they collaborated? To raise these questions is not to assume that somewhere out there lies an unvarnished truth or that, as the cliché has it, knowledge is power. Verne Harris and Christopher Merrett remind us that to know is not necessarily to gain mastery over the past. 'Knowledge does not equal power,' they say, 'but power cannot be exercised without it.'[11] How, then, can South Africans exercise power as citizens if they have little or no knowledge of this part of their past? These questions have no easy answers. Gregory Sibusiso Radebe says, 'Some people expect that "here's a question; here's an answer".'[12] But, as he points out, life does not work like that. Life is not a series of clear questions followed by a series of neat answers. Life is messy. But does the messiness of life mean that we should let apartheid's secrets go to the grave?

David Xiao has written, 'A secret is like a knife which severs the flow of time, leaving a scar which will sometimes masquerade as the secret itself.'[13] Xiao's point calls to mind the ease with which whispers about who might have been a collaborator are used in post-apartheid South Africa to silence political rivals; it reminds one of the manner in which rivals are delegitimised with claims that they bear scars of collaboration that render them morally suspect and politically unreliable in a democracy. In both cases, those subjected to such whispers and claims are victims of secrets that refuse to be revealed.

Instead of allowing for a full reckoning with the messy business of collaboration, South Africans have allowed the secrets of the past to gain an afterlife. Instead of the nation using the secrets of the past to come to grips with the pervasiveness of complicity, some are using these secrets to fight contemporary political battles. In the course of writing this book, I have been intrigued by the number of people who, whispering almost, told me how stunned I would be if I were to discover who the 'real' apartheid collaborators were. None of them would give me the names, supposedly hidden in plain sight. For these whisperers, it always seemed enough to them to pass on the secret without really saying who the collaborators were. It was as if they knew that the power of the secrets they were purporting to share resided, not in the content of the secrets themselves, but in the mere hint that there were secrets.

* * *

Sometime in 1994 or shortly thereafter, someone in the just-renamed South African Police Service produced a report about the whole business of askaris.[14] The top-secret report was in effect a post-mortem on the askari project. Written in point form, it opened with the question: how many askaris were there? According to the report, there were 103 South African and 14 Namibian askaris in April 1993. Of the South Africans, 86 were 'rationalised on the 30th April 1993 by the SAP.'[15] The date referred to F.W. de Klerk's decision to put a stop to Vlakplaas. The state paid out about R17.5 million in retrenchment packages to black and white Vlakplaas members.[16] The popular belief is that the operatives walked off into the sunset with big packages. Gregory Sibusiso Radebe commented, 'When the farm was shut down, we were given lump sums. I got R100,000. I used some of that money to start that thing.' Radebe was in detention at the Johannesburg Central Prison when I spoke to him in May 2013, and 'that thing' was a pyramid scheme named Miracle 2000, for which he had been convicted, fined and given a suspended sentence in the year 2000.[17]

The secret police report also suggests that the popular story about askaris and their white commanders – that they were all paid off and then went their separate ways – might not be true.[18] According to the report, of the 86 askaris 'rationalised' on 30 April

1993, 80 were appointed members of the SAP; six were 'employed by the SAP but not appointed due to medical or other reasons (e.g. AIDS, etc.)'. Thirty-one askaris were excluded from the rationalised group: 11 because they had died and 20 because they had deserted or been discharged. With regard to how many operatives were stationed at Vlakplaas, the report stated, 'The numbers fluctuated over the years. At one stage there were 144 members at Vlakplaas – Askaris, handlers and labourers (black and white). When the unit was rationalised on the 30th of April 1993, only 7 whites, 1 black handler and 12 labourers remained.' By the time the report was drawn up, six former Vlakplaas unit members were stationed in the police's Criminal Investigation Service (CIS) at the police head office in Pretoria; five were working for the CIS in the Northern Transvaal; one was working for the CIS in the Northern Cape; one was with the CIS in Pietermaritzburg; one was with the CIS on the Witwatersrand; one was stationed at the CIS in Durban; three were with the CIS in Mossel Bay; one was with the CIS in Bloemfontein; and one with the CIS in Nylstroom. The report alluded to the continuities between apartheid and post-apartheid security services. 'In the new dispensation the G.N.U. [Government of National Unity] has also started with the recruitment of askaris.' It did not elaborate.

At least two white Vlakplaas operatives, Charlie Kloppers and Willie Nortje, were working directly for the police, while three (Coetzee, Van Heerden and Geldenhuys – no first names given) were listed as 'sources'. The report continued, 'Others are in the process of recruitment or are being handled clandestinely which of course does not entirely meet with the prerequisites of transparency, responsibility and control.' The report concluded: 'Other [government] departments have also controlled askaris and most likely still do.' Although it has been 20 years since the report was drawn up, it is likely that some of these askaris remain within the police and intelligence services, as well as in other state agencies.

* * *

South Africa has yet to find a proper legal method of addressing collaboration under apartheid. The TRC flagged the issue but could not face it, locked as the commission was into a moral framework in which the story of apartheid South Africa was one of victims and perpetrators. One legal inquiry into collaboration came about in 2003, when President Thabo Mbeki appointed a commission headed by Judge Joos Hefer to probe claims that Bulelani Ngcuka, then national director of public prosecutions, was an apartheid spy. Judge Hefer concluded that there was no evidence for this allegation. 'I have not found anything, as a matter of probability, that [Ngcuka] was a pre-1994 government agent. On the contrary, the probabilities heavily favour the opposite conclusion.'[19]

However, the Hefer Commission was compromised from the beginning because Ngcuka's main accusers – Mac Maharaj, Ranjeni Munusamy and Moe Shaik – were acting out of questionable motives, rather than a desire to uncover secrets of the past. Maharaj, a senior member of the ANC who had previously served as minister of transport, was under investigation by Ngcuka's office for corruption, as was Jacob Zuma, then deputy president. To many observers, it was apparent that Maharaj and Zuma, with the help of their allies Shaik, a ministerial adviser, and Munusamy, a journalist, sought to derail the corruption investigations by calling Ngcuka's integrity and motives into question. What better way to do that than to call Ngcuka a collaborator? Referring to Shaik, Hefer pointed to his 'motive for raking up old scores'.[20] Among those being investigated for corruption were Shaik's brother Schabir, who had benefited from government contracts issued by the Department of Transport, while Maharaj, who was a friend of the Shaik brothers, was minister of transport in Nelson Mandela's government. The Hefer Commission showed that, aside from the lingering effects of South Africa's failure to deal fully with collaboration, the leaking of politically sensitive (and often false) information about individuals was driven by vendettas.

* * *

Speaking of the selective unmasking of collaborators in Hungary, Istvan Rev remarked, 'My agent only served the public good, while your agent was a morally corrupt traitor.'[21] Rev's remark calls to mind a South African story worthy of Jorge Luis Borges.

In 'Theme of the traitor and the hero', Borges tells the story of Fergus Kilpatrick, leader of an Irish revolutionary group supposedly killed by the police in 1824.[22] The story takes place in 1924, the centenary of Kilpatrick's death, and his great-grandson Ryan is writing a book about his martyred forebear. As Ryan does his research, he is struck by the fact that details of Kilpatrick's death combine many elements, from Julius Caesar's Rome to Shakespeare's *Macbeth.* Delving deeper, he discovers that the old man was in fact a traitor and that when his comrades discovered his treachery, they killed him – but made it look as if the police had done it. In fact, Ryan discovers, Kilpatrick himself authorised his execution. 'He signed his own sentence, but begged that his punishment not harm his country.'[23] His comrades went along with this because, as the narrator says, 'Ireland idolised Kilpatrick; the most tenuous suspicion of his infamy would have jeopardised the revolt'. Ryan also finds out that James Nolan, one of Kilpatrick's comrades, planned the execution: Kilpatrick was to be killed by an unknown assassin in dramatic circumstances that would 'remain engraved in the imagination of the people and would hasten the revolt'. Kilpatrick, hoping to redeem himself and serve again the revolution he had betrayed, went along with the plot.[24] Ryan discovers all this. 'After a series of hesitations, he resolves to keep his discovery silent. He publishes a book dedicated to the hero's glory; this, too, perhaps, was foreseen.'[25]

In the South African story that parallels this tale, the traitor was not killed. As the journalist and former activist Gavin Evans told it in an article of 1994 titled 'Secret histories', the traitor was Peter Mokaba, charismatic leader of the South African Youth Congress and member of the ANC underground in the Northern Transvaal in the 1980s and 1990s.[26] According to Evans, when the ANC found out that Mokaba was an apartheid agent, the ANC security department detained him in Zambia, and through interrogation, which very likely involved torture, he confessed. However, the ANC president, Oliver Tambo, 'did not want Mokaba to be held in a detention camp', and the ANC decided not to publicise Mokaba's confession 'as this would cause disillusionment among the youth'.

Evans said that incontrovertible evidence against Mokaba included a 'claim by a fellow Northern Transvaal student that Mokaba had tried to recruit him for the security police, and another by an activist who said that Mokaba had set him up to be collected at a particular spot for training by Umkhonto we Sizwe, but in fact it was the police who arrived'. Instead of acting against Mokaba, the ANC allowed him to return to South Africa, 'subject to certain conditions'. When he died in 2002, he was one of the ANC's leading lights. In 2012 the ANC government posthumously conferred on Mokaba the Order of Luthuli, one of South Africa's most prestigious awards, for his contribution to the struggle for democracy.

Who said irony was dead?

* * *

As the narrator says in Gillian Slovo's novel *Red dust*, South Africa does not offer a 'story with a beginning, a middle and its own neat ending'.[27] There is nothing neat about the history presented here. Sedibe's story is not the whole story. The experience of one man can only be understood in a wider context. Many of these stories exist in a world of shadows that has yet to be explored. There are stories that continue to refuse to be told. How might we go beyond that refusal? One way, it seems to me, is to engage honestly with the 'fatal intimacy' at the heart of human relations in South Africa.[28] It is in our persons that the secrets of the past have found a home. We must open up these archives and tell these stories.

Anticipating the mixed reception he expected for his book *Stones against the mirror*, Hugh Lewin offered the following advice: 'Well, Dear Reader, treat it as fiction. That's what I'd advise.'[29] Well, dear reader, let me tell you a story you would be best advised to treat as fictional.[30] The setting is a ritual ceremony at a family home in Katlehong. A boy has lost his favourite aunt. She just keeled over and died. She was 34, overweight, and came from a family with a history of heart disease. Years later, when the boy is an adult, he will think that the aunt's death was a straightforward case of a heart attack. But that is not how, at the moment of the aunt's passing, death is rationalised or how her family understands her death. In a (cultural) context where things happen for a reason, poor health is not reason enough to die. The aunt's death must have come from some malevolent source. The boyfriend who left the aunt for one of her friends shortly before the aunt's death – that's him. He is the cause. He must pay. An uncle of dubious occupation calls a family meeting on the day of the funeral. Only men are invited. They resolve to punish the ex-boyfriend. The boyfriend is indeed punished. But the boy, who is excused from the business of men, is not brave enough to ask the men what form the punishment took. All he knows is that the dodgy uncle took the lead.

This uncle has been known to tell people that he's a cop, yet no one can claim to have seen him in a police uniform. He is a charmer and a ladies' man. He is also a storyteller and a boaster. Once, during another ritual ceremony, the only occasions during which the boy would meet the uncle, the uncle says, '*Bengikhona*' (I was there), when the subject of Sam Ntuli's death comes up. A trade unionist and anti-apartheid civic leader, Ntuli was assassinated on 29 September 1991 outside his home in Thokoza, west of Katlehong.[31] The boy is sitting with the men, as befits the social architecture at these ritual gatherings, and he is certain he heard the uncle say: 'I was there.' But it is not his place to ask: 'What do you mean you were there? There in the vicinity or at the killing itself?' It is possible that the uncle, who lives not far from Ntuli's house, was in the neighbourhood when the assassination took place. But the boy does not say much. He stores the uncle's story in his memory bank.

Years later, the boy, now a young man keen on history, is at another family gathering when he overhears a cousin talking about the uncle. The uncle's criminal friends have been complaining about how their plots always seem to go pear-shaped when the uncle is around. The young man takes this as his cue. When he bumps into the uncle on the street one day, he confronts him. Have you ever worked for the police? When did you start? What was your rank? Have you ever spied for the police? Perhaps to call this a confrontation is an overstatement. The exchange, although it takes place on the street, is polite, friendly even. But the uncle is clearly taken aback. This is not what he was expecting from his nephew, whom he had not seen in a while. 'Ja, eish,' says the uncle. He hems. He haws. He is rushing somewhere, he says. Perhaps he and the nephew should set up an appointment for a proper chat. He goes his way.

Later that day, the young man tells his closest cousin, who also has his doubts about the uncle, about the exchange. The cousin asks: 'Why? How could you? Why do you want to know?' As the questions, more like arrows hitting a bullseye, threaten to overwhelm the young man, he is forced to confront a number of uncomfortable questions. Why indeed did he confront his uncle? What was he hoping to gain? Who wants to know? To what end?

As the young man takes these questions in his head in turn, he finds himself face to face with the notion of a legitimate secret. Can there ever be a life without secrets? Does the young man, and by extension his family, really want to know if there is a collaborator in their midst? Does the family want to know if one of their own was an informer for the apartheid police? Would knowledge of the uncle's past, if he had been an informer or agent of some sort, change the uncle's standing in the family? The young man decides, after a struggle with himself, that he does not want to know. He decides that maybe some things are not worth knowing.

There ends our fiction.

* * *

When Václav Havel became president of Czechoslovakia in 1989, someone gave him a list of individuals who had informed on him to the secret police during his days as a dissident. Havel not only lost the list the same day it was given to him, but he promptly forgot whose names were on the list. 'That simply means that I personally am inclined rather to let it go. I keep my distance from it because I'm familiar with those meat grinders and I know how they can destroy people,' Havel said years later by way of explanation.[32] It should not surprise us, perhaps, that Havel was the one to lose the list and forget its contents. He was, after all, the world's most reluctant politician. But to how many of us mere mortals is it given to forget so thoroughly, as Havel claims to have done, that the question of forgiveness does not even arise?

Should South Africans push for disclosure about collaboration? Should we be asking who, besides the askaris, collaborated with the apartheid state and in what ways? Should we be purging our public life of known and suspected collaborators? Antjie Krog asks, 'What are the invisible links between being tortured into breaking your own moral codes and later corruption, between giving up everything in the fight for freedom and eventual greed?'[33] South Africans, feeling increasingly overwhelmed by corruption and greed, and seeing the dream of liberation threaten to turn into yet another postcolonial nightmare, would do well to think seriously about this question. We would do well to consider the sources of corruption and the apparent ease with which many of yesterday's liberators have become today's looters, and to think seriously about the continuities and discontinuities between apartheid and democratic South Africa. That means thinking critically about the ways in which apartheid corruption and inefficiencies have seeped into post-1994 society and poisoned the way we lead our lives, conduct our politics and think about the future. That is also the only way we can challenge those who would have us believe that corruption is a post-apartheid phenomenon.

The legacies of the past haunt our present. We could of course deal with these legacies through lustration or 'the thick line', another of the options tried in Eastern Europe to come to terms with the effects of collaboration.[34] The idea of a 'thick line' was first suggested by Tadeusz Mazowiecki, Poland's first post-Communist prime minister, who sought to 'draw a thick line between the past and the present and to say that the only criterion for judging bureaucrats would be their competence and their loyalty to the new order'.[35] This attempt came to naught as opponents accused Mazowiecki of trying to shield criminals from a reckoning with the past. South Africa seems to have adopted the idea of the 'thick line' by default (leaving aside the issue of 'competence' for purposes of this discussion). Together with the 'sunset clause', which guaranteed public servants their jobs and pensions in return for supporting reform, South Africans seem to have let apartheid collaborators slip seamlessly into the new order.

To borrow Havel's words from a different context, 'That really means that we didn't cut out the abscess that was infecting the whole body. The abscess kept decaying and kept producing poisons. So it seems to me that the need for some kind of excision to achieve justice is fully understandable and natural.'[36] But Havel warned against using the 'excision' as an excuse for 'unlawful revenge' and the hounding of individuals. He counselled against resorting to the denunciatory politics that marked authoritarianism.

The struggle against apartheid was, above all, a struggle for justice. That means that, even if South Africans do agree to have a frank conversation about collaboration and complicity under apartheid, that conversation can only be meaningful if it is guided by the principle of justice. Knowing who the collaborators were and where the askaris are today need not mean the violation of individual rights and human dignity.

I have tried to treat Sedibe with dignity, to tell his story as part of a series of stories about collaboration and complicity under apartheid. By telling his story as just one among many, I hope I have shown those with similar stories to tell that it can be done.

The life of Glory Sedibe highlights something of the 'fatal intimacy' at the heart of human relations. To say that apartheid generated an unwanted intimacy between individuals, and to challenge the false claim that the struggle against apartheid was simply a racial war, is not to say that 'race' did not matter or that race thinking had no salience. Race obviously mattered a great deal. But it would be wrong to think that race determined the allegiances and loyalties of individuals in any simplistic way. Race might have been handy in the work of askaris, but far more potent was the personal and social intimacy that askaris could call on and generate in order to carry out their missions.

It was intimacy (his love of his brother) that drew Sedibe into the struggle against apartheid; it was intimacy (his familiarity with the ANC) that made Sedibe an effective askari; it was intimacy (his closeness to Military Intelligence operatives) that made Sedibe vulnerable to elimination once he had reached his sell-by date. True, Sedibe's is but one story. But it complicates how we think about apartheid and its legacies, and reminds us of the stories that still refuse to be told. As a nation, we would do well to examine the taboos, the secrets and the disavowals at the core of our collective memories.

Notes

Introduction

1 Glenn Moss, 'The strange saga of Mr X1', *Work in Progress*, 54 (June–July 1988), 13–17.

2 *State* vs *Maseko and two others*, HGH CC319/87, vols. 43–53, National Archives, Pretoria.

3 Conny Braam, *Operation Vula* (Johannesburg: Jacana Media, 2004), 101.

4 Njabulo Ndebele, Foreword, in Megan Jones and Jacob Dlamini (eds.), *Categories of persons: Rethinking ourselves and others* (Johannesburg: Picador Africa, 2013).

5 My thinking on this is inspired by Paul Gilroy's work, notably his book *Against race: Imagining political culture beyond the color line* (Cambridge: Harvard University Press, 2000).

6 Eugene de Kock, personal interview, 24 February 2013.

7 I borrow the notion of 'archival slivers' from Verne Harris, 'The archival sliver: Power, memory, and archives', *Archival Science*, 2 (2002).

8 Terry Bell and Dumisa Ntsebeza, *Unfinished business: South Africa, apartheid and truth* (London: Verso, 2003), 9.

9 Ibid.

10 Achille Mbembe, 'The power of the archive and its limits', in Carolyn Hamilton, Verne Harris, Jane Taylor, Michele Pickover, Graeme Reid and Razia Saleh (eds), *Refiguring the archive* (Boston: Kluwer Academic Publishers, 2002), 23.

11 Allan Sekula, 'The body and the archive', *October*, 39 (Winter 1986), 17.

12 Lalla, personal interview, 26 January 2014.

13 See, for a sample, journalist Zanele Vutela's article 'Notorious askari "September" dies', in *City Press*, 3 April 1995; Jacques Pauw, *In the heart of the whore: The story of apartheid's death squads* (Halfway House: Southern Book Publishers, 1991), 86; Jacques Pauw, *Into the heart of darkness: Confessions of apartheid's assassins* (Johannesburg: Jonathan Ball, 1997), 73; Ronnie Kasrils, *Armed and dangerous: From undercover struggle to freedom* (Johannesburg: Jonathan Ball, 1998), 182; and Elias Masilela, *Number 43 Trelawney Park: KwaMagogo* (Claremont: David Philip, 2007), 152.

14 Masilela's *Number 43 Trelawney Park*. On page 124, Masilela says our subject died in April 1994; on page 151, he says the subject died in December 1993.

15 Moss, 'The strange saga of Mr X1'.
16 Testimony in *State* vs *Maseko and two others*, HGH CC 319/87.
17 Istvan Rev, 'The man in the white raincoat', in Oksana Sarkisova and Peter Apor (eds), *Past for the eyes: East European representations of communism in cinema and museums after 1989* (Budapest: Central University Press, 2008), 30.
18 Ibid., 29.
19 Jean-Paul Sartre, 'Paris under the occupation', in *The aftermath of war* (New York: Seagull Books, 2008), 14.
20 Gillian Slovo, *Red dust* (London: Virago Press, 2000), 257.
21 Mark Sanders, *Complicities: The intellectual and apartheid* (Durham: Duke University Press, 2002), 1.
22 Tina Rosenberg, *The haunted land: Facing Europe's ghosts after communism* (New York: Vintage Books, 1996), 5.
23 Jacklyn Cock, 'The role of violence in current state security strategies', in Mark Swilling (ed.), *Views on the South African state* (Pretoria: HSRC, 1990), 94.
24 Hermann Giliomee, *The Afrikaners: Biography of a people* (Cape Town: Tafelberg, 2003), 666.
25 Ibid., 625.
26 Ibid., 624.
27 Ibid., 652.
28 Albert Grundlingh, *The dynamics of treason: Boer collaboration in the South African War of 1899–1902* (Pretoria: Protea Book House, 2006), 298.
29 Raymond Suttner, *The ANC underground in South Africa, 1950–1976* (Johannesburg: Jacana Media, 2008), 103.
30 Sartre, 'Paris under the occupation', 32.
31 Ibid., 33.
32 Rosenberg, *The haunted land*, 400.
33 Ibid., 399.
34 Ibid.
35 Ibid.
36 Ibid.
37 Ibid.
38 Julia Hornberger, *Policing and human rights: The meaning of violence and justice in the everyday policing of Johannesburg* (New York: Routledge, 2011), 33.
39 Ibid., 33.
40 Nofomela, personal interview, Soshanguve, January 2014.
41 TRC Amnesty Committee hearing into the abduction of Glory Sedibe, Pretoria, February 2000.
42 Mary Douglas, *Purity and danger* (London: Routledge and Kegan Paul, 1966), 36–165.
43 Sharika Thiranagama and Tobias Kelly (eds), *Traitors: Suspicion, intimacy, and the ethics of state-building* (Philadelphia: University of Pennsylvania Press, 2010), 11.
44 Wally Serote, *Revelations* (Johannesburg: Jacana Media, 2010), 217.
45 ANC pamphlet, 'MK strikes against impimpis' (n.d.).

46 *Sechaba* (December 1986).
47 Giliomee, *The Afrikaners*, 666.
48 Keith Breckenridge, 'Verwoerd's bureau of proof: Total information in the making of apartheid', *History Workshop Journal*, 59 (Spring 2005), 83–108.
49 Jacobo Timerman, *Prisoner without a name, cell without a number* (New York: Knopf, 1981), 108–9.
50 Giliomee, *The Afrikaners*, 625.
51 Pauw, *In the heart of the whore*, 64.
52 The story is recounted in Pieter Wolvaardt's memoirs *A diplomat's story: Apartheid and beyond* (Alberton: Galago Books, 2005), 131.
53 TRC's Amnesty Committee, case no. AC/2001/094.
54 Deborah Posel, 'The TRC report: What kind of history? What kind of truth?' in Deborah Posel and Graeme Simpson (eds), *Commissioning the past: Understanding South Africa's Truth and Reconciliation Commission* (Johannesburg: Wits University Press, 2002), 167–8.
55 Vusi Pikoli and Mandy Wiener, *My second initiation: The memoir of Vusi Pikoli* (Johannesburg: Picador Africa, 2013), 122.
56 Antjie Krog, *Conditional tense: Memory and vocabulary after the South African Truth and Reconciliation Commission* (New York: Seagull Books, 2013), 30.
57 Rorty is quoted in Peter Wagner, *Modernity: Understanding the present* (Cambridge: Polity, 2012), 120–1. Although a consistent supporter of apartheid, Buckley made his case in an editorial titled 'What would you do if you were they?' *National Review*, 24 October 1986, quoted in Thomas J. Redden Jnr's article 'The US Comprehensive Anti-apartheid Act of 1986: Anti-apartheid or anti-African National Congress?', *African Affairs*, 87, 349 (October 1988), 595–605.
58 Patrick Flanery, *Absolution* (New York: Riverhead Books, 2012), 161.

Chapter 1

1 Albert Camus, *The fastidious assassins* (London: Penguin, 2008), 90.
2 Kaborone KK Sedibe, personal interview, Edenvale, 27 February 2013.
3 We must resist the temptation to call Ephraim Sedibe 'elite'. As Peter Limb shows, 'the mere accretion of literacy [did] not guarantee membership of a privileged elite' in colonial South Africa. In fact, Limb says, some African primary teachers earned less than factory workers. See Peter Limb, *The ANC's early years: Nation, class and place in South Africa before 1940* (Pretoria: Unisa Press, 2010), 12.
4 The claim that Ephraim quit teaching in 1949 comes from Kaborone Sedibe's evidence in the BPC–SASO Trial in 1976. See KK Sedibe's testimony, vols. 100 and 101, Reel 6, Wits Historical Papers, 5871. However, the claim is contradicted by David Mokwena, who says Ephraim Sedibe taught him in the 1950s. Personal interview with David Mokwena, Penge, February 2013.
5 These were not the only names Sedibe used.
6 Masilela, *Number 43 Trelawney Park*, 121.
7 Ebrahim Ebrahim, telephonic interview, 2 May 2013.

8 George Nene, personal interview, Pretoria, January 2013.
9 Sam Mtileni, telephonic interview, 16 January 2014.
10 Humphrey Mkhwanazi, personal interview, Johannesburg, 17 May 2013.
11 Eugene de Kock, personal interview and email correspondence, 24 February 2013.
12 *State* vs *Mandla Acton Maseko, Simon Dladla and Ebrahim Ismail Ebrahim*, HGH CC 319/87.
13 Elzbieta Matynia (ed.), *An uncanny era: Conversations between Václav Havel and Adam Michnik* (New Haven: Yale University Press, 2014), 119.
14 KK Sedibe, personal interview, Edenvale, 2014.
15 KK Sedibe, vols. 100 and 101, reel 6, Wits Historical Papers, 5871.
16 Ibid., 5846.
17 Ibid., 5846–7.
18 Ibid., 5847.
19 KK Sedibe, Plea, reel 10, Wits Historical Papers.
20 Luisa Passerini, *Autobiography of a generation: Italy, 1968* (Middletown: Wesleyan University Press, 1996), 81.
21 KK Sedibe, Plea, reel 10, Wits Historical Papers.
22 Mr X1's testimony, *State* vs *Maseko, Dladla and Ebrahim*, HGH CC 319/87, 2331.
23 KK Sedibe, personal interview, Edenvale, 27 February 2013.
24 Kirsten Weld, *Paper cadavers: The archives of dictatorship in Guatemala* (Durham: Duke University Press, 2014), 233.
25 Confidential source.
26 Weld, *Paper cadavers*, 6.
27 Ibid., 6.
28 Thula Simpson, '"The bay and the ocean": A history of the ANC in Swaziland: 1960–1979', *African Historical Review*, 41, 1 (2009), 90. Simpson's essay offers a vivid description of how an MK recruit like Sedibe would have travelled from South Africa to Swaziland to Mozambique and, from there, to Angola.
29 ANC, Second submission to the TRC, www.anc.org.za.
30 David Bunn, 'The museum outdoors: Heritage, cattle, and the permeable borders in the southwestern Kruger National Park', in Ivan Karp, Corinne A. Kratz, Lynn Szwaja and Tomas Ybarra-Frausto (eds), *Museum frictions: Public cultures, global transformations* (Durham: Duke University Press, 2006), 374.
31 *State* vs *Maseko, Dladla and Ebrahim*, HGH CC 319/87, 2339.
32 Mzwakhe Ndlela, *For the fallen: Honouring the unsung heroes and heroines of the liberation struggle* (Johannesburg: KMM Review Publishing, 2013), 8.
33 Moss, 'The strange saga of Mr X1', 13–17.
34 Ebrahim Ebrahim profile in Goolam Vahed (ed.), *Muslim portraits: The anti-apartheid struggle* (Durban: Madiba Publishers, 2012), 110.
35 Simpson, '"The bay and the ocean"', 90–117.
36 Ibid., 104–10.
37 Ibid., 107.
38 James Ngculu, *The honour to serve: Recollections of an Umkhonto soldier* (Claremont: David Philip, 2009), 79–90.

39 Sello letter to AAM in Anti-Apartheid Movement Archives, Rhodes Library, Oxford University, MSS AAM 922.
40 See ANC's Second submission to the TRC, www.anc.org.za, as well as, for example, Ndlela's *For the fallen*, Ngculu's *The honour to serve*, and Peter Harris's *In a different time: The inside story of the Delmas Four* (Johannesburg: Umuzi, 2008). For a critical study of ANC camp life in Angola, see Paul Trewhela's *Inside Quatro: Uncovering the exile history of the ANC and Swapo* (Johannesburg: Jacana Media, 2009). As Trewhela makes clear, the ANC camps in Angola were also places of tremendous brutality and violence.
41 Sam Mtileni, telephonic interview, 16 January 2014.
42 Harris, *In a different time*, 71.
43 James Ngculu, *The honour to serve*, 90.
44 Shubin, 'Comrade Mzwai', in Arianna Lissoni, Jon Soske, Natasha Erlank, Noor Nieftagodien and Omar Badsha (eds), *One hundred years of the ANC: Debating liberation histories today* (Johannesburg: Wits University Press, 2012), 264.
45 Ngculu, *The honour to serve*, 90.
46 Ray Lalla, personal interview, Pretoria, 14 March 2013.
47 Michael Wolfers, 'Background to the Nkomati Accord', in Ben Turok (ed.), *Witness from the frontline* (London: Institute for African Alternatives, 1988), 48–9.
48 Ibid., 49.
49 Ibid.
50 Ngculu, *The honour to serve*, 79.
51 De Kock, personal interview, Pretoria, 24 February 2013.
52 Pauw, *Into the heart of darkness*, 69.
53 Maria da Conceição, interview with Nadja Manghezi, '"They were part of us and we were part of them": The ANC in Mozambique' (online, n.d.), 189.
54 Humphrey Mkhwanazi, personal interview, Johannesburg, 17 May 2013.
55 Kaborone Sedibe, personal interview, Edenvale, 27 February 2013.
56 Ibid.
57 Ebrahim Ebrahim, telephonic interview, 2 May 2014.
58 Kaborone Sedibe, personal interview, Edenvale, 27 February 2013.
59 Delilah Rekisa (not her real name), personal interview, Pretoria, 24 January 2014. See also Zanele Vutela, 'Notorious askari "September" dies', *City Press*, 3 April 1994.
60 Kaborone Sedibe, personal interview, Edenvale, 27 February 2013; Delilah Rekisa, personal interview, Pretoria, 24 January 2014.
61 De Kock, personal interview, Pretoria, 24 February 2013.

Chapter 2

1 The exchange took place in a political case named *State* vs *Dudu Buthelezi and eleven others*. The trial began in the Pietermaritzburg Supreme Court on 3 November 1986. The 11 accused were students at the University of Natal Medical School and the University of Durban-Westville. The students

were charged with terrorism. Two of the accused, Phumezo Nxiweni and Sipho Bhila, were acquitted for lack of evidence. The Security Branch killed Nxiweni in 'revenge'.

2 For the record, Sedibe was not South Africa's first Mr X. Bruno Mtolo, a founder member of MK who defected to the Security Branch in 1963, served as Mr X in the Rivonia Trial against Nelson Mandela and others. Mtolo was followed on the stand by Mr Y (real name Cyril Davids) and Mr Z (real name Patrick Mthembu), both defectors.

3 Paddy Hillyard and Jane Percy-Smith, 'Converting terrorists: The use of supergrasses in Northern Ireland', *Journal of Law and Society*, 11, 3 (Winter 1984), 336.

4 Ibid., 338.

5 Bruno Mtolo, *Umkhonto we Sizwe: The road to the left* (Durban: Drakensberg Press, 1966), 130.

6 Hillyard and Percy-Smith, 'Converting terrorists', 336 and 340–1.

7 Ibid., 341.

8 Ibid.

9 Personal communication, May 2014.

10 Stephen Ellis, 'The historical significance of South Africa's Third Force', *Journal of Southern African Studies*, 24, 2 (June 1998), 268.

11 The different figures for askaris come from, one, a secret report obtained from a confidential source, as well as Ellis, 'The historical significance of South Africa's Third Force', 269, and Kevin O'Brien, *The South African Intelligence Services: From apartheid to democracy, 1948–2005* (London: Routledge, 2011), 187.

12 See, among others, Howard Barrell's 'The turn to the masses: The African National Congress' Strategic Review of 1978–79', *Journal of Southern African Studies*, 18, 1, 75 (March 1992); Hugh Macmillan's *The Lusaka years: The ANC in exile in Zambia, 1963–1994* (Johannesburg: Jacana Media, 2013), and Stephen Ellis's *External mission: The ANC in exile, 1960–1990* (Johannesburg: Jonathan Ball, 2012), for information (or lack thereof) about the number of ANC members in exile.

13 Even though Vlakplaas itself began life as the base of police death squads in 1979, the South African police had been 'turning' insurgents into counterinsurgents since the 1960s. See, for example, Madeleine Fullard's essay, 'State repression in the 1960s', in SADET (ed.), *The road to democracy in South Africa*, vol. 1 (1960–1970) (Cape Town: Zebra Press, 2004), 341–91.

14 Dirk Coetzee, *Hit squads: Testimony of a South African security policeman: The full story*, unpublished memoir, Wits Historical Papers, A2790F.

15 Mfalapitsa's testimony to TRC Amnesty Committee hearing into Cosas Four case, 4 May 1999, Johannesburg, available online.

16 Jacques Pauw, *In the heart of the whore*, 35.

17 *TRC Final Report*, vol. 2, chapter 1, 30.

18 *TRC Final Report*, vol. 6, chapter 1, section 3, 217.

19 Twala's state witness testimony in *State* vs *Mncube and Nondula*, HGH CC 449/87, vol. 9, 862.

20 Nofomela testimony to Harms Commission of Inquiry, Wits Historical Papers.
21 Ibid.
22 *TRC Final Report*, vol. 6, chapter 1, section 3, 218.
23 Judas Mpho Tladi (not his real name), conversation, Letlhabile, 23 January 2014.
24 I tell the story of the protests in *Native nostalgia* (Johannesburg: Jacana Media, 2009) and, with colleagues, in *The smoke that calls: Insurgent citizenship, collective violence and a struggle for a place in the new South Africa* (Johannesburg: SWOP, 2011).
25 De Kock, personal interview, Pretoria, 24 February 2013.
26 Delilah Rekisa (not her real name), personal interview, Pretoria, 24 January 2014.
27 Gregory Sibusiso Radebe, email exchange, 9 May 2013.
28 Nofomela, personal interview, Soshanguve, 18 January 2014.
29 Confidential source, email exchange, 7–8 March 2014.
30 Ibid.
31 Almond Nofomela, personal interview, 18 January 2014.
32 Thabo Shenge Luthuli, *The spilling of blood* (Cape Town: Gariep Publishing, 1999), 249.
33 Gregory Sibusiso Radebe, personal interview, Johannesburg, 8 May 2013.
34 Mfalapitsa's testimony in TRC Amnesty Committee hearing into the case of the Cosas Four, 4 May 1999.
35 Ibid.
36 Oscar Linda Moni's testimony in TRC Amnesty Committee hearing into the matter of Cassius Nceba, Caswell Khumalo and Richard Ngwenya, Johannesburg, 28 October 1999.
37 Ibid.
38 Eugene de Kock with Jeremy Gordin, *A long night's damage: Working for the apartheid state* (Johannesburg: Contra Press, 1998), 96.
39 Ibid., 290.
40 Johan van der Merwe, *Trou tot die dood toe: Die Suid-Afrikaanse Polisiemag* (Pretoria: Praag, 2010), 316.
41 *TRC Final Report*, vol. 6, chapter 1, section 3, 218.
42 *TRC Final Report*, vol. 2, chapter 1, 132.
43 De Kock's testimony during TRC Amnesty Committee hearing into the killing of Goodwill Sikhakhane, 20 September 1999.
44 *TRC Final Report*, vol. 6, chapter 1, section 3, 218.
45 De Kock and Gordin, *A long night's damage*, 103.
46 Gregory Sibusiso Radebe, personal interview, Johannesburg, 8 May 2013.
47 A Vlakplaas document in my possession lists the askaris' pager numbers. Confidential source.
48 De Kock offered a useful explanation of how askaris worked during his testimony in the TRC's Amnesty Committee hearings into Sedibe's abduction, Pretoria, February 2000.
49 Mfalapitsa's evidence during TRC Amnesty Committee hearing, 4 May 1999.
50 Gregory Sibusiso Radebe, personal interview, Johannesburg, 8 May 2013.

51 David Beresford gives a moving account of this story in *Truth is a strange fruit: A personal journey through the apartheid war* (Johannesburg: Jacana Media, 2010), 284.
52 David Beresford tells of Skhosana's life and murder in *Truth is a strange fruit.*
53 Mbelo gives details of the operation in his amnesty application for his role in the case. See his application, AM3785/96, available online.
54 The details of these incidents are recorded in the TRC's *Final Report.*
55 Gregory Sibusiso Radebe, personal interview, Johannesburg, 8 May 2013.
56 Ndlela, *For the fallen*, 135.
57 Antjie Krog, *Country of my skull: Guilt, sorrow, and the limits of forgiveness in the new South Africa* (New York: Three Rivers Press, 1998), 232.
58 Confidential source.
59 Nicky Rousseau, 'The farm, the river and the picnic spot: Topographies of terror', *African Studies,* 68, 3 (December 2009), 361.
60 Ibid., 361–2.
61 Gregory Sibusiso Radebe, personal interview, Johannesburg, 8 May 2013.
62 The above details come from a report written by the Missing Persons Task Team.
63 See De Kock's testimony to TRC Amnesty Committee hearing into Sedibe's abduction, February 2000.
64 Gregory Sibusiso Radebe, personal interview, Johannesburg, 8 May 2013.
65 Ibid.
66 Personal communication, May 2013.
67 De Kock's testimony to TRC Amnesty Committee hearing into Sedibe's abduction, February 2000, 34.
68 Gregory Sibusiso Radebe, personal interview, Johannesburg, 8 May 2013.
69 Bernard Malope, personal interview, Matibidi, January 2013.
70 Mpho Tladi, conversation, Letlhabile, 23 January 2014.
71 Letlapa Mphahlele, *Child of this soil: My life as a freedom fighter* (Cape Town: Kwela Books, 2002), 79.
72 Gregory Sibusiso Radebe, personal interview, Johannesburg, 8 May 2013.
73 'Spy scare sequel', *Times of Swaziland*, 21 July 1987.
74 *New Nation*, 30 July – 5 August 1987.
75 Barry Gilder, personal interview, Pretoria, 20 February 2013.

Chapter 3

1 Rousseau, 'The farm, the river and the picnic spot', 362.
2 See Pauw's *In the heart of the whore*, 47, and Phumla Gobodo-Madikizela's *A human being died that night: A South African story of forgiveness* (Boston: Houghton Mifflin, 2003), 104, for descriptions of Vlakplaas.
3 See Johan van der Merwe's *Trou tot die dood toe*, 314.
4 Ellis, 'The historical significance of South Africa's Third Force', 267.
5 Van der Merwe, *Trou tot die dood toe*, 314–15.
6 Pauw, *In the heart of the whore*, 47.
7 Ibid., 48.

8 Ibid., 47.
9 Coetzee, *Hit squads*, 73.
10 Pauw, *In the heart of the whore*, 50.
11 See Julia Hornberger's *Policing and human rights*, 22–37; Anita Gossman's essay 'The South African military and counterinsurgency: An overview', in Deane-Peter Baker and Evert Jordaan (eds), *South Africa and contemporary counterinsurgency: Roots, practices, prospects* (Claremont: UCT Press, 2010), 86–99.
12 See South African Police (SAP) booklet celebrating 70 years of the SAP (Pretoria: Government Printers, n.d.).
13 Peter Goodwin, 'If only Smith had shown some imagination', *The Guardian*, 25 November 2007.
14 Ibid.
15 Michael Morris, *Terrorism: The first full account in detail of terrorism and insurgency in southern Africa* (Cape Town: Howard Timmins, 1971), 126.
16 See Caroline Elkins's *Imperial reckoning: The untold story of Britain's gulag in Kenya* (New York: Henry Holt, 2005) and David Anderson's *Histories of the hanged: The dirty war in Kenya and the end of empire* (New York: W.W. Norton, 2005) for excellent accounts of how the British used 'pseudo-gangs', what we would call askaris, to destroy the Mau Mau.
17 Hugh Macmillan offers an excellent account of the campaigns in *The Lusaka years*.
18 Van den Bergh, quoted in Morris, *Terrorism*, 175. Constand Viljoen, a general in the South African Defence Force who had wanted to send the army and not the police into Rhodesia, said the following about South Africa's deployments in Rhodesia: 'I wanted to give my people the experience of fighting that kind of war because we all knew it was going to come South Africa's way.' 'I believe it was because of their involvement in Rhodesia that the police became a type of militia using crude methods not within the principles of the Geneva Convention or the principles of a just war.' See Hilton Hamann, *Days of the generals: The untold story of South Africa's apartheid-era military generals* (Cape Town: Zebra Press, 2001), 7–9.
19 Kevin O'Brien, 'Counter-intelligence for counter-revolutionary warfare: The South African Police Security Branch, 1979–1990', *Intelligence and National Security*, 16, 3 (2001), 40.
20 Mark Phillips, 'The nuts and bolts of military power: The structure of the SADF', in Jacklyn Cock and Laurie Nathan (eds.), *War and society: The militarisation of South Africa* (Cape Town: David Philip, 1989), 27.
21 De Kock, personal interview, Pretoria, 24 February 2013.
22 De Kock and Gordin, *A long night's damage*, 96.
23 *TRC Final Report*, vol. 2, chapter 1, 5.
24 De Kock and Gordin, *A long night's damage*, 96.
25 Morris, *Terrorism*, 124, 125, 202.
26 O'Brien, 'Counter-intelligence for counter-revolutionary warfare', 37.
27 Gregory Sibusiso Radebe, personal interview, Johannesburg, 8 May 2013.
28 Chiara Lepora and Robert E. Goodin, *On complicity and compromise* (Oxford: Oxford University Press, 2013), 43.

29 Ibid.
30 Ibid.
31 Ibid.
32 The reconstruction of the events detailed in this chapter is based on personal interviews with two of the participants, Almond Nofomela and Eugene de Kock. I interviewed De Kock in February 2013, and spoke to Nofomela over several days in January 2014. In addition to these interviews, I have also relied on three primary sources. The first is Almond Nofomela's affidavit to the Harms Commission of Inquiry 'into certain murders' in February 1990. The affidavit is part of the Independent Board of Inquiry Collection at Wits University's Historical Papers archives, AG2543. The second source is the court records of the treason trial *State* vs *Maseko and two others*, held at the National Archives in Pretoria, HGH CC319/87, vols. 43–53. The third source is the record of a special three-day hearing by the TRC's Amnesty Committee into the abduction of Glory Lefoshie Sedibe/Comrade September from Swaziland in August 1986. The hearing took place in Pretoria on 14, 15 and 16 February 2000. The committee's decision, delivered on 16 March 2001, is numbered AC/2001/094. The transcripts from the Amnesty Committee's hearing come in three batches. The batch from the first day numbers 45 pages, 82 pages for the second day, and 37 pages for the third day. I have retained these page lengths to indicate from which batches the quotes used come.
33 In fact, Christo Deetlefs was already in Swaziland waiting for his seven colleagues. The seven drove to Swaziland, rendezvoused with Deetlefs at a hotel for a final briefing and planning session, and then drove from there to the prison for the attack. See the men's testimonies to the Amnesty Committee hearing into Sedibe's abduction.
34 See, for example, report of Phumi Nxumalo's arrest and court appearance in *Times of Swaziland*, 4 December 1986.
35 See *TRC Final Report*, vol. 2, chapter 2, 129.
36 The ruse worked. Years later, the ANC leader Mathews Phosa told Christo Deetlefs, a former security police officer, that the ANC believed initially that its operatives had sprung Sedibe from prison. See Deetlefs's testimony to the Amnesty Committee hearing into Sedibe's abduction, 14 February 2000, 10 of 45. To show just how confused the ANC was by the abduction, an ANC spokesman told the *Swazi News*, 16 August 1986: 'The ANC does not usually free its men like that in independent countries. What we usually do is talk to the authorities responsible or make it official if we want any of our men held by the police to be freed.'
37 Thula Simpson and Elias Masilela provide details of the role of Swaziland in the struggle against apartheid. See Simpson's '"The bay and the ocean"', 90–117, and Masilela's *Number 43 Trelawney Park*.
38 Robert M. Price, *The apartheid state in crisis: Political transformation in South Africa, 1975–1990* (Oxford: Oxford University Press, 1991), 92.
39 Gobodo-Madikizela, *A human being died that night*, 18.
40 Breyten Breytenbach, *The true confessions of an albino terrorist* (Emmarentia: Taurus, 1984), 27–8.
41 Personal interview with Eugene de Kock, Pretoria, 24 February 2013.

42 Pauw, *Into the heart of darkness*, 72.
43 Confidential source.
44 Barry Gilder confirmed this during a personal interview in Pretoria, 20 February 2013.
45 Nofomela's affidavit is in the Independent Board of Inquiry Collection at Wits University's Historical Papers archives, AG2543, 172.
46 Veena Das, *Life and words: Violence and the descent into the ordinary* (Berkeley: University of California Press, 2007), 7.
47 Masilela, *Number 43 Trelawney Park*, 151. Philipos Mamabolo Nwedamutswu, Masilela's source for this claim, told me the same thing through intermediaries in February 2014.
48 Elaine Scarry, *The body in pain: The making and unmaking of the world* (New York: Oxford University Press, 1985), 35.
49 Ibid., 28.
50 Ibid., 28–9.
51 Ibid., 35.
52 Ibid.
53 Whitehead, personal interview, Midrand, 20 February 2013.
54 Masilela, *Number 43 Trelawney Park*, 152.
55 Alfred W. McCoy, *A question of torture: CIA interrogation from the Cold War to the war on terror* (New York: Metropolitan Books, 2006), 80.
56 Amnesty Committee hearings, De Kock's testimony into Glory Sedibe's abduction, 29 of 82.
57 Amnesty Committee hearings, Pienaar's testimony into Glory Sedibe's abduction, 32 of 45.
58 Amnesty Committee hearings, De Kock's testimony into Glory Sedibe's abduction, 29 of 82.
59 Ibid., 30 of 82.
60 Amnesty Committee hearings, Fourie's testimony into Glory Sedibe's abduction, 7 of 37.
61 Ibid., 2 of 37.
62 Amnesty Committee hearings, De Kock's testimony into Glory Sedibe's abduction, 30 of 82.
63 Ibid., 30 and 31 of 82.
64 Amnesty Committee hearings, Deetlefs's testimony into Glory Sedibe's abduction, 9 of 45.
65 Amnesty Committee hearings, Visser's testimony into Glory Sedibe's abduction, 21 of 82.
66 Whitehead, personal interview, Midrand, 20 February 2013.
67 Nofomela, personal interview, Soshanguve, 18 January 2014.
68 Nyanda, quoted by Zanele Vutela in *City Press*, 3 April 1994.
69 *TRC Final Report*, vol. 2, chapter 1, 28.
70 Peter Polack, *The last hot battle of the Cold War: South Africa vs Cuba in the Angolan civil war* (Havertown, PA: Casemate, 2013), 47 and 57.
71 *TRC Final Report*, vol. 2, chapter 1, 28.
72 Iain Guest, *Behind the disappearances: Argentina's dirty war against human rights and the United Nations* (Philadelphia: University of Pennsylvania Press, 1990), 229.

73 Leigh A. Payne, *Unsettling accounts: Neither truth nor reconciliation in confessions of state violence* (Durham: Duke University Press, 2008).
74 Wolvaardt, *A diplomat's story*, 153–5.
75 Nofomela, personal interviews, Soshanguve, 18 and 20 January 2014.
76 Scarry, *The body in pain*, 3.
77 Leigh A. Payne, 'Collaborators and the politics of memory in Chile', *Human Rights Review* (April–June 2001), 14.
78 Stephen Ellis and Tsepo Sechaba, *Comrades against apartheid: The ANC and the South African Communist Party in exile* (Bloomington: Indiana University Press, 1992), 168.
79 O'Brien, 'Counter-intelligence for counter-revolutionary warfare', 50.
80 Vladimir Shubin, *ANC: A view from Moscow* (Bellville: Mayibuye Books, 1999), 249.
81 Ebrahim Ebrahim, telephonic interview, 2 May 2014.
82 See Don Foster, Dennis Davis and Diane Sandler, *Detention and torture in South Africa: Psychological, legal and historical studies* (Cape Town: David Philip, 1987) for an excellent comparative study of apartheid South Africa's ranking in the world of torture.
83 The Directorate Security Legislation file was a document opened as a matter of course by a directorate within the Department of Justice on any detainee or political prisoner detained or arrested under any of South Africa's security laws.
84 The material for this section comes from the declassified portions of Sedibe's Directorate of Security Legislation file, no. 2/3/2/7992. The material is available upon request from the National Archives in Pretoria.
85 Foster, Davis and Sandler, *Detention and torture in South Africa*, 36.
86 Lawrence Baxter, 'Section 29 of the Internal Security Act and the rule of law', *Reality,* 17, 6 (1985), 4–7.
87 Ibid.
88 Ibid.
89 Claim made on his wife's behalf by the lawyer Percy Makgotshe Leopeng on 14 February 2000 at Amnesty Committee hearing into Sedibe's abduction, 20 of 45.
90 Amnesty Committee hearings, De Kock's testimony into Glory Sedibe's abduction, 46 of 82.

Chapter 4

1 Nadine Gordimer, *The late bourgeois world* (Harmondsworth: Penguin, 1983), 80.
2 Kaborone Sedibe, personal interview, Edenvale, 27 February 2013.
3 Nofomela, personal interview, Soshanguve, 18 January 2014; testimony given in *State* vs *Maseko, Dladla and Ebrahim*, HGH CC 319/87.
4 Kaborone Sedibe, personal interview, Edenvale, 27 February 2013.
5 Ibid.
6 Ibid.
7 Confidential source. H referred to Harbour, which was one of the ANC's secret codes for Mozambique; Bay referred to Swaziland; while Ocean

referred to South Africa. However, as Thula Simpson points out, these were just some of the many codes used by the ANC in exile. See Simpson's '"The bay and the ocean"', 90–117.

8 Manghezi, '"They were part of us and we were part of them", 188.
9 Ibid.
10 Ibid.
11 Ray Lalla, personal interview, 14 March 2013.
12 Manghezi, '"They were part of us and we were part of them"', 187.
13 De Kock, personal interview, February 2013.
14 Manghezi, '"They were part of us and we were part of them"', 187.
15 Ibid., 188.
16 Gregory Sibusiso Radebe, personal interview, May 2013.
17 Amnesty Committee hearings, Pienaar's testimony into Glory Sedibe's abduction, 34 of 45.
18 Manghezi, '"They were part of us and we were part of them"', 188.
19 Amnesty Committee hearings, De Kock's testimony into Glory Sedibe's abduction, 33 of 82.
20 Ibid., 38 of 82, and personal interview with De Kock, Pretoria, 24 February 2013.
21 Manghezi, '"They were part of us and we were part of them"', 188.
22 Amnesty Committee hearings, Pienaar's testimony into Glory Sedibe's abduction, 34 of 45.
23 Amnesty Committee hearings, De Kock's testimony into Glory Sedibe's abduction, 41 of 82.
24 Confidential source.
25 Ibid.
26 Ibid.
27 Mr X1's testimony, *State* vs *Maseko and two others*, HGH CC319/87.
28 Ebrahim Ebrahim, telephonic interview, 2 May 2014.
29 *TRC Final Report*, vol. 2, chapter 2, and vol. 6, chapter 2.
30 *KUBARK counter-intelligence interrogation manual*, July 1963. I am grateful to the National Security Archive in Washington DC for granting me access to its holdings, which include the KUBARK manual as well as its 1983 update.
31 Ebrahim Ebrahim, telephonic interview, 2 May 2013.
32 Ibid.
33 See *State* vs *Sheila Mathabe Nyanda*, 1989 in Wits University's Historical Papers, AK2377.
34 Ibid.
35 Mr X1's testimony, *State* vs *Maseko and two others*, HGH CC319/87.
36 Braam, *Operation Vula*, 65.
37 Confidential source.
38 Whitehead, personal interview, Midrand, 20 February 2013.
39 Nyanda, quoted by Zanele Vutela in *City Press*, 3 April 1994.
40 Kasrils, *Armed and dangerous*, 182.
41 Masilela, *Number 43 Trelawney Park*, 122.
42 Ibid., 121.
43 Ibid., 122.

44 Barry Gilder, personal interview, Pretoria, 20 February 2013.
45 Van der Merwe, *Trou tot die dood toe*, 332.
46 Ibid.
47 Amnesty Committee hearings, De Kock's testimony into Glory Sedibe's abduction, 33, 34 and 35 of 82.
48 Ibid., 33 of 82.
49 Macmillan made the point during a talk I gave on Sedibe at Oxford University on 23 May 2013.
50 Whitehead, personal interview, Midrand, 20 February 2013.
51 Ibid.
52 Pillay, personal interview, Pretoria, 14 March 2013.
53 Ellis and Sechaba, *Comrades against apartheid*, 168.
54 Ibid., 169.
55 This claim comes from the ANC's Second submission to the TRC, available at www.anc.org.za.
56 Whitehead, personal interview, Midrand, 20 February 2013. Whitehead said Chris Hani, MK's chief of staff at the time, told him this in person.
57 Ibid.
58 Lalla, personal interview, Pretoria, 14 March 2013.
59 Confidential source.
60 Ibid.
61 De Kock, personal interview, Pretoria, 24 February 2013.
62 Ebrahim Ebrahim, telephonic interview, 2 May 2014.
63 Ibid.
64 Ibid.
65 Pauw, *Into the heart of darkness*, 73.
66 Eugene de Kock, Delilah Rekisa, Almond Nofomela and a Military Intelligence (MI) operative who worked with Sedibe at a secret MI base called Fontana, north of Pretoria, confirmed this.
67 Nene, personal interview, Pretoria, January 2013. Nene acted as intermediary between me, Nyanda and Shoke, and he and I also communicated by telephone, January 2013.
68 Miriam Phumla Williams, personal correspondence, November 2013.
69 *New Nation*, 30 July – 5 August 1987.
70 See court transcripts of *State* vs *Maseko and two others*, HGH CC319/87.
71 Moss, 'The strange saga of Mr X1', 13–17.
72 Whitehead, personal interview, Midrand, 20 February 2013.
73 Ibid.
74 Masilela, *Number 43 Trelawney Park*, 152.
75 Kasrils, *Armed and dangerous*, 182. Kasrils misspelt Sedibe's surname ('Sedebe', he called him). A former ANC operative who knew and worked with both Sedibe and Kasrils in exile said, contrary to Kasrils's harsh views about Sedibe in his memoirs, that Kasrils actually liked and favoured Sedibe and Cyril Raymonds. It was only when the two men's stars waned within the ANC that Kasrils changed his views.
76 Ibid.
77 See court transcripts of *State* vs *Maseko and two others*, HGH CC319/87.
78 Whitehead, personal interview, Midrand, 20 February 2013.

79 Ibid.
80 Gabriella Turnaturi, *Betrayals: The unpredictability of human relations* (Chicago: University of Chicago Press, 2007), 13.
81 Ibid., 43.
82 Ibid., 30.
83 Barry Gilder, personal interview, Pretoria, 20 February 2013.

Chapter 5

1 Hein Grosskopf, *Artistic graves* (Johannesburg: Ravan Press, 1993), 74.
2 Dante, *The divine comedy: The inferno*, Canto XXXII, 363, translated by Mark Musa (New York: Penguin Books, 1984).
3 The five women's harrowing stories are recounted in Munu Actis et al., *That inferno: Conversations of five women survivors of an Argentine torture camp* (Nashville: Vanderbilt University Press, 2006).
4 Firmenich's career as a double agent is detailed in Martin Edwin Andersen's *Dossier secreto: Argentina's desaparecidos and the myth of the dirty war* (Boulder: Westview Press, 1983), 71–321. See Martin A. Miller, *The foundations of modern terrorism: State, society and the dynamics of political violence* (Cambridge: Cambridge University Press, 2013), 208–9, for the number of people killed by Argentina's military junta.
5 Andersen, *Dossier secreto*, 321.
6 Ibid., 257.
7 Ibid., 319.
8 Michael J. Lazzara (ed.), *Luz Arce and Pinochet's Chile: Testimony in the aftermath of state violence* (New York: Palgrave Macmillan, 2011).
9 Quoted in Payne, 'Collaborators and the politics of memory in Chile', 18.
10 See Peter Wyden's biography of Stella Goldschlag, titled *Stella: One woman's true tale of evil, betrayal, and survival in Hitler's Germany* (New York: Simon & Schuster, 1992). Claudia Card, drawing on Wyden's book, mentions her story in her essay 'Women, evil, and gray zones', *Metaphilosophy*, 31, 5 (2000), 509–28.
11 Betsy Konefal, *For every Indio who falls: A history of Maya activism in Guatemala, 1960–1990* (Albuquerque: University of Mexico Press, 2010), 136.
12 Thean Potgieter, 'COIN in Africa: The colonial experience', in Baker and Jordaan, *South Africa and contemporary counterinsurgency*, 79.
13 Caroline Elkins, 'The wrong lesson', *Atlantic Monthly* (July–August 2005).
14 Ibid.
15 Laleh Khalili, *Time in the shadows: Confinement in counterinsurgencies* (Stanford: Stanford University Press, 2013), 5.
16 Ibid.
17 *The US Army and Marine Corps counterinsurgency field manual*, no. 3–24 (Chicago: University of Chicago Press, 2007).
18 Stathis Kalyvas, 'Review of the new U.S. Army/Marine Corps counterinsurgency field manual', *Perspectives on Politics*, 6, 2 (June 2008), 351–3.
19 Hans Joas and Wolfgang Knobl (eds), *War in social thought: From Hobbes*

to the present (Princeton: Princeton University Press, 2013), 2.
20 Anthony Giddens, *The nation-state and violence*, vol. 2 of *A contemporary critique of historical materialism* (Cambridge: Polity Press, 1985), 223.
21 Ibid., 301.
22 Price, *The apartheid state in crisis*, 92.
23 Samuel P. Huntington, 'Reform and stability in South Africa', *International Security*, 6, 4 (1982), 6.
24 Ibid., 8.
25 Ibid., 9.
26 Ibid.
27 Ibid., 19.
28 *Foreign Relations of the United States*, 1969–1976, vol. 28, Southern Africa, xxxi–xxxii. According to Lesley Gill, Kennedy was 'fascinated' by the doctrine of counterinsurgency. See Lesley Gill's *The school of the Americas: Military training and political violence in the Americas* (Durham: Duke University Press, 2004), 75.
29 See memo dated 9 March 1962 from Office of the Assistant Secretary of Defence to the Department of State, copy available at the National Security Archive, George Washington University, Washington DC, SA00002, 4.
30 Ibid.
31 Ellis, 'The historical significance of South Africa's Third Force', 269.
32 This is not to suggest that Botha or indeed Malan personally ordered Sedibe's abduction. It is to say, rather, that Total Strategy created the environment in which such actions were not only sanctioned implicitly but deemed by apartheid's foot soldiers to be both legitimate and necessary.
33 Andrew Boraine, 'The militarisation of urban controls', in Cock and Nathan, *War and society*, 160.
34 See Mark Swilling and Mark Phillips, 'State power in the 1980s: From "total strategy" to counter-revolutionary warfare', in Cock and Nathan, *War and society*, 144.
35 De Wet Potgieter, *Total onslaught: Apartheid's dirty tricks exposed* (Cape Town: Zebra Press, 2007), x.
36 Maritz Spaarwater, *A spook's progress: From making war to making peace* (Cape Town: Zebra Press, 2012), 48.
37 Ibid.
38 On J.J. McCuen's ideas, see Swilling and Phillips, 'State power in the 1980s', 144.
39 See Julia Hornberger's useful critique of Total Strategy and Wham in *Policing and human rights*, 26.
40 Khalili, *Time in the shadows*, 5.
41 Hamann, *Days of the generals*, 49.
42 Spaarwater, *A spook's progress*, 89.
43 Ibid., 48.
44 Hamann, *Days of the generals*, 62.
45 Like most commentators, Davidson and Filatova say Total Strategy actually worsened the political crisis in southern Africa. See Irina Filatova and Apollon Davidson, *The hidden thread: Russia and South Africa in the Soviet era* (Johannesburg: Jonathan Ball, 2013), 207.

46 Gossman, 'The South African military and counterinsurgency', 98–9.
47 Jacklyn Cock, 'The role of violence in current state security strategies', in Mark Swilling (ed.), *Views on the South African state* (Pretoria: Human Sciences Research Council, 1990), 101.
48 Brian Pottinger, *The imperial presidency: P.W. Botha, the first 10 years* (Johannesburg: Southern Book Publishers, 1988), 75.
49 Magnus Malan, *My life with the South African Defence Force* (Pretoria: Protea Book House, 2006), 205.
50 Annette Seegers, 'South Africa's National Security Management System, 1972–1990', *Journal of Modern African Studies*, 29, 2 (1991), 253–6.
51 Ibid., 253–73.
52 F.W. de Klerk, *The last trek* (London: Macmillan, 1999), 115.
53 Ibid.
54 Ibid., 116.
55 Boraine, 'The militarisation of urban controls', 159.
56 Ibid.
57 De Klerk, *The last trek*, 116.
58 Ibid., 122.
59 CIA, 'South Africa: Weathering the storm', National Intelligence Estimate, June 1992, copy available at the National Security Archive, George Washington University, SA21740.
60 Annette Seegers, 'Making sense of counterinsurgency', in Baker and Jordaan, *South Africa and contemporary counterinsurgency*, 15.
61 Ibid., 18.
62 Kevin O'Brien, 'The use of assassination as a tool of state policy: South Africa's counter-revolutionary strategy, 1979–92', parts one and two, *Terrorism and Political Violence*, 10, 2 (1998) and 13, 2 (2001).
63 Anita M. Gossman, 'Insurgency and counterinsurgency: An introduction', in Baker and Jordaan, *South Africa and contemporary counterinsurgency*, 33.
64 Ibid., 34.
65 Annette Seegers, 'Covert operations: Three-and-a-half moral arguments', in Charl Schutte, Ian Liebenberg and Anthony Minnaar (eds.), *The hidden hand: Covert operations in South Africa* (Pretoria: Human Sciences Research Council, 1998), 81–2.
66 Ibid.
67 Vincent Crapanzano, *The Harkis: The wound that never heals* (Chicago: University of Chicago Press, 2011), 69.
68 Ibid.
69 Spaarwater, *A spook's progress*, 90.
70 See Hugh Macmillan's *The Lusaka years* for an excellent account of the Morogoro conference.
71 See Morogoro documents at www.anc.org.za.
72 Nhlanhla Ndebele and Noor Nieftagodien provide an insightful analysis of the significance of the conference and its resolutions in their essay 'The Morogoro conference: A moment of self-reflection', in SADET, *The road to democracy in South Africa*, vol. 1 (1960–1970), 573–99.
73 Spaarwater, *A spook's progress*, 89.
74 O'Brien, *The South African Intelligence Services*, 169.

75 Botha, preface to 1973 White Paper on Defence and Armaments Procurement, National Parliament Archives, Cape Town.

Chapter 6

1 Istvan Rev, 'In mendacio veritas', *Representations*, 35, Special issue: Monumental histories (Summer, 1991), 17.

2 Behr's confession is contained in a speech titled 'South Africa: Living in the faultlines', *Common Sense*, 11, 1 (October 1996).

3 O'Donnell's response to Behr's 'confession' is in a letter to the editor, *Common Sense*, 11, 2 (November 1996).

4 O'Donnell's letter to the editor, *Common Sense*, 11, 2 (November 1996).

5 See Luz Arce's memoirs *The inferno: A story of terror and survival in Chile* (Madison: University of Wisconsin Press, 2004), and Michael Lazzara's *Luz Arce and Pinochet's Chile*.

6 Barbara Miller, *Narratives of guilt and compliance in unified Germany* (London: Routledge, 1999), 4–5.

7 Ibid., 14.

8 Ibid., 54.

9 Rosenberg, *The haunted land*, 180.

10 Sedibe's security police file. Confidential source.

11 Trevor-Roper quoted in Gerard R. Hughes and Len Scott, '"Knowledge is never too dear": Exploring intelligence archives', in Gerard R. Hughes, Peter Jackson and Len Scott (eds), *Exploring intelligence archives: Enquiries into the secret state* (London: Routledge, 2008), 26.

12 See Eugene Fourie's testimony to TRC Amnesty Committee hearing into Sedibe's abduction, 16 February 2000, 2–11 of 37.

13 *TRC Final Report*, vol. 2, chapter 1, 5.

14 Bell and Ntsebeza, *Unfinished business*, 9. See also Verne Harris's essay '"They should have destroyed more": The destruction of public records by the South African state in the final years of apartheid, 1990–1994', in Richard J. Cox and David A. Wallace (eds), *Archives and the public good* (Westport: Quorum Books, 2002).

15 Bell and Ntsebeza, *Unfinished business*, 9.

16 Ibid.

17 Harris, *In a different time*.

18 Vlakplaas personnel file. Confidential source.

19 Manghezi, '"They were part of us and we were part of them"', 189.

20 Bell and Ntsebeza, *Unfinished business*, 16.

21 Ibid.

22 Vlakplaas personnel file. Confidential source.

23 Barry Gilder, personal interview, Pretoria, 20 February 2013.

24 Kaborone Sedibe, personal interview, Edenvale, 27 February 2013.

25 The structure of Sedibe's file bears an uncanny resemblance to the structure of a Stasi file. See Miller, *Narratives of guilt and compliance in a unified Germany*, 12, and Timothy Garton Ash's description in *The file: A personal history* (London: Atlantic Books, 2009) for the structure of the file the Stasi kept on him.

26 See Eugene Fourie's testimony to TRC's Amnesty Committee hearing into Sedibe's abduction for an explanation and description of the album, 16 February 2000, 2–11 of 37.
27 Breytenbach, *The true confessions of an albino terrorist*, 27–8.
28 Ibid.
29 The ANC's intelligence section mentioned the album in a report titled 'Some aspects of enemy counter-guerrilla tactics compiled from our own experience'. Confidential source.
30 Breytenbach, *The true confessions of an albino terrorist*, 27–8.
31 Mwezi Twala, *Mbokodo! Inside MK: A soldier's story* (Johannesburg: Jonathan Ball, 1994), 149.
32 Hugh Lewin, *Bandiet: Seven years in a South African prison* (London: Heinemann, 1981), 25. Piet Beyleveld, a white anti-apartheid activist who turned against his former comrades and testified against Bram Fischer, used the police's alleged omnipotence to justify his reason to collaborate. Beyleveld said the 'shock to me was that the police knew as much as they did'. See Madeleine Fullard's essay 'State repression in the 1960s', 372.
33 Rev, 'The man in the white raincoat', 11.
34 Sedibe's security police file. Some of the dirt Sedibe dished up included claims about extramarital affairs and domestic abuse. Confidential source.
35 Rev, 'The man in the white raincoat', 27.
36 All the entries in this section are drawn from Sedibe's security police file. Confidential source.
37 Mtolo, *Umkhonto we Sizwe*, 118–19.
38 Sedibe security police file, 131. Confidential source.
39 Ibid. The fact that Fourie could not spell such a common name as Nyerere is instructive of how we might want to think about the 'intelligence' of the South African security establishment.
40 Sedibe's security police file, 38. Confidential source.
41 Weld, *Paper cadavers*, 6.
42 Ray Lalla, personal interviews, Pretoria, 16 March 2013 and 26 January 2014.
43 Garton Ash, *The file*, 91.
44 See *Times of Swaziland*, 10 July 1987.
45 O'Brien, 'Assassinations as a tool of state policy', 50.
46 Whitehead, personal interview, Midrand, 20 February 2013.
47 O'Brien, 'Assassinations as a tool of state policy', 50.
48 Ibid., 103.
49 Ibid., 108.
50 Ibid., 109.
51 Ibid.
52 Ibid.
53 An askari named Mpho Tladi (not his real name) told me that Sedibe participated in the assassination of ANC members. Conversation, Letlhabile, 23 January 2014.
54 Ebrahim Ebrahim, telephonic interview, 2 May 2014.
55 Mpho Tladi, conversation, Letlhabile, 23 January 2014.
56 Mr X2's testimony in *State* vs *Maseko and two others*, HGH CC319/87.

57 Information about the askari Chris Makgopa comes from his former wife Delilah Rekisa, personal interview, Pretoria, 24 January 2014.
58 Mpho Tladi, conversation, Letlhabile, 23 January 2014.
59 See TRC Amnesty Committee decision AC/2000/230.
60 Mpho Tladi said during our conversation that Sedibe took part in his interrogation, encouraging him to turn. Conversation, Letlhabile, 23 January 2014.
61 Ibid.
62 Ibid.
63 O'Brien, *The South African Intelligence Services*, 82.
64 Swilling and Phillips, 'State power in the 1980s', 143.
65 Ibid.
66 CIA Intelligence memo dated 28 August 1992. Copy available at the National Security Archive, SA 21740, George Washington University, Washington DC.
67 Potgieter, *Total onslaught*, 12.
68 O'Brien, *The South African Intelligence Services*, 69.
69 Ibid., 68.
70 Ibid., 169.
71 Miller, *Narratives of guilt and compliance in unified Germany*, 131.
72 Potgieter, *Total onslaught*, 142.
73 James Sanders tells this story in his book *Apartheid's friends: The rise and fall of South Africa's secret service* (London: John Murray, 2006), 338.
74 In fact, Kevin O'Brien and James Sanders claim that South Africa's 'viability as a country and a society has been – to varying degrees over the period 1910 to 2005 – dictated and influenced by its intelligence dispensation', and that 'Since the early 1960s, South Africa has been a land infested with spies'. See O'Brien's *The South African Intelligence Services*, 2, for the first quote, as well as Sanders's *Apartheid's friends,* 1, 2 and 7, for the second quote. Sanders's quote is also repeated in *The South African Intelligence Services*, 2.

Chapter 7

1 De Kock's testimony to TRC Amnesty Committee hearing into abduction of Glory Sedibe, Pretoria, 15 February 2000.
2 A number of people remarked on this during my interviews with them. Totsie Memela, personal interview, Randburg, January 2013; George Nene, personal interview, Pretoria, January 2013; and Eugene de Kock, personal interview, Pretoria, 24 February 2013. See also Masilela, *Number 43 Trelawney Park*, 121.
3 Totsie Memela, personal interview, Randburg, January 2013; Masilela, *Number 43 Trelawney Park*, 121.
4 Kaborone Sedibe, personal interview, Edenvale, 27 February 2013.
5 Diana Wylie, *Art and revolution: The life and death of Thami Mnyele* (Johannesburg: Jacana Media, 2008), 1.
6 Mr X1's testimony in *State* vs *Maseko and two others*, HGH CC 319/87, 2753.

7 Kevin O'Brien, 'A blunted spear: The failure of the African National Congress/Communist Party revolutionary war strategy, 1961–1990', *Small Wars and Insurgencies*, 14, 2 (2003), 27–70.
8 I am grateful to Jacklyn Cock for insisting and reminding me that I need to make this point unequivocally. See Howard Barrell's 'The turn to the masses', 77, and Tom Lodge's 'The African National Congress in South Africa, 1976–1983: Guerrilla war and armed propaganda', *Journal of Contemporary African Studies*, 3, 1–2 (1983), 169, for an examination of the propaganda value of the ANC's armed struggle.
9 Barrell, 'The turn to the masses', 72.
10 Thula Simpson, 'The making (and remaking) of a revolutionary plan: Strategic dilemmas of the ANC's armed struggle, 1974–1978', *Social Dynamics*, 35, 2 (2009), 316.
11 O'Brien, 'A blunted spear,' 27–70.
12 Lodge, 'The African National Congress in South Africa', 155.
13 Francis Meli, *South Africa belongs to us: A history of the ANC* (Harare: Zimbabwe Publishing House, 1988), 191.
14 Ellis, *The external mission*, 243–4.
15 Lodge, 'The African National Congress in South Africa', 153.
16 Barrell, 'The turn to the masses', 76.
17 Stephen R. Davis, '"Voices from without": The ANC, its radio, its allies and exile, 1960–84', in Liz Gunner, Dina Ligaga and Dumisani Moyo (eds), *Radio in Africa: Publics, cultures, communities* (Johannesburg: Wits University Press, 2011), 223.
18 *TRC Final Report*, vol. 2, chapter 1, 10.
19 Stephen Ellis, 'The genesis of the ANC's armed struggle in South Africa, 1948–1961', *Journal of Southern African Studies*, 37, 4 (2011), 657.
20 Scott Everett Couper, '"An embarrassment to the Congresses"? The silencing of Chief Albert Luthuli and the production of ANC history', *Journal of Southern African Studies*, 35, 2 (2009), 341 n.46.
21 *Foreign Relations of the United States series*, 1961–1963, vol. 21, Africa, Memo from Department of State Executive Secretary Battle to Bundy, 13 November 1961, 612, National Archives of the United States, Maryland.
22 Ibid.
23 See Luthuli's Nobel Peace Prize speech at www.nobelprize.org.
24 See *Foreign Relations of the United States*, 1969–1976, vol. 28, Southern Africa, xxxi.
25 Ibid., xxxi–xxxii.
26 Ibid.
27 Filatova and Davidson, *The hidden thread*, 200–1 and 227.
28 Ibid., 414.
29 Ibid., 41–2.
30 Ibid., 200.
31 Ibid., 200–1 and 227.
32 Zoë Wicomb, *David's story* (New York: The Feminist Press at CUNY, 2001), 196.
33 Ted R. Gurr, *Why men rebel* (Princeton: Princeton University Press, 1970), 358.

34 Ted R. Gurr, 'Some observations on resistance and revolution in contemporary Africa', *Journal of Asian and African Studies*, 47, 3 (2012), 282.
35 Ibid., 280.
36 Ibid., quoting Michael Lobban, 280.
37 Ibid., 280.
38 Ibid., 284.
39 Gurr, *Why men rebel*, 359.
40 See report by the Centre for Sustainability in Mining and Industry for the Asbestos Relief Trust, 'The future of Penge: Prospects for people and the environment', Final report, July 2008. The report provides a detailed history of Penge and of the history of mining in the area.
41 Stander and La Grange, 'Investigation reports on the processing of certain minerals in the Republic of South Africa and in South West Africa', National Resources Development Council, vol. III, House of Assembly Annual Report for 1964, National Parliament Archives, Cape Town, 891–917.
42 Asbestos Relief Trust, 'The future of Penge', 15.
43 Stander and La Grange, 'Investigation reports on the processing of certain minerals in the Republic of South Africa and in South West Africa'. See also Asbestos Relief Trust, 'The future of Penge', 9.
44 Asbestos Relief Trust, 'The future of Penge', 9.
45 Ibid.
46 Ibid., 9–10.
47 Ibid., 10.
48 Ibid.
49 Ibid.
50 Kaborone Sedibe, personal interview, Edenvale, 27 February 2013.
51 Asbestos Relief Trust, 'The future of Penge', 11.
52 Stander and La Grange, 'Investigation reports on the processing of certain minerals in the Republic of South Africa and in South West Africa'.
53 I was unable to determine from my interviews when the whole family moved to Penge.
54 David Mokwena, personal interview, Penge, January 2013.
55 Miriam Mashego, personal interview, Mpumalanga, January 2013.
56 Asam Phiri, personal interview, Penge, January 2013.
57 Ibid. Phiri called Sedibe '*morupa*', Pedi slang for dead wood.
58 I am grateful to David Mokwena for giving me a guided tour of Penge in January 2013.
59 One can still see the two doors at the post office and the butcher. Of course, the old apartheid notices are long gone.
60 David Mokwena, personal interview, Penge, January 2013.
61 Asbestos Relief Trust, 'The future of Penge', 11.
62 Ibid.
63 David Mokwena, personal interview, Penge, January 2013.
64 Kaborone Sedibe, personal interview, Edenvale, 27 February 2013.
65 Ibid.
66 Bernard Malope, personal interview, Matibidi, January 2013.

67 The reconstruction of Sedibe's schooling is based on his security police file. Confidential source.
68 Baruch Hirson, *Year of fire, year of ash* (London: Zed Press, 1979), 7.
69 The reconstruction of Sedibe's schooling is based on his security police file. Confidential source.
70 Mr X1's testimony in *State* vs *Maseko and two others*, HGH CC 319/87, 2331.
71 The reconstruction of Sedibe's movements after matric is based on his security police file. Confidential source.
72 Lillian Sedibe, personal interview, Matibidi, January 2013.
73 David Mokwena, personal interview, Penge, January 2013.
74 Kaborone Sedibe, personal interview, Edenvale, 22 January 2014.
75 Lillian Sedibe, personal interview, Matibidi, January 2013.
76 Ibid.
77 Ibid.
78 Kaborone Sedibe, personal interview, Edenvale, 27 February 2013.
79 Ibid.
80 Ibid.
81 Sedibe's security police file. Confidential source.
82 Colin Bundy, 'Street sociology and pavement politics: Aspects of youth and student resistance in Cape Town, 1985', *Journal of Southern African Studies*, 13, 3 (1987), 321.
83 Sedibe's security police file. Confidential source.
84 Ibid. See also Thula Simpson's essay '"The bay and the ocean"', as well as Masilela's *Number 43 Trelawney Park* for biographical sketches of Mabizela.
85 Sedibe's security police file. Confidential source.
86 Ibid.
87 Tim Gibbs, 'Chris Hani's "country bumpkins": Regional networks in the African National Congress underground, 1974–1994', *Journal of Southern African Studies*, 37, 4 (2011), 679. See also Mzwakhe Ndlela's memoir *For the fallen* for an insightful account of the role of Mziwonke Mganu, a Ciskei 'diplomat', in the ANC underground in Cape Town and the Eastern Cape, 107–12.
88 Mark Orkin, '"Democracy knows no colour": Rationales for guerrilla involvement among black South Africans', *Journal of Southern African Studies*, 18, 3 (1992), 643.
89 Ibid., 642.
90 Ibid., 667.
91 Ibid.
92 Gibbs, 'Chris Hani's "country bumpkins"', 683.
93 Orkin, '"Democracy knows no colour"', 667.
94 Ibid., 667–8.
95 Ibid., 668.
96 Ibid., 669.
97 See Deborah Posel's *The making of apartheid, 1948–1961: Conflict and compromise* (Oxford: Clarendon Press, 1991) and Paul Maylam's *South Africa's racial past: The history and historiography of racism, segregation,*

and apartheid (Farnham: Ashgate, 2001).

98 P.C. Swanepoel, *Really inside BOSS* (Derdepoortpark: The author, 2007), 53.

99 Jonny Steinberg is doing some insightful and excellent work on Verwoerd as a failed high modernist who could not come to terms with the fact that reality would not bend to his will. Steinberg gave a seminar on this topic at the University of Barcelona in 2012.

100 See De Klerk's memoirs *The last trek*; Herman Stadler's *The other side of the story: A true perspective* (Pretoria: Contact Publishers, 1997); and Maritz Spaarwater's *A spook's progress*.

101 I am thinking here of Giliomee's *The Afrikaners*.

102 See Nicoli Nattrass and Jeremy Seekings, *Class, race, and inequality in South Africa* (New Haven: Yale University Press, 2005).

103 Eugene de Kock, personal interview, Pretoria, 24 February 2013.

104 See Hannah Arendt's *Eichmann in Jerusalem: A report on the banality of evil* (Harmondsworth: Penguin, 2006).

105 Ibid. To be fair to Arendt, she does not minimise Eichmann's crimes. It is her 'explanation' for why he did what he did, her claims about his alleged thoughtlessness, that are problematic.

106 David Cesarini, *Eichmann: His life and crimes* (London: William Heinemann, 2004), 6.

107 I am grateful to Beatriz Silva Pinochet for challenging me to think more critically and expansively about the meaning of 'choice' when one is forced to 'choose' to collaborate.

108 Asbestos Relief Trust, 'The future of Penge'.

109 Ibid.

110 Radebe, personal interview, Johannesburg, March 2013.

Chapter 8

1 Mr X1's testimony in *State* vs *Maseko and two others*, HGH 319/87, 2328.

2 Ibid., 2563–4.

3 Ngculu, *The honour to serve*.

4 Ibid.

5 Mr X1's testimony in *State* vs *Maseko and two others*, HGH 319/87, 2579.

6 Ibid., 2564.

7 Ibid., 2563.

8 Sedibe's security police file. Confidential source.

9 Ebrahim Ebrahim, telephonic interview, 2 May 2014.

10 This is what Sedibe told the court in his turn as Mr X1 in *State* vs *Maseko and two others*, HGH 319/87, 2374. However, Francis Meli claimed that the ANC resolved at its conference at Morogoro, Tanzania, in 1969 to prioritise the 'adoption of a code and oath which all revolutionaries in the ANC and MK should be governed and bound by'. See Meli's *South Africa belongs to us*, 168. Ironically, Meli was later exposed as an apartheid spy. He died mysteriously in South Africa in the early 1990s shortly after the ANC's unbanning and his return from exile.

11 Ngculu, *The honour to serve*.

12 Stephen Ellis, 'Mbokodo: Security in ANC camps, 1961–1990', *African Affairs*, 93 (1994), 283.
13 Dick Lord, *From fledgling to eagle: The South African Air Force during the border war* (Johannesburg: 30 Degrees South Publishers, 2008), 109. The attack was so precise that it raised suspicions that spies in the camp had given the attackers the camp's geographic coordinates. The camp was abandoned and residents moved elsewhere.
14 Ellis, 'Mbokodo', 289.
15 See Swanepoel's *Really inside BOSS* for an account of the reorganisation.
16 *Sechaba* editorial, 3 (9 September 1969).
17 Ellis, 'Mbokodo', 287.
18 Pillay, personal interview, Pretoria, 14 March 2013.
19 Mr X1's testimony in *State* vs *Maseko and two others*, HGH 319/87, 2785.
20 Mkhwanazi, personal interview, Johannesburg, 17 May 2013.
21 Ibid.
22 Ibid.
23 Ibid.
24 Ibid.
25 Ibid.
26 Mr X1's testimony in *State* vs *Maseko and two others*, HGH 319/87, 2786. The exchange between Gering and Sedibe is taken from 2786–840.
27 Ibid., 2328.
28 Mkhwanazi, personal interview, Johannesburg, 17 May 2013.
29 Van der Merwe, *Trou tot die dood toe*, 332.
30 Lalla, personal interview, Pretoria, 14 March 2013.
31 Delilah Rekisa (not her real name), personal interview, Pretoria, 24 January 2014.
32 Mpho Tladi (not his real name), personal interview, Letlhabile, 23 January 2014.
33 Ibid.
34 Ibid.
35 Mr X4's testimony in *State* vs *Maseko and two others*, HGH 319/87, 3684–9.
36 Sekula, 'The body and the archive', 17–46.

Chapter 9

1 Rev, 'In mendacio veritas', 6.
2 Mr X1's testimony in *State* vs *Maseko and two others*, HGH 319/87, 2527.
3 Ibid.
4 Ibid.
5 Ibid., 2527–830.
6 De Kock, personal interview, Pretoria, 24 February 2013.
7 Kaborone Sedibe, personal interview, Edenvale, 27 February 2013.
8 De Kock, personal interview, Pretoria, 24 February 2013.
9 Ibid.
10 Maseko letter, 5 March 1990. Confidential source.

11 Ibid.
12 De Kock, personal interview, Pretoria, 24 February 2013.
13 Mkhwanazi, personal interview, Johannesburg, 17 May 2013.
14 Van der Merwe, *Trou tot die dood toe*, 328.
15 De Kock, personal interview, Pretoria, 24 February 2013.
16 Ibid.
17 Ibid.
18 Ibid.
19 Mr X1's testimony in *State* vs *Maseko and two others*, HGH 319/87, 2567.
20 Ibid., 2569.
21 Ibid., 2527–814.
22 Nofomela confirmed this story during a personal interview, Soshanguve, 18 January 2014.
23 Nofomela affidavit in Harms Commission Collection in Wits Historical Papers, AK2300.
24 Ibid., 170.
25 Ibid.
26 Ibid., 172.
27 Ibid., 172–3.
28 Ibid.
29 Vlakplaas personnel file. Confidential source.
30 Posel, 'The TRC report', 157.
31 Potgieter, *Total onslaught*, 190.
32 Deetlefs's testimony to TRC Amnesty Committee hearing into Sedibe's abduction, 14 February 2000, 3 of 45.
33 Pienaar's testimony to TRC Amnesty Committee hearing into Sedibe's abduction, 14 February 2000, 28 of 45.
34 Ibid., 29 of 45.
35 Madeleine Fullard and Nicky Rousseau, 'Truth, evidence and history: A critical review of aspects of the amnesty process', in Charles Villa-Vicencio and Erik Doxtader (eds), *The provocations of amnesty: Memory, justice and impunity* (Claremont: David Philip, 2003), 195–217.
36 Leopeng's introduction at TRC Amnesty Committee hearing into Sedibe's abduction, 14 February 2000, 1 of 45.
37 De Kock's testimony to TRC Amnesty Committee hearing into Sedibe's abduction, 15 February 2000, 33 of 82.
38 Deetlefs's testimony to TRC Amnesty Committee hearing into Sedibe's abduction, 14 February 2000, 9 of 45.
39 Ibid., 3 of 45.
40 Ibid., 9 of 45.
41 Manghezi, '"They were part of us and we were part of them"', 188.
42 De Kock's testimony to TRC Amnesty Committee hearing into Sedibe's abduction, 15 February 2000, 36 of 82.
43 Ibid., 35 of 82.
44 Ibid., 34 of 82.
45 Ibid., 33 of 82.
46 Ibid., 34 of 82.
47 John D. Battersby, 'Afrikaner paper urges talks with Mandela', *New York*

Times, 17 January 1989.
48 The Boeremag trial involved a secret Afrikaner organisation whose members tried to start a 'racial war' by killing black South Africans.
49 De Kock's testimony to TRC Amnesty Committee hearing into Sedibe's abduction, 15 February 2000, 41–2 of 82.
50 Phumla Williams, personal communication with author, 2013.
51 Phumla Williams, email correspondence, 2013.
52 De Kock's testimony to TRC Amnesty Committee hearing into Sedibe's abduction, 15 February 2000, 35 of 82.
53 *TRC Final Report*, vol. 2, chapter 1, 129.
54 Posel, 'The TRC report', 148.
55 Ibid., 167–8.

Chapter 10

1 Wally Serote, *To every birth its blood* (Johannesburg: Ravan Press, 1981), 29.
2 The details in this section of the chapter come from Alan Morris's informative essay 'The South African state and the Oukasie removal', *Transformation*, 8 (1989), 24–46.
3 Ibid., 25.
4 Ibid., 42.
5 Twala, personal interview, Letlhabile, 23 January 2014.
6 Manghezi, '"They were part of us and we were part of them"', 189.
7 See Peter Harris's *In a different time*, 179, for example.
8 Delilah Rekisa (not her real name), personal interview, Pretoria, 24 January 2014.
9 Manghezi, '"They were part of us and we were part of them"', 189.
10 Ibid.
11 Nofomela, personal interview, Soshanguve, 18 January 2014.
12 See De Kock and Jeremy Gordin's *A long night's damage* for an informative account of De Kock's upbringing.
13 Mr X1's testimony, *State* vs *Maseko and two others*, HGH CC 319/87, 2569–70.
14 See, for example, Munu Actis et al., *That inferno*, 163.
15 Confidential source.
16 Manghezi, '"They were part of us and we were part of them"', 188–9.
17 Ibid., 189.
18 Delilah Rekisa, personal interview, Pretoria, 24 January 2014.
19 Stephen Phiri, personal interview, Pretoria, 20 January 2014. Jan Anton Nieuwoudt was among the Military Intelligence personnel responsible for the training of the Caprivi trainees, Inkatha hit squads responsible for hundreds of deaths in the 1980s and 1990s.
20 Gregory Sibusiso Radebe, personal interview, Johannesburg, 10 May 2013.
21 Mpho Tladi (not his real name), conversation, Letlhabile, 23 January 2014. Tladi said Sedibe took part in his police interrogation, and that Chris Makgopa was among those who 'helped' him return to South Africa.
22 Harris, *In a different time*, 179.

23 Evidence for this comes from conversations with Sedibe's relatives and from policeman Freek Pienaar's testimony to the TRC Amnesty Committee hearings into Sedibe's abduction.
24 Gregory Sibusiso Radebe, personal interview, Johannesburg, 8 May 2013.
25 Nofomela, personal interview, Soshanguve, 18 January 2014.
26 Ray Lalla, personal interview, Pretoria, 26 January 2014.
27 Tlhomedi Ephraim Mfalapitsa testimony at TRC Amnesty Committee hearing into the case of the Cosas Four, Johannesburg, 4 May 1999.
28 Oscar Linda Moni testimony at TRC Amnesty Committee hearing, Johannesburg, 28 October 1999.
29 Ibid.
30 Nofomela, personal interview, Soshanguve, 18 January 2014.
31 Twala, personal interview, Letlhabile, 23 January 2014.
32 Ibid.
33 Gregory Sibusiso Radebe, personal interview, Johannesburg, 10 May 2013.
34 Mpho Tladi, conversation, Letlhabile, 23 January 2014.
35 Gregory Sibusiso Radebe, personal interview, Johannesburg, 8 May 2013.
36 Mpho Tladi, conversation, Letlhabile, 23 January 2014.
37 See Pauw's *Into the heart of darkness*. Pauw says on page 61 that De Kock once beat up Chappies Klopper, a white member of his unit, after catching Klopper with a (black) prostitute in a Johannesburg hotel. De Kock himself told me during an interview on 24 February 2013 that he had to beat up some of his white members to keep them away from Sedibe's wife.
38 Gregory Sibusiso Radebe, personal interview, Johannesburg, 8 May 2013.
39 Ibid.
40 Nofomela, personal interview, Soshanguve, 18 January 2014. Nofomela's claim must be taken with a pinch of salt. By all accounts, De Kock was not one to argue with on any subject.
41 Twala, personal interview, Letlhabile, 23 January 2014.
42 Delilah Rekisa, personal interview, Pretoria, 24 January 2014.
43 Ibid.
44 Nofomela, personal interview, Brits, 23 January 2014.
45 Ibid.
46 Joe Mamasela debriefing by Independent Board of Inquiry into Informal Repression, Wits Historical Papers.
47 Mpho Tladi, conversation, Letlhabile, 23 January 2014.
48 Joe Mamasela debriefing by Independent Board of Inquiry into Informal Repression, Wits Historical Papers.
49 Delilah Rekisa, personal interview, Pretoria, 24 January 2014.
50 Mamasela, SABC TRC special report, section 3, episode 37. Available at sabctrc.saha.org.za.
51 Delilah Rekisa, personal interview, Pretoria, 24 January 2014.
52 Ibid.
53 Ibid.
54 Ibid., and follow-up telephonic interviews in January, February and March 2014.
55 Evidence for this comes from interviews and conversations with Nofomela and the askaris interviewed for this book.

56 Pauw mentions Shosha in his book *In the heart of the whore*, 81. According to Pauw, Shosha joined the ANC in 1980, was trained in Angola, East Germany and Libya, and was captured by the South African Police in 1984.
57 Ibid.
58 Jacklyn Cock, *Women and war in South Africa* (Cleveland: Pilgrim Press, 1993), viii.
59 Delilah Rekisa, personal interview, Pretoria, 24 January 2014.
60 Ibid.
61 Ibid.
62 Nofomela, personal interviews, January 2014.
63 Delilah Rekisa, personal interview, Pretoria, 24 January 2014.
64 Ibid.
65 Card, 'Women, evil, and gray zones', 512.
66 Delilah Rekisa, personal interview, Pretoria, 24 January 2014.
67 Ibid.
68 Ibid.
69 See, for example, Masilela's *Number 43 Trelawney Park*; and policeman Christo Deetlefs's testimony to TRC Amnesty Committee hearing into Sedibe's abduction.
70 See Kerry Bystrom, 'The public–private sphere: Family narratives and democracy in Argentina and South Africa', *Social Dynamics*, 31, 1 (2010), 139–52, for a thoughtful examination of some of these masculinist narratives. Bystrom says: 'Apartheid itself can be seen as a schizophrenic attempt to turn South Africa into an "ordered family", with the white male as head of the family', 142.
71 Delilah Rekisa, personal interview, Pretoria, 24 January 2014.
72 Ibid.
73 Manghezi, '"They were part of us and we were part of them"', 190.
74 *Government Gazette*, 'Notice to creditors in deceased estate', 17 June 1994.
75 Manghezi, '"They were part of us and we were part of them"', 190.
76 Humphrey Mkhwanazi, personal interview, Johannesburg, 17 May 2013.

Chapter 11

1 Jean-Paul Sartre, 'What is a collaborator?', in *The aftermath of war*, 42. I am grateful to Gerard Rosich for finding me the English translation of this text.
2 Gregory Sibusiso Radebe, personal interview, Johannesburg, 8 May 2013.
3 It is not surprising that askaris used this line. The police themselves believed it. See police propagandist Herman Stadler's *The other side of the story*. Stadler says: 'It has to be emphasised that the South African Police never had any policy or agenda to perpetuate crime or violence' (4).
4 Mbanda's claim echoed a statement made by Johann Hans Breyer, a former Nazi guard at Auschwitz who claimed in 2012 to have had nothing to do with what went on inside the concentration camp as he only did guard duties outside. See Scott Neuman's report, 'Onetime Auschwitz guard arrested in Philadelphia on German warrant', www.npr.org, 18 June 2014.

5 Mbanda, telephonic conversation, 14 May 2013.
6 Pillay's story is detailed in the TRC's *Final Report*.
7 Nofomela and Rekisa, personal interviews, January 2013.
8 Mbembe, 'The power of the archive and its limits', 19.
9 These details and the following dialogue are reconstructed from the transcripts of *State* vs *N.J. Lubisi and others*, CC 167/80, vols. 6–9, National Archives, Pretoria.
10 Twala, personal interview, Letlhabile, 23 January 2014.
11 Twala's testimony and Black's objection are reconstructed from *State* vs *Mthetheleli Zephania Mncube and Mzondeleli Euclid Nondula*, HGH CC 449/87, vol. 9, National Archives, Pretoria.
12 Twala, personal interview, Letlhabile, 23 January 2014.
13 Makuleni's testimony is reconstructed from *State* vs *Mthetheleli Zephania Mncube and Mzondeleli Euclid Nondula*, HGH CC 449/87, vol. 9.
14 Cock, 'The role of violence in current state security strategies', 100.
15 Ibid., 100.
16 Achmat Dangor, *Bitter fruit* (New York: Black Cat 2001), 102.
17 See Mr X2's testimony in *State* vs *Maseko and two others*, HGH CC 319/87.
18 See Mr X4's testimony in *State* vs *Maseko and two others*, HGH CC 319/87, 3691.
19 Mr X1's testimony in *State* vs *Maseko and two others*, HGH CC 319/87, 2569.
20 Alan Furst, *Night soldiers* (London: Phoenix, 2005), 300.
21 Mr X1's testimony in *State* vs *Maseko and two others*, HGH CC 319/87, 2570.
22 Gregory Sibusiso Radebe said Sedibe would never think twice about buying 15 men drinks. Personal interview, Johannesburg, 8 May 2013.
23 Delilah Rekisa (not her real name), personal interview, Pretoria, 24 January 2014.
24 Manghezi, '"They were part of us and we were part of them"', 190.
25 Goodman Twala, personal interview, 23 January 2014.
26 Mfalapitsa's testimony at TRC Amnesty Committee hearing in Cosas Four case, 4 May 1999.
27 Ibid.
28 Oscar Linda Moni's testimony to TRC Amnesty Committee, 28 October 1999.
29 *TRC Final Report*, vol. 6, chapter 1, section 3, 217.
30 Mfalapitsa's testimony at TRC Amnesty Committee hearing in Cosas Four case, 4 May 1999.
31 Natoo Babenia, *Memoirs of a saboteur* (Bellville: Mayibuye Books, 1995), 106. Joel Joffe, one of the defence lawyers in the Rivonia Trial, said the following about Mtolo's testimony: 'His evidence was an interwoven mixture of fact and fiction, moments of truth between downright lies. The lies were so neatly tailored to suit the state's case that I do not believe Mtolo could have invented them for himself. Most of the [state witnesses] lied shamelessly, purposefully and apparently to order.' Quoted in Madeleine Fullard's essay 'State repression in the 1960s', 370.

32 Babenia, *Memoirs of a saboteur*, 112.
33 Kasrils, *Armed and dangerous*, 30.
34 Francis Meli, writing in *South Africa belongs to us*, 191, said: 'The ANC, like any African elephant, has demonstrated a long historical memory in such cases.' The irony, of course, is that Meli himself was an apartheid agent within the ANC.
35 Mtolo, *Umkhonto we Sizwe*, 73.
36 Ibid., 130.
37 Ibid., 161.
38 Ibid., 177.
39 Thula Bopela and Daluxolo Luthuli, *MK: Fighting for a divided people* (Alberton: Galago, 1999), 246.
40 Ibid., 247.
41 Ibid., 254.
42 Gerard Ludi, *Operation Q-018* (Cape Town: Nasionale Boekhandel, 1969), 7.
43 Ibid., 9.
44 Ibid.
45 *Sechaba* editorial, 3 (9 September 1969).
46 See Bell and Ntsebeza, *Unfinished business*, 44.
47 Gerard Ludi, *The communistisation of the ANC* (Alberton: Galago, 2011), 292.
48 *Sechaba* editorial, 3 (9 September 1969).
49 Twala, *Mbokodo!*
50 The question of torture in ANC camps was a serious matter for the organisation. Hugh Macmillan's *The Lusaka years* records a heated ANC executive meeting on 23 August 1993 during which Pallo Jordan chided some of his ANC colleagues for trying to excuse 'ANC torture'.

Chapter 12

1 Lazzara, *Luz Arce and Pinochet's Chile*, 160–1.
2 One of these comrades, now an officer in the South African Intelligence Services, confirmed the meeting to me through an intermediary, January 2014.
3 Humphrey Mkhwanazi said he met Sedibe in Pretoria sometime in 1992. Personal interview, 17 May 2013.
4 Masilela, *Number 43 Trelawney Park*, 151. Nwedamutswu, who refused to meet me in person, confirmed this exchange through an intermediary, January 2014.
5 Ibid.
6 Ibid., 122; Barry Gilder, personal interview, Pretoria, 20 February 2013.
7 Masilela, *Number 43 Trelawney Park*, 151–2.
8 Ibid.
9 Mbembe, quoted in David Attwell's *Rewriting modernity: Studies in black South African literary modernity* (Pietermaritzburg: University of KwaZulu-Natal Press, 2005), 14.
10 Sobukwe's, Mandela's and Mahlangu's speeches are available online.

11 Mr X1's testimony in *State* vs *Maseko and two others*, HGH CC 319/87, 2563.
12 Humphrey Mkhwanazi said Sedibe told him the following sometime in 1992: 'To be honest with you, I never really wanted to work for these guys. But I guess I was a coward.' Personal interview, 17 May 2013.
13 Details of what happened to Ndwandwe are contained in her killers' amnesty applications.
14 See Beresford's *Truth is a strange fruit*, 74; Albie Sachs's *The strange alchemy of life and law* (Oxford: Oxford University Press, 2011); and Judith Mason's personal website, www.judithmason.com.
15 Judith Mason's personal website, www.judithmason.com.
16 Richard Lyster, a former official of the TRC who participated in Ndwandwe's exhumation, said the story about the plastic underwear came from one of the policemen who killed her.
17 The story is told on Judith Mason's personal website, www.judithmason.com.
18 Sachs, *The strange alchemy of life and law*, vii.
19 Amnesty Committee's decision.
20 Ibid.
21 Munu Actis et al., *That inferno*, xvii.
22 Ibid., xvi.
23 Ibid.
24 Ibid., xvii.
25 Ibid., 100.
26 Ibid., 163.
27 Ibid., 51.
28 Ibid., 59.
29 Ibid., 52.
30 Ibid., 56.
31 Ibid., 57–8.
32 Ibid., 67.
33 Ibid.
34 Dirección de Inteligencia Nacional.
35 Arce, *That inferno*, 142–3.
36 Arce recounts this story in *That inferno*, her memoir.
37 Lazzara, *Luz Arce and Pinochet's Chile*, 79.
38 Ibid., 5.
39 Ibid., 6.
40 Ibid., 160.
41 Ibid., 81.
42 Ibid., 156.
43 Ibid., 81.
44 Ibid., 83.
45 Ibid., 87.
46 Ibid., 86.
47 Ibid., 85.
48 Ibid., 160.
49 Chris Mosiane's testimony to TRC Amnesty Committee hearing, Durban, 16 October 2000.

Chapter 13

1 Hugh Lewin, *Stones against the mirror: Friendship in the time of the South African struggle* (Cape Town: Umuzi, 2011), 98.
2 Sartre, 'What is a collaborator?', 49 and 51.
3 Ibid., 52 and 53.
4 Ibid., 54.
5 Nofomela, personal interview, Soshanguve, 18 January 2014.
6 Sartre, 'What is a collaborator?', 54 and 56.
7 To mention just one source: Sam Mtileni, a former ANC operative who knew Sedibe, said: 'He would go back to Swaziland to terrorise his former comrades.' Telephonic interview, 16 January 2014.
8 Lillian Sedibe, personal interview, Matibidi, January 2013.
9 Ibid.
10 Ibid.
11 Ibid.
12 Miriam Mashego, personal interview, Mpumalanga, January 2013.
13 I am grateful to Jonny Steinberg, Rommy Morales, Beatriz Silva Pinochet and Gerard Delanty for encouraging me to think seriously about this question.
14 Adri Kotze, '"September" was nie bloot 'n lakei', *Beeld*, 24 January 1994.
15 Mr X1's testimony in *State* vs *Maseko and two others*, HGH CC 319/87; Kaborone Sedibe, personal interview, Edenvale, 27 February 2013.
16 Lazzara, *Luz Arce and Pinochet's Chile*, 74.
17 Jean Amery, *At the mind's limit: Contemplations by a survivor of Auschwitz and its realities* (Bloomington: Indiana University Press, 1980), 40.
18 Ibid., 34.
19 De Kock, personal interview, Pretoria, 24 February 2013.
20 Barry Gilder, personal interview, 20 February 2013.
21 Thomas Blass, 'The Milgram paradigm after 35 years: Some things we now know about obedience and authority', *Journal of Applied Social Psychology*, 25, 5 (1999), 958.
22 Ibid., 959.
23 I am grateful to Professor Kurt Danziger for sharing this with me. Email exchange, November 2013.
24 Ibid.
25 Ibid.
26 Lewin, *Bandiet*, 18.
27 Evans, obituary of Adrian Leftwich, www.independent.co.uk, 28 May 2013. Leftwich himself referred to the judge's words in his essay 'I gave the names', *Granta*, 78 (Summer 2002), 22.
28 Evans, obituary of Adrian Leftwich, www.independent.co.uk, 28 May 2013.
29 Leftwich, 'I gave the names', 11.
30 Ibid., 17.
31 Ibid., 19.
32 Ibid., 18.
33 Ibid.

34 Ibid., 21.
35 Lewin, *Stones against the mirror*, 179.
36 Ibid., 47–8.
37 Ibid., 99.
38 Ibid., 102.
39 Personal communication.

Chapter 14

1 In Matynia, *An uncanny era*, 98.
2 Pikoli and Mandy Wiener, *My second initiation*, 79.
3 Quoted in Istvan Rev's essay 'The man in the white raincoat', 6. Another version of the essay can be found in Thiranagama and Kelly, *Traitors*, 200–27.
4 Hans-Jürgen Becken, '"Give me water, woman of Samaria": The pilgrimage of southern African blacks in the 1980s', *Journal of Religion in Africa*, 14, 2 (1983), 115.
5 Quoted in Becken's essay 'The mother of Cancele', *Journal of Religion in Africa*, 13, 3 (1982), 190.
6 Becken, '"Give me water, woman of Samaria"', 118.
7 No relation to the author.
8 Becken, '"Give me water, woman of Samaria"', 118–19.
9 Kaborone Sedibe, personal interview, Edenvale, 27 February 2013. Delilah Rekisa (not her real name) confirmed the story of Sedibe's interest in the Zion Christian Church, which is the largest Christian church in southern Africa. Personal interview with Rekisa, Pretoria, 24 January 2014.
10 Kaborone Sedibe, personal interview, Edenvale, 27 February 2013.
11 Verne Harris and Christopher Merrett, 'Toward a culture of transparency: Public rights of access to official records in South Africa', *American Archivist*, 57 (Fall 1994), 681.
12 Gregory Sibusiso Radebe, personal interview, Johannesburg, 8 May 2013.
13 David Xiao, 'Why I came to write', in Linny Stovall (ed.), *Secrets* (Hillsboro: Blue Hill Publishing, 1996), 104.
14 Confidential source. A former senior police officer told me in January 2014 that, in fact, the ANC conducted a number of such post-mortems when it took over government in 1994.
15 Kevin O'Brien and Stephen Ellis say there were 300 askaris by the time Vlakplaas was shut down in April 1993. Their figures might be inflated by the possible inclusion of fighters from the rest of southern Africa who had joined the South African security establishment. See Ellis's essay 'The historical significance of South Africa's Third Force', 269, and O'Brien's book *The South African Intelligence Services*, 187.
16 O'Brien, *The South African Intelligence Services*, 187.
17 Gregory Sibusiso Radebe, personal interview, Johannesburg, 8 May 2013. Radebe was in detention and on trial because he had revived his pyramid scheme, thereby violating the terms of his suspended sentence for the first offence.
18 Confidential source.

19 Hefer Commission report, 51. The report is available online.
20 Ibid., 57.
21 Rev, 'The man in the white raincoat'. The most shameful aspect of the attempt by Maharaj and Shaik to destroy Ngcuka was their paid use of Gideon Nieuwoudt, a former apartheid security policeman, to back them up. Nieuwoudt was responsible for, among his many crimes, the murder of Steve Biko.
22 Jorge Luis Borges, 'Theme of the traitor and the hero', in *Labyrinths: Selected stories and writings*, ed. by Donald A. Yates and James E. Irby (New York: New Directions, 1964), 73–4.
23 Ibid.
24 Ibid.
25 Ibid., 75.
26 Gavin Evans, 'Secret histories', *Leadership* magazine, 13, 5 (1994).
27 Slovo, *Red dust*, 337.
28 Ndebele, Foreword, in Jones and Dlamini, *Categories of persons*.
29 Lewin, *Stones against the mirror*, 187.
30 I shared this fiction in the form of a keynote address at the biennial conference of the Southern African Historical Society at the University of KwaZulu-Natal, Durban, in June 2011.
31 Details of Sam Ntuli's assassination are contained in the Independent Board of Inquiry Collection in Wits Historical Papers, AG2543.
32 In Matynia, *An uncanny era*, 39.
33 Krog, *Conditional tense*, 170.
34 Matynia, *An uncanny era*, 33.
35 Ibid.
36 Ibid., 33–4.

Acknowledgements

This book recounts a particular kind of collaboration, one that scarred the world, corrupted individuals and destroyed lives. But the book itself is the product of another type of collaboration, one that was collegial, nurturing and supportive. I am certain that those who helped make this a better book will not mind my calling them my kind of collaborators. Sharon Chetty, Ivor Chipkin, Jacklyn Cock, Carli Coetzee, Antjie Krog, Gerry Maré, Thembisa Waetjen, Peter Wagner and Vron Ware read various drafts of the manuscript, making each draft better than the last one. My heartfelt thanks to them for their generosity and insightful comments. I do not expect them to agree with everything in the previous pages. But I hope they will recognise the imprint of their counsel in the book. I would also like to thank the following for their help: Tyrone August, Barbara and Terry Bell, Catherine Burns, Mbongiseni Buthelezi, Keith Breckenridge, Selina and Robin Cohen, Piet Croucamp, Kurt Danziger, Gerard Delanty, Saul Dubow, Ebrahim Ebrahim, Madeleine Fullard, Angela Lorena Fuster, Barry Gilder, Jeremy Gordin, Robert Harms, Shireen Hassim, Stephen Hubbell, Nathalie Karagiannis, Jose Katito, Ruben Lo Vuolo, Richard Lyster, Edgar Manjarin, Elzbieta Matynia, Patricia Sue McGaughey, Rommy Morales, Hlonipha Mokoena, Aurea Mota, Steve Naidoo, Sifiso Ndlovu, Sarah Nuttall, Piers Pigou, Adam Radwan, Gerard Rosich, Nicky Rousseau, Sam Sadian, Christina Seisun, Beatriz Silva, and Jonny Steinberg.

Kaborone Gilbert Sedibe and his mother, Lillian Mamoedi Sedibe, gave of their time without any expectations. I thank them for that.

Louis Kumayl Molantoa and Simphiwe Ngwane, my research assistants, went beyond the call of duty. They tracked down obscure sources, found interview subjects, traipsed from archive to archive and offered cheerful company, all the while challenging and questioning me about everything from my assumptions to my research methods. This was a learning experience for the three of us and we are, I believe, the richer and wiser for it.

Of course, my work, as well as Louis's and Simphiwe's, would have got nowhere without the archivists and librarians who were with us every step of the way. We owe thanks to the staff at the National Archives of South Africa, the Defence Archives, the Foreign Affairs Archives, Wits Historical Papers, the Johannesburg Public Library, the South African National Library, the South African Parliamentary Archives, the Bodleian Library at Oxford University, the US National Archives, and the National Security Archives in Washington DC.

When Greg Rosenberg, my friend and editor, received the first draft of the manuscript, it was a beast of a thing. But Greg, in his sharp and unsentimental ways, tamed the beast. He gave it focus and structure, and made sure that the book told its story without bells and whistles. *Ngiyabonga*. Russell Martin, my editor and publisher, believed in this book long before I had anything on paper. If Greg tamed the beast, Russell domesticated it. I thank him for that. I also thank the Jacana family for taking me in: special thanks to Bridget Impey and Maggie Davey.

This publication was supported by a grant from the Open Society Fellowship. I would also like to recognise the support of TRAMOD, my intellectual home at the University of Barcelona. TRAMOD, funded by the European Research Council under Advanced Grant no. 249438, gave me the space to test my ideas and provided a mentor (in Peter Wagner) and interlocutors (in my colleagues) to help me tell this as part of a bigger story about the modern world.

JACOB DLAMINI

Index